EFFANBEE
Dolls That Touch Your Heart

by Patricia R. Smith

EFFANBEE
Dolls That Touch Your Heart

by Patricia R. Smith

Cover:
Large *Bubbles*, small 14″ *Charlie McCarthy*, and
18″ *Suzie Sunshine* from the Ship Ahoy Collection.
(Courtesy Diane Hoffman & Martha Gragg)

COLLECTOR BOOKS
P.O. Box 3009
Paducah, Kentucky 42001

Searching for a Publisher?

We are always looking for knowledgeable people considered experts within their fields. If you feel that there is a real need for a book on your collectible subject and have a large comprehensive collection, contact Collector Books.

Additional copies of this book may be ordered from:

Collector Books
P.O. Box 3009
Paducah, KY 42002-3009

@ $19.95. Add $2.00 for postage and handling.

Copyright © 1983 by Patricia R. Smith
Updated Values, 1998

This book or any part thereof may not be reproduced without the written consent of the Author and Publisher.

Printed by IMAGE GRAPHICS, INC., Paducah, Kentucky

DEDICATION

This book is dedicated to a dear friend who loved Effanbee dolls that were made of composition. She appreciated all other dolls from this company, but the composition were the dolls of her childhood and each and every one of them brought back memories of that beautiful fleeting time in all our lives. Her name was Thelma Flack, a great lady who passed out of this world making it a happier place to live for the people who knew her.

CREDITS

We wish to thank the following for their help in compiling this book on Effanbee dolls. All photos are by Dwight F. Smith unless noted.

Hazel Adams.
Rose Albanese, photos by Fay Rodolfos.
Ruth Arent, photos by Margaret Mandel.
Lilah Beck, photos by Renie Culp.
Shirley Bertrand, of Shirley's Doll House.
Kay Bransky, photos by her husband.
Dorothy Cameron, of Cameron Doll Museum.
Pearl Clasby.
Renie Culp, photos by Renie Culp.
Sally Freenman, photos by Sally Freenman.
Joleen Flack, photos by Joleen Flack.
Martha Gragg.
Eloise Godfrey, photos by Robert Walker.
Beverly Harrington.
Eileen Harris.
Naomi Hennig, photos by Joe Morrison.
Marilyn Hitchcock, photos by Frank Prochillo.
Diane Hoffman, photos by Diane Hoffman.
Bee Johnson, photos by Bea Johnson.
Virginia Jones.
Miriam Knox, photos by Miriam Knox.
Nancy Lucas, photos by Sally Freenman.
Barbara Jean Male, photos by Michael Male.
Margaret Mandel, photos by Margaret Mandel.
Jeannie Mauldin, photos by Jeannie Mauldin.

Billie McCabe of Marianne's Doll House.
Marge Meisinger, photos by David Miller.
Joan Meivose, photos by June Schultz.
Elizabeth Montesano, of Yesterday's Children.
Dottie Mulholland, by Dottie Mulholland.
Pam Ortman, photos by Pam Ortman.
Shirley Pascuzzi, photos by Shirley Pascuzzi.
Doris Richardson, photos by Doris Richardson.
E. Samec, photos by E. Samec.
Jimmy & Fay Rodolfos, photos by Fay Rodolfos.
Sheryl Schmidt, photos by Sheryl Schmidt.
June Schultz, by June Schultz.
Carol Stephens, photos by Sally Freenman.
Mary Stolzenberg, photos by Mary Stolzenberg.
Mary Sweeney, photos by Mary Sweeney.
Marjorie Uhl, photos by Marjorie Uhl.
Glorya Woods, photos by Glorya Woods.
Rilla M. Van Zandt, photos by Rilla M. Van Zandt.

Our extra special thanks go to two very generous people, who certainly helped a great deal by loaning us their valuable Effanbee Catalogs: 1965, 1967, 1970, 1972, 1973, 1974, & 1977. Arthur Keller, Vice President of the Effanbee Corporation, and Mrs. Marge Meisinger, a long time friend. Also, for her help, Lisa Feldmann.

CONTENTS

EFFANBEE . . . A CHRONOLOGY
Composition Dolls (1912-1949)

By the year 1903 and 1904 the psychology of childhood had become of interest to many the world over, and the child's emotional involvement with toys began raising questions. Toy makers gave a long, hard look at the idol they had created and felt some changes were necessary.

The actual "revolution" began in Munich by the designer, Marion Kaulitz. Her dolls were modelled by Paul Vogelsanger, and made of composition and/or all fabric. These dolls are now referred to as "Munich Art Dolls", and a sample is very difficult to find except scattered around the world in various museums. These dolls looked like real children and their first success came about in 1909 when an exhibition was arranged in a warehouse of Hermann Tietz. Herr Tietz had never heard of Marion Kaulitz, and after seeing the dolls describes them as, "Full of individuality and character, yet remaining childish, so true hearted and bright, so charmingly pert and rakish." The Munich Art dolls were important as they were the foundation for the portrayal of true-to-life children, rather than the dream of what a child was like, imposed by the doll makers.

As the psychology of doll and toy making drove the manufacturers to new ideas, two men had met and enjoyed being business neighbors in Atlantic City, New Jersey. Bernard E. Fleischaker had moved from Louisville, Kentucky to run a shop selling furniture, while his neighbor, Hugo Baum, operated a store selling shopping bags. Hugo Baum was a native of Germany, the land of the toymakers, and had come to the United States 12 years before meeting Bernard Fleischaker. The two became good friends, and as their friendship reflected trust they decided to become partners, and in 1910 the firm of Fleischaker and Baum was created.

The first two years were difficult and the two men spent most of their time finding toys to buy (jobbing) and the retail markets to sell them in. They had learned a great deal about selling toys when, in 1912 they decided to manufacture their own dolls. Their dolls would be made in America for American children, and they took great pride in selecting the trademark that their products would be famous for: EFF-for Fleischaker and BEE-for Baum, thereby known as Effanbee.

Since this writing is a chronology, the following listing will be done by the year and the story of the company will continue under the year certain events took place.

There has been a great amount written about the Effanbee Doll Company and many photographs appear in print, therefore we have listed for your reference, these books.

Anderton, Johana Gast, *Twentieth Century Dolls*, 1971; *More Twentieth Century Dolls*, 1974.

Axe, John, *Collectible Patsy Dolls & Patsy Types,* 1978.

Cooper, Marlowe, *Dimples and Sawdust*, Vol. 2, 1968.

Ellenburg, M. Kelly, *Effanbee, The Dolls With The Golden Heart*, 1973.

Foulke, Jan, *Blue Book of Doll Values*, Vol. 1, 1975; Vol. 2, 1976; Vol. 3, 1978. Focusing on Effanbee Composition Dolls.

Leuzzi, Marlene, *Antique Doll Price Guide*, Vol. 4, 1978; *Composition to Vinyl*, Vol. 1, 1973.

Selfridge, Madalaine, *Wendy and Friends*, 1969; *Images of Love*, Vol. 1.

Shoemaker, Rhoda, *Composition Dolls, Cute and Collectible*, Vol. 1, 1971; Vol. 2, 1973; Vol. 3, 1979.

Smith, Patricia R., *Modern Collector's Dolls*, Vol. 1, 1973; Vol. 2 1975; Vol. 3, 1976, Vol. 4, 1979; *Doll Values*, Vol. 1, 1979, Vol. 2, 1980, Vol. 3, 1982; *Standard Modern Price Guide*, 1976.

Stewart, Ethel & Dennis, Katherine, *Collector's Guide to Patsy Dolls.*

There is also an Effanbee Fan Club, and following is the address:

Effanbee Fan Club
Dee Carson, President
P.O. Box 1430
Barstow California 92311

Yearly Chronology

1912: Fleischaker and Baum imported a series of molds from a German maker and had the heads made by Fredrick Devoll of Providence, R.I.. It was from the German brothers of Heubach (Gebruder) they bought the molds to dolls called *Naughty Marietta,* but Ideal Doll Company put out a doll called *Naughty Maritta* at the same time, so Fleischaker and Baum changed their doll's name to *Miss Coquette* and *Laughing Mariertta.* She was a little 12" doll with molded hair, modeled hair ribbon and hair bows on the side. The eyes are painted to the side and the head is slightly tilted. She was offered as a premium for eighty-five cents and one subscription to the *People's Home Journal* in December, 1912. For this magazine, she was dressed in check dress with drop waist and had circular lined cloth legs with sewn on shoes of felt.

Other heads (molds) were bought with Devoll providing the composition and bodies, and one, *Baby Dainty,* was Fleischaker & Baum's first real taste of success. She has a cloth body, is a toddler with composition shoulder head and was to become a part of the Effanbee line through 1925. *Johnny Tu-Face,* a cloth bodied doll with composition head with a laughing face on one side, and a crying face on the other. The company mold for this doll was purchased from an unknown, but that company marketed their version of the same doll as *Soozie Smiles,* 'the doll that made a Queen smile'. It came dressed in a linen romper dress with border and pocket print of running rabbits, with hat to match. *Little Boy Blue* was 12" tall and dressed in a blue Russian style outfit with belt and tape trim of red with white stripes. The hair was molded, head and hands were composition and the legs had circular bands and sewn on shoes. He was offered for selling subscriptions to *The People's Home Journal,* December 1912. Also, for the same publications the dolls named *Tiny Tads* were made. 12" tall and look very much like the *Campbell Kids,* with molded hair, and came as a boy or a girl. They were dressed in blue and white check material. The name of *Tiny Tads* was used again in 1916 - 1918. Another doll this year was *Little Walter,* a sleeping baby from a mold purchased from the Devoll company.

1913: A few dolls a day were made by Fleishacker and Baum in the beginnings of their own factory, and during the course of 1913 it was still necessary for them to have much of the composition heads made elsewhere. They introduced *Betty Bounce,* with molded hair and painted eyes, which came in 11" and 15" sizes, and was cloth and composition. The boy version was called *Bobby,* and *Bobby Bounce,* dressed in romper suits.

In 1913 the *Baby Dainty* had a closed mouth, but was sold with a pacifier and came with molded hair, or a wig. *Baby Huggins* was 9" - 10" tall, all composition with molded hair and painted eyes.

The two men made another good selection, which meant a greater success to their small business. They were able to purchase the German made *Grumpy* molds in six sizes, and these first *Grumpy* dolls will only be marked with: 171, 172, 173, 174, 175, or 176. The *Grumpy* dolls were so welcomed by the public the manufacturer of them continued into the 1930's. They came in the same six different sizes, and some were Black. The body and legs were stuffed cloth, the arms, with composition hands. The eyes are painted to the side, and the mouth is closed and very pouty. The hair is molded with the modeling dropping down on the foreheads. The black version was called *Snowball.*

All these early ones had circular striped cloth legs. Some of these early dolls were also marked with a number, and perhaps a light mark *Deco,* which stands for the company that made the composition these first years. (Fredrick Devoll Co.) Also marketed this year was a doll called *Pa jama Baby.*

1914: Fleischaker and Baum continued to grow by adding more employees, and by the end of 1913 they had begun to use the trademark: *Eff* and *Bee.* Some early examples will be marked: *Eff And Bee.* During 1914 they introduced a line made entirely in their own factory called *Tango Kiddies,* with closed mouths, painted eyes, and cloth bodies that were plush covered. These dolls came with the novel idea of red, green or blue molded hair. To make the *Tango Kiddies,* the *Betty Bounce* doll was used. A *Nun* doll was also marketed during 1914, along with the rest of the 1913 line.

1915: New dolls for this year were: *Baby Bodkins,* in 11" and 15" sizes, painted hair and eyes. *Baby Bright Eyes, Jr.* with painted eyes. *Baby Grumpy, Jr., Betty Bounce* in 11" and 15". *Billy Boy,* 11" and 15", also with painted eyes. Black doll line included: *Aunt Dinah, Baby Snowball* (Grumpy) and *Uncle Mose. Jumbo Infant* was made from 1915 into 1920 and was all cloth with stitched fingers and composition heads. *School Girl,* came in 11" and 15" with molded hair and painted eyes.

1916: *Bright Eyes* came only in the 15" size this year. *Dorothy Dainty,* with open mouth/pacifier. *Tiny Tad,* all cloth with composition head, molded hair, painted eyes. This year Hugo Baum designed two dolls for the line: *Uncle Sam* and *Columbia.* These two new additions brought the number of dolls that Effanbee had to offer the public to over one hundred models, which included twelve differently dressed, and sized, *Baby Grumps* and *Baby Grumps, Jr.* The regular *Grumps* had straight legs, while the "Jr" had slight curved legs.

1917: *Baby Bunting,* cloth body, composition head with wig, came dressed in "Teddy Bear" suit. *Mary Jane* to 1923. *Our Baby,* cloth with composition head and hands to wrist, wig or molded hair and painted eyes.

1918: As World War I raged in Europe, the doll and toy industry in America and Japan grew, as all imports from Germany and France stopped. To meet the demands American makers added a great many new items to their doll lines. Fleischaker and Baum were no exception with over one hundred and fifty models available during 1918 season. *Baby Blanche,* 15" and *Baby Catherine,* 12", 14", 16" & 20", came with sleep or painted eyes, open mouth/pacifier. *Baby Daintie* with cloth body and limbs with composition hands and head, painted eyes, wig and pacifier. *Brother* with painted eyes and wig, (same doll as used for *Lady Grumpy). Christening Baby,* which were large dolls and made in 25", 27" and 29" sizes, open mouths/ pacifiers. *Coquette,* with painted eyes and molded hair. *Dolly Dumpling* (also called Baby Dumpling), cloth with composition head, painted eyes and came with molded hair or wig. *Jumbo Infants,* 16", 20" and 22", same as *Christening Babies,* and same sizes. *Katie Kroose,* 15" fabric doll with painted eyes, wigs and dressed in foreign style costumes. *Lady Grumpy.* Young girl Grumpy with wig and painted eyes. *Red Cross Nurse* in 12", 15", 18" & 25" sizes. *Soldier, The Sweethearts,* boy and girl with wigs and painted eyes. *Romper Babies, Tiny Tads,* 7" & 11", small versions of *Betty Bounce, Coquette, Billy Boy* and *Bright Eyes*.

1919: During the years of the first World War the supply of bisque dolls had been totally cut off from the European makers, and it was at this point that Japan entered the bisque doll field. The Fulper Company, in the U.S.A., made some bisque heads for the Horsman Doll Company, and during this same time Fleischaker and Baum commissioned bisque heads to be made by the Lenox Pottery Company of Trenton, N.J.. Apparently the dolls were either made in a very small amount, or they were never marketed. Composition heads on ball jointed bodies made from the Lenox molds did appear on the market and are considered to be very rare. During 1919 Effanbee began using the slogan "American Dolls Are Now The World's Standard". The *Mary Jane* doll was available in sizes 16", 18", 20" and 24" (made from 1917 to 1923). In 1919 the *Mary Jane* came on a German style kidelene body with composition/wood arms and legs with extra joints. Effanbee introduced a line of dolls called *Novelty Art Dolls*, which included *Baby Buds*, as *Riding Hood Bud, Valentine Bud*, and others. These were composition dolls molded in one piece with jointed shoulders only. Two other dolls were called *Airman* and *Teddy Bear*. These were cloth and composition and dressed in knit outfits. Also this year was *Baby Blue* and *Baby Pink* with molded hair, painted eyes, cloth with composition heads and dressed in knit sweaters and booties. Effanbee offered over three hundred models to the market in 1919 and among these were a completely new line of *Christening Babies* and *Mama* crying dolls. It must also be noted that they handled stuffed animals, such as cats and Teddy bears. *Cunning Baby*, 12", 16" & 19", molded & wigs, sleep eyes, open mouth. "Fat" style baby, both large toes molded up and almost separate. Jointed wrists.

1920: *Mary Jane*, along with many, many other boys and girls, as well as babies were offered during the 1920 season. Dolls made of all cloth, some with cotton stuffed bodies and composition heads, and a re-introduction of the *Baby Grumpy* took place this year. The *Novelty Art* dolls (*Baby Buds*) came with modeled on costumes, as well as with removable clothes. They were 7" - 8" tall with painted eyes and some had wigs. They were Eskimos, Orientals, Hawaiians and Indians. All had dark skin tones. The all cloth dolls were advertised as being cotton stuffed and without pins used on the clothes. Ads in magazines such as *Good Housekeeping* carried Effanbee ads showing a pin (tin) with a blue bird at the top and the words: Effanbee Dolls. The ads stated: Look for this button on each doll.

1921: One of the highly advertised new dolls for this year was *Margie* with a cork stuffed body. New, also was *Salvation Army Lass*, a "mama" style doll that said "papa", and a delightfully named doll: *Trottie Truelife*.

1922: Was a repeat of 1921 with over three hundred models for their customers to choose from. It was this year that Effanbee began using the trademark: "They Walk and They Talk", and the ads read that the voice boxes were made of metal, not rubber, so would not rot. Most of the dolls being offered this year were in the 12" to 16" range.

1923: On June 12, 1923 Effanbee took out the Trademark-Register #181,883 for *Buttons Monk*. The trademark was stamped on buttons that were attached to the dolls. This year Hugo Baum also copyrighted the *Baby Grumpy*. The copyright says the design of the doll was by Ernesto Peruggi. Mr. Peruggi was an Italian citizen residing in New York City, and he is credited with designing dolls for a number of manufacturers with two for Effanbee, *New Born*

Baby in 1925, and the 1923 *Baby Grumps*. Mr. Peruggi's actual "design" was in reality a re-design of old molds. Effanbee began extensively using sleep eyes during 1923 and now their ads read: "They walk, They sleep". This trademark has been found on dolls that do none of these things, as well as dolls that perhaps only one part of the trademark fits. A button with the name "Effanbee" was pinned to all the dolls. The Nancy Ann and Mary Ann models were made into a new line named the "Dolls with The Golden Heart", and all wore a heart shaped pendant. There was also a *Betty Lee* that was sold through the October 1924 *Good Housekeeping* magazine that has a composition shoulder head with full composition limbs and a cloth body. She has a "mama" *Cryer And Sleep Eyes With Lashes*. Her cheeks are dimpled and has a wig. She is shown wearing the golden heart. The *Nancy Ann* was 23" tall and the *Mary Ann* was 20", both were also offered through the *Ladies Home Journal* in 1923, plus readers could send for a free booklet called '*How to Select The Proper Doll To Suit Your Child's Age*'. Other dolls this year were: *Beach Baby* and *Honey Bunch*, and a completely new line of large, "mama" type dolls.

1924: *Alice Lee*, 23" tall with sleep eyes and wig, *Barbara Lee*, who was 29", *Betty Lee* was 20" - 21" and *Marilee* who was 24" and 27". All the *Lee* dolls had cloth bodies, sleep eyes, cheek dimples, and real eyelashes. There was a complete line of babies and toddlers that came either black or white. *Mary Lou* has a cloth body with a "mama" cryer, straight legs and used the Marilee head. *Harmonica Joe* was a black doll with composition head and cloth body. There was a tube from the open mouth to a rubber ball in the stomach and by pressing the doll he played the harmonica. Introduced as a black child, the doll was also made as white. Joseph L. Kallus assisted Hugo Baum in an advisory capacity this year, but in what area is not known. One new feature this year, beside the real eyelashes was the full composition arms that are jointed at the shoulders. *Bubbles* came into being this year, was nationally advertised, and was a very successful doll for Effanbee.

This first year, the Bubble line included 13" - 14" *Dolly Bubbles*, 20" *Charlotte Bubbles*, and 22" *Betty Bubbles*. Some *Bubbles* will be marked: 1924, but were not on the market until 1925. It is interesting to note that Bubbles was not registered until December 17, 1926 (241,611). This doll was so well loved by the public that she sold into the late 1930's. A few *Bubbles* were made black, but the majority were white.

1925: Ernesto Peruggi of New York City designed *New Born Baby* for Effanbee. The design was copyrighted by Fleischaker, and since they were late in producing their version of the Bye-Lo Baby, they called their's *Baby Dainty* and *Baby Effanbee* (name they had already used). To compete, Effanbee used two innovations and marketed *Baby Dainty* (New Born Baby) as twins and triplets, and also as *Pat-O-Pat*, when the stomach was pressed the doll clapped its hands. *Baby Grumpy* was also put out as singles, or twins this year. The *Baby Evelyn* of this year was marked with her name, but also just with the "Effanbee". She had cloth body, composition head and limbs, came with molded hair as well as wigs. *Baby Huggins*, composition and cloth. *Rosemary* in 14", 18", 20", 26" and 28" sizes. She came with cloth body, straight composition legs and full composition arms.

1926: *Bubbles* was registered December 17, 1926 (241,611). See 1926 section of this book for *Baby Gloria*, the doll *Bubbles* was molded from. The 13" *Dolly Bubbles* came with both painted eyes as well as sleep eyes. This early size of 13″ - 14″ also came with an open/closed mouth, painted teeth. These early production *Bubbles* had very fat legs with modeled wrinkles and two deep knee dimples. This year a 24″- 25″, and a 18″ size was added to the line. Also this year Effanbee introduced a line of "*Walking Bubbles*". These had toddler type legs of all composition with thinner legs and much less dimple and wrinkle detail than the regular Bubbles models. All the Bubbles had cloth bodies, full composition arms and legs, and a one piece shoulder and head composition. Except for the 13″-14″ with the open/closed mouth, they all had slightly open mouths, and the arms are modeled bent at the elbows that allowed the hand to be placed to the mouth. These dolls came with celluloid, modeled/painted composition, and inset teeth. A few dolls were produced in black. *Rosemary* was once again a popular doll this year. One of the new dolls was *Catherine*, all composition with large round eyes painted to the side and molded red hair, and on a *Patsy* body with bent arm.

Patsy, the first model used the Baby Dainty head and came in sizes 14″- 15″ with a cloth body. Along with the ads for Bubbles were ads for *Lovey Mary*, which came in sizes 13″-14″, 16″-17″, 19″-20″, 22″-23″, 25″-26″. She is the Rosemary type doll with cloth body and straight legs and full composition arms. The ads say you can teach her to walk and even dance the Charleston. Sleep eyes with real eyelashes and the wig is brown with its style rolled into ear length bob, and full bangs. Dressed in organdie short dress that came in purple, pink or blue, matching organdy bonnet with rosette and black velvet ribbon tie, and tie black patent shoes. This doll was named for Bessie Love in the Metro-Goldwyn-Mayer moving picture called "*Lovey Mary*" which was made in 1926 (see ad in this book). *Just Me*, forerunner to *Patsy Doll* (see 1926-this book).

1927: *Bubbles* came in sizes of 16″, 18″, 22″, and 24″. All with cloth bodies, and full composition legs and arms. Each were packaged with six photographs of the doll. It must be noted that composition shrunk many times when taken from the molds and there can be as much as 1″ difference in size. *Naughty Eyes* as advertised through Montgomery Wards in 1927. She is a Rosemary style doll that came in sizes 14½″, 16″, 18″, and 21″. She had flirty eyes, open mouth with teeth, mohair "bobbed" wig and a cloth body. She also came as a blonde or a brunette. Another Rosemary style doll offered was called *Rose Mary*, and came with dark brown long curls, and the same ad states that her sister is *Mary Sue*, which is the same doll only she has golden wig in a short, fluffy bob. Both dolls came in sizes of 18″, 21″, 23″, and 26″. Each came with six photographs of the doll.

Patsy was introduced this year, and the **name**, not the design was registered on October 14, 1927. (256,080). The body used for the Patsy was used one year earlier (1926) for the *Catherine* doll. The *Patsy* and the Armand Marseille doll *Just Me* are almost identical. It is known from original owners, and from ads that the *Just Me* (310 mold number) was made as early as 1922. These dolls have bisque heads and were made in Germany by the Armand Marseille firm. The distribution of the dolls was turned over to George Borgfeldt in 1928. Mr. Borgfeldt registered the name in the United States on January 22, 1929 (278,429), and in Berlin on January 22, 1929 (397339). These later *Just Me* dolls were of painted bisque and were sold by Borgfeldt into the early 1930's.

The *Patsy* is reported to have been designed by Bernard Lipfert who was a trained sculptor and a fourth generation toymaker. Herr Lipfert had worked in his native Germany for Goebel, Kestner and Armand Marseille (who made the *Just Me* dolls). After coming to the United States he worked for E. I. Horsman, and soon was working for many manufacturers. To quote an authority on Bernard Lipfert, Joan Amundsen (Lipfert article appears in the Antique Trader of July 2, 1974), "Lipfert grew tired of making only baby dolls, the kind other people told him to make. He felt there was a need for something new and different. In 1928 he took it upon himself to design the *Patsy* doll, a toddler doll he always considered his biggest and best creation. He had some difficulty persuading a manufacturer to buy his model. After all, the doll wasn't a baby and couldn't say mama. Effanbee Doll Company finally decided to take a chance on its salability. Patsy was an instant success, and was followed by a complete family of dolls." Herr Lipfert died in 1974 at the age of 87. He was the designer of many famous dolls, besides the *Patsy*, such as the *Shirley Temple, Dionne Quints* and the original *Dy-Dee* of which he said in a thick German accent, "had the dumbest face I have ever designed." In fact, Lipfert didn't want to sell the doll but Effanbee insisted on buying it and apparently knew what they were doing for the doll became one of their largest sellers over a great many years. There is a life-size model of the *Patsy* doll in Lipfert's attic, along with hundreds of his other designs. It is a shame that someone did not think to ask Herr Lipfert if he continued to design for Armand Marseille (Germany), and if he actually did pattern the *Patsy* after the *Just Me*.

The *Patsy* came in 14″, all composition with painted eyes, and a small "rosebud" closed mouth. The *Patsy* was an important part of doll development in the U.S., as she was the first major doll that came with, or had available extra clothes. She was the first member of a large family which included: 5½″ *Wee Patsy*, 8″ *Babyette*, 9″ *Patsyette*, 11″ *Patsy Jr.*, 13″ *Patsy Baby*, 14″ *Patricia*, 16″ *Patsy Joan*, 18″ *Patsy Ann*, 22″ *Patsy Lou*, 26″ *Patsy Ruth* and 30″ *Patsy Mae*. The 8″ *Patsy Babyette* with molded hair or wigs, and sleep eyes was first introduced in 1927, also. This same doll was used for many years and was reintroduced in 1940 in composition and in 1950 with a hard plastic head.

One other item should be mentioned, and that is that B. E. Fleischaker's brother Walter had joined the firm early in its career and had helped the company grow. Hugo Baum brought his son Bernard into the business, and in 1923 he brought in Morris Lutzman who became as a second son to him.

The forerunner to the *Patsy* was the 1926 *Catherine*, and it is most interesting that the body was in use before the *Patsy* head. The same design (or head) of the *Catherine* by Effanbee was used as the *Mitzi* made by the Maxine Doll Company. Both were designs of Bernard Lipfert. Effanbee sued the Maxine Company to try and obtain an injunction to stop the doll as they felt it infringed on their own *Catherine* and *Patsy* dolls. It was in July of 1928 that the Supreme Court of the State of New York ruled that the Maxine Company could continue to make and sell their *Mitzi*. An appeal court (Appellate) later reversed the decision and granted Effanbee the exclusive right "to a doll having the features, characteristics and general appearance, as well as the trade name." It would be impossible to straighten out what really took place, at this late date, and not being able to talk to the actual people involved.

There is another item of importance, in relation to the year 1927. On October 14, 1927, a Registered Trademark

258,079 was taken out for the name *Mimi*. John Axe in his book *"Collectable Patsy Types"* states the doll was featured in the 1927 issue of *"Playthings"* Magazine and advertised as *"IT"*. Mr. Axe also states that the January, 1928 ad in *"Playthings"* now has named the doll *Patsy* (Mimi-It). The doll marked *"It"* was actually made by Louis Amberg and Sons in 1928. They sold "blanks" (dolls without their name) to other doll companies, and some of these dolls were sold to the Alexander Doll Company as late as 1934. The Alexander doll was marketed as "Betsy" with tagged clothes and the doll is only marked *"It"*. The *"It"* girl was Clara Bow, this name was dubbed for her by the screen writer Madame Elinor Glyn. To date, there is actually no information on the *Mimi* doll by Effanbee and we do not know if the doll was really marketed, nor if marked *"It"*, or not.

1928: *Mary Ann*, with open mouth, cloth body and composition head and limbs. 1928 to 1937. *Lovums*, with open mouth and two upper and lower teeth. With molded hair, or caracul wig (also ads read "Touslehead"). Came in sizes 15", 22" and 28" this first year. The name was registered on November 2, 1928 (274,713) and the doll was made to 1939. One *Lovums* was made with a mechanism that was key wound to make the heart "beat". The Lovums shoulder plate and body was used with different heads, thereby creating other dolls. *Mae Starr*, 28"-29" cloth body with phonograph that takes wax cylinders. The doll could talk and sing. The doll was marketed through the regular channels, as well as being a premium for selling subscriptions to the *"Philadelphia Ledger"*. *Bubbles* for 1928 came in sizes 16", 18", 20", 22", and 24". The two larger sizes had "mama" voices, where the others just had cryer. Bubbles was offered in a variety of costumes and the more elaborate the clothing, the higher the price. *Skippy* was new this year and came on the *Patsy* body, blonde painted hair with a molded curl down the forehead, and blue painted eyes. The character of *Skippy* originated with the comic strip by P. L. Crosby (later played in movie by Jackie Cooper, see 1931). *Patsy* really came on the market this year and the early *Patsy* dolls have a molded headband with most being red heads. A great amount have various shades of red with brown being very rare. The eyes on the majority are painted brown, with blue eyes being rare. The eyes are painted to the side, with the center painted ones being rare. The heads are unmarked. And marked on the backs: Effanbee/Patsy/Pat.Pend./Doll. *Skippy* was advertised as the "boyfriend of *Patsy*".

1929: *W. C. Fields*, puppet, 18". Ads in magazines appeared where any child could get a "golden" metal heart shaped necklace marked Effanbee by sending in the coupon and six cents. 19" *Patsy Ann*. She has molded, painted red hair, or unpainted with wig, both human and mohair, sleep eyes made both in tin and glass. The eye colors can be brown, green or blue. Marks are: Effanbee/ "Patsy-Ann"/ Pat. #1283558. Called the "Open Mouth Patsy Ann" are the dolls using the regular Patsy Ann all composition body with the Lovums head. They came with caracul "tousle" wigs, as well as human hair wigs. Sleep eyes and smiling open mouth with six upper teeth. *Patsy Lou* is 22" tall with molded red hair, and also came with wigs. Sleep eyes can be green, brown or blue. Marks: Effanbee/"Patsy Lou". The *Patsy Lou* can also be found on the Lovums body that is cloth with shoulder plate that will be marked Lovums body that is cloth with shoulder plate that will be marked "Lovums". *Joan Carol* with cloth body and composition limbs, and 20" tall. Also a *Jan Carol* is advertised as being

24" tall.
1930: *Wee Patsy* was 5"-5½" tall and all composition. Came as both a girl or boy. *Lamkin*. 16". *Patsy, Jr.*, also called *Patsykins*. 11½"-12". *Patsy Joan*. 16". Both *Patsy Joan* and *Patsy Jr.* (Patsykins) came with molded hair and wigs. It must be noted that almost every member of the Patsy family came as either a boy or a girl. *Mary Lee*. 21" Open mouth, sleep eyes with lashes, cloth body and full composition limbs.
1931: Some animals were added to the regular doll line this year and included *Puss N Boots*, with a composition cat head on a regular Patsy body and is 11" tall, there was also an 11" rabbit. *Patsyette*. 9"-9½" and was put out as girl, boy and as twins. Painted eyes can be brown or blue and the hair is molded. There are brown skin toned *Patsyettes*. The *Patsyette* also was marketed with a wig with a hole in the middle of the head that the wig is attached to.

Bubbles was offered as a premium doll for selling three subscriptions to the *"Junior Home"* magazine. This was a 14" size, and in the November issue the choice of three dolls were given, Bubbles, Patsy or Baby Lamkin. *Skippy* becomes even more popular this year when the movie "Skippy" starring Jackie Cooper is introduced. The 1930's *Skippy* will have a cloth body with either the full composition legs or the kind that "swing" with painted on shoes and socks. There are some, rather rare, brown skin toned *Skippys*.
1932: *Patricia*. 14"-15" All composition and both arms are slightly curved. Came with both human and mohair wigs, and the sleep eyes can be green, blue or brown. She will be marked: Effanbee/Patricia on the back. *Mary Lee* came in 15"-16"-17" size and used the Patsy Joan all composition body, and also with a cloth body using the full composition arms and legs. She came with caracul and human hair wigs. The mouth is open with four upper teeth, and the sleep eyes can be green, blue, or brown. *Patsy Baby-Kin*. 8"-9", 10", all composition with bent baby legs. Will be marked: Patsy Baby, Baby Tinyette and Patsy Babyette, but all advertised as *Patsy Baby-kin*. Came with molded hair as well as caracul wigs. Brown or blue glass or tin eyes. Came as twins, and as girl or boy. There are also black *Patsy Baby-kins*, especially in 1936 (see that year). *Patsy Fluff* and *Patriciakin*. There is no information on these dolls, and the name just shows up in 1932 ads with no pictures. *New Bubbles*. With all rubber body, bent baby style legs and both arms slightly curved. The doll was strung so she had posable limbs. The head was composition with open mouth, molded hair and sleep eyes and uses the Lovums style head rather than the conventional Bubbles head. This would be a rare find, indeed. As rubber does not keep well, so few may have survived. *"Home Magazine"* of December, 1932 shows a *Patsy* in riding habit, jodhpurs, jacket and brimmed cap. Snow suit with zipper boots and cap for *Patsy Ann*. Also white fur coat, fur hat and white zipper boots on a *Patsy*. *Wee Patsy* in Naval officer's uniform and with sewing machine. *Patsy Ann* in a jumper dress, wide collar, short sleeved blouse and *Patsy Joan* in pleated skirt and knit sweater and bonnet. Both *Patsy Ann* and *Patsy Joan* were also available in a trunk with a wardrobe.
1933: *Popeye*. 16" all cloth. *Betty Brite* 16" all cloth. *Betty Brite* 16½" all composition, straight leg girl with curly caracul wig. *Kali-Ko-Kate*. All cloth with painted features (flat face). *Baby Tinyette*. 8" All composition. Straight or bent legs, painted eyes and molded hair. *Baby Bubbles*. 11" to 18" with all rubber body and limbs and composition head. Molded hair and brown sleep eyes, open mouth. *Dy-*

Dee Baby with rubber bodies by Miller Rubber Co. *Dy-Dee Wee*-9", *Dy-Dee-Ette*-11", *Dy-Dee-Kin*-13", *Dy-Dee Baby*-15" and *Dy-Dee Lou*-20".

The December, 1936 "*Fortune Magazine*" had an article about dolls in which is said, "Effanbee, which has been selling *Dy-Dees* by the carload for the past two years (it didn't get really started the first year) and doing a smart business in layettes and appurtenances right along. Dydee's rubber parts are made in Akron by the Miller Rubber Company, Inc., with soft rubber for the body and hard rubber for the head. Inside, Dydee works somewhat more simply than the infant it mimics (drink and wet feature). The bottle empties into a tube through which the water is pulled by suction when the stomach is pressed; the exit is a valve, which holds the water back for a while so as not to confuse the young mother about nature's tempo. A Miss Marie Wittman, middleaged language teacher in Brooklyn, got the idea from no one knows where, brought it in to Mr. (Hugo) Baum, who fell for it at once. Not everyone does. In England some Dy-Dees were put on display at Harrod's and promptly removed when patrons pronounced them vulgar. But the Duchess of Kent came in and asked for one soon after, whereupon they began to go very well.

Mr. Baum who takes joy in being referred to as "the Ziegfeld of the doll industry", thinks *Dy-Dee* embodies a basic advance...and there is Effanbee's merchandising, probably the most consistent in the business. He helps Aunt Patsy send out 250,00 copies of a *Patsytown News* promotion piece four times a year and in between times gives parties in department store toy sections.

Dy-Dee gets competition from three or four dolls cast in it's general type, but mostly from one put out by American Character Doll Company, Inc. That company began by calling it's doll *Wee Wee*. Outraged by what they considered plagiarism, Messrs. Fleischaker and Baum marched into court. *Dy-Dee* won. *Wee Wee* was changed to *Bottletot*. This year (1936) American Character has *Marvel-tot*, which justifies its name by twisting its mouth into a grin or pout along with looking normally dumb and wetting its pants" ...end of quote from "*Fortune Magazine*".

1934: The *Patsy Mae* was introduced in 1934 and can be 28" or 30" tall. She has the regular Patsy style composition head with sleep eyes and has a wig. The body is cloth with a composition shoulder plate that is marked: Effanbee/Lovums/Pat. No. 1283558 and the head is marked: Effanbee/Patsy Mae. This year *Patsy* was issued dressed as Red Riding Hood, and using the *Patsy* body with a composition head, both a *Wolf*, and *Grandma*, were available. The *Three Pigs* came out this year also.

1935: *Baby Wonder*, was new this year. All composition baby with sleep eyes and molded hair. Came with celluloid hand/bottle, as well as with composition hands. *Judy Doll*, no information. *Mary Lee*- (Anne of Green Gables) *Anne Of Green Gables* in 14"-22" and 28" sizes. This is the real Anne Shirley doll. *Anne Shirley* (Patricia-*Little Lady* marks). This first year she came in 9"-12" and 15. *Fairy Princess* (Wee Patsy). 5"-5½"- all composition. The *Wee Patsy* was never meant to represent the Princess of the Colleen Moore Castle, but the tie in was effective as the doll was to scale. The *Fairy Princess* doll came packaged in a replica castle and also with a cardboard case with change of clothes. Each wore a pin stating: Colleen Moore/Fairy Princess/An Effanbee/Doll. Colleen Moore was a movie star of the silent era that moved into "talkies" successfully. The famous doll house castle took from 1928 to 1935 to complete, and wanting to share the beauty with the public, Miss

Moore used it in many fund raising affairs and then moved it on permanent loan to the Museum of Science and Industry in Chicago in 1949. She presented it as a gift to the same museum in 1976.

1936: *Patsy Ruth* was added to the Patsy family this year and will be found from 25" to 27" tall, all composition in the taller size, and with a cloth body with a composition shoulder plate in the smaller sizes. Sleep eyes and wigs, and will be marked on head: Effanbee/Patsy Ruth. Will be marked: Effanbee/Lovums/Pat No. 1283558, on the shoulder plate. *Patsy, Patsy Joan* and *Patsy Ann* were all available with a small insert of celluloid on the fingers, so that they could be polished. This may have been exclusive to FAO Schwarz. *Sugar Baby* came in 20", 23"-24" with a cloth body and composition head and limbs. Had a caracul wig, and an open mouth with two upper teeth.

Amosandra was "born" to Amos and Ruby of the famous Amos and Andy radio show during the 1936 season, and gifts from listeners were showered on the shows stars. Effanbee made *Patsy Baby-kin* and *Baby Grumpy* into a black doll with three tufts of yarn hair. The doll must be marked Effanbee to be real Amosandra, as there were many dolls introduced at this time (see photo in this book). *River Brethren* and *Pennsylvania Dutch* dolls of the 7"-9" and 12" are all composition with painted eyes and are made from the *Grumpy* molds. Through gift shops the following are known to have been available: Pennsylvania Dutch family of mother, father and boy and girl. Amish, Mennonite were also available as a family group, or sold separately. These dolls are also called "The Plains Group". (Focusing). Effanbee signs Dewees Cochran to a contract to do four models that would be 15", 18" and 21" tall. This group is to be called *America's Children*, and were advertised as such, but also as *Portraits Of America's Children*, *American Children* and *Portrait Children*. Dewees Cochran was a remarkable lady for the times, and right into today. Recommended reading is her own book "As If They Might Speak" printed in 1979. During 1934 Dewees perfected her six basic types. During 1934 "*Harpers's Bazaar*" carried a photograph of one of her dolls in the shopping section, and soon after she met and went to work for Madame Alexander designing doll heads, soft body dolls, original characters, costumes and animals. This was a short term contract, and Dewees continued in other areas of her doll making. In December of 1934 Dewees was introduced to Messrs. Fleischaker and Baum of Effanbee by the Vice President of FAO Schwarz, and she signed a contract for three years, soon after that meeting. She was to make up sample complete dolls before the March 1935 toy fair, and working many hours a day completed the task. She immediately began work on the four chosen models and making the 21" bodies as well. She made and delivered the first four plaster models in mid-May. Effanbee had completed this line by June of 1936. These Portrait Dolls of American Children came in 21" size, all composition with the special material arms and hands designed by Dewees Cochran with wide open fingers, and the first dolls to be able to wear gloves. They came with sleep eyes and painted eyes. All these dolls are fully marked. Of the four models, the one with painted eyes, a full mouth and rather sad expression was marketed as *Peggy Lou*. One model with sleep eyes and thinner closed mouth was called *Gloria Ann*. The *Barbara Lou* model came with closed, as well as open mouth (1939) and the other model was called *Ruth Ann*.

1937: *Charlie McCarthy.* Ventriloquist doll. Marionettes: *Clippo Clown, Emily Ann. Lucifer, Liza Lee, Poochie (dog).*

These marionettes were designed by the famous puppeteer Virginia Austin, and founded the "Clippo Club" as part of the promotion. *Mary Ann* in 14", 16", 20" and 22" sizes. All composition, open mouth and wig. The *American Children* came in 17"-18" and 20"-21".

1938: 19" *Sweetie Pie* with flirty eyes in 2-piece plush snowsuit. Has hood with high peaked cap - maribou fur at neck, around sleeves and collar. 11" *Nurse.* An order of these same dolls were made for the Alexander Doll Company during 1936-37 when Alexander's own plants could not handle the amount of orders for their dolls. *American Children* in four models in 15"-18" and 21" sizes. These dolls were produced to 1940. *Ice Queen,* marketed also as *Betty Ann,* came in 15" size with open mouth and inset teeth. The sleep eyes and open mouth of this doll caused a lot of problems, and production was not as great as in the other models. Dewees Cochran also designed a man and woman that was 12" tall for Effanbee this year. 8" *Button Nose* - all composition, painted eyes to side, molded hair, dressed in various International outfits. 1938 Ward's show 15", 17½" and 21" *Ann Shirley* (Little Lady) with blonde hair in coronet braids around head, curls in front, pink straw hat. Dewees Cochran designed arms and wide spread fingers and she is dressed in sheer pink and blue dotted swiss short dress, blue dimity pinafore with pocket and scalloped ruffles and pink side high button shoes. *N. Shure Co.* Catalog of 1938 shows Boudoir Dolls: *Ella*-24", *Marietta*-27", *Ginger Curls*-23", *Florence*-31", *Bride*-28" and *Elizabeth*-29". Also a 16"-*Sonja On Skates* with caption "Effanbee has captured the very expression of her famous namesake". She has human hair wig, white taffeta skate outfit with maribou trim.

1939: Catalogs carried the 11¼" *Suzette* in check gingham dress and bonnet with both the names of *Susie* and *Sunbonnet Sue.* Suzette was used for a series of Internationals, including a molded head Hawaiian. 7"-11" *Grumpy* as *Plains People/River Brethern. Sweetie Pie.* 16", 19"-20", 24". Cloth and composition baby with closed mouth and molded or caracul wig and flirty eyes. Also advertised as *Touslehead. Mickey Baby.* 15", 18", 20", 24". Cloth and composition with straight legs. Closed mouth and came with molded hair as well as caracul wigs. *Patsy Ann* in the 18" that is composition and cloth with key wind music box that plays "Happy Birthday". *Boo-Hoo* and *Ha-Ha,* all rubber squeeze toys with molded on clothes. *Pat-O-Pat,* all cloth. 15"-16" and 18" with painted eyes to the side, little girl. *Suzette,* 11". All composition, painted eyes to the side, and also sleep eyes. Came with molded hair, as well as a wig. *Little Lady* with and without the Dewees designed hands. Came in 15", 19", 22", 27", 29". All composition and marked *Anne Shirley,* or just Effanbee on back. *Little Lady* to 1949 in the 14"-15" size was packed in suitcase with 19 piece wardrobe. The doll came dressed in a striped dimity evening dress. The right arm is slightly bent at the elbow, and each finger is separated, but are shorter and fatter than the "Dewees hands". *Dy-Dee* with hard rubber head and soft rubber body and limbs came in 11", 15", and 20" sizes. A 19-piece layette was available for the doll. *Touslehead* with cloth body, composition head and limbs, sleep eyes, caracul wig. Came in the 18" size with an automatic mechanism phonograph that plays "Now I Lay Me Down To Sleep". List of additional records included with each doll. Dressed in pajamas and flowered flannel bathrobe. *Portrait doll (American Children* design), and called "Magazine Cover Doll". 20", sleep eyes with hair lashes. Human hair blonde wig in page boy set, composition with the arms and

hands of hard rubber, and separate fingers. Came in pink velvet dress with small white collar, white imitation leather shoes, rayon hose and large hair bow. This doll is same "face" that appeared on the cover of the April 3, 1939 "*Life Magazine*", and still being called "Cover Doll" in 1940. The arms are composition, but smaller hands with the second and third fingers together and curled into the palm. *Birthday Doll.* Swiss music box in body, 17" and composition. Sleep eyes, closed mouth Ice Queen face, with the Dewees hard rubber arms and hands that will take gloves. Blue velvet dress and hat, lace trim and four pearl buttons. *Historical Sets.* There were three sets with thirty dolls to each set. The sets depicted fashions from an Indian maid of 1492 through the "sophisticate" of 1939. The sets were 20"-21", all composition with hard rubber arms and marked "*Ann Shirley*".

The eyes are painted with dots around the edges of the lashes, and the brows are dotted. The materials used were very elaborate with the use of velvets, satins and beautiful laces. These sets were displayed across the U.S. in department stores, and at the same time 14" replicas of each of the historical dolls were sold. Lesser, but still fine materials were used on the smaller dolls. The 14" has the *Little Lady* head, and marked "Anne Shirley" body, along with the Dewees Cochran hard rubber arms with separate fingers. The eyes are also painted.

1940: *Dy-Dee's* names are by sizes: *Dy-De Kins, Dy-Deette, Dy-Dee Jane, Dy-Dee Louise, Dy-Dee Ellen.* Hard molded rubber heads with rubber body and limbs. Molded or caracul hair. Came in many ways, such as in trunk, suitcase, play pen, etc. *Tommy Tucker,* all composition, and also cloth and composition, flirty eyes, closed mouth and caracul wig. (Baby Bright Eyes mold). 17" *River Brethern/Plains Doll* were available again this year. The *Baby Bright Eyes* came with flirty eyes, was 20" and all composition with molded hair or caracul wigs. (Tommy Tucker). *Suzanne.* 14", all composition with sleep eyes. Some used by F.A.O. Schwarz to have magnets placed in hands to hold different items. Schwarz also used *Skippy* and *Patricia* with magnets this year. Also available this year: *Patsy Baby, Patsy Joan, Sugar Baby, Little Lady. Portrait Dolls.* 12" All composition with sleep eyes and wigs. Came as Ballerina. Little Bo Peep, Gibson Girl, Bride and Groom and Kate Greenaway style boy and girl. *Babykin.* All composition from 9" to 12" with molded hair. Came as boy and girl, and twins. (to 1949). *Babykin* and *Suzette* (both with molded hair) were sold in 1940 John Plain's catalog in a trunk and called "*Baby And Big Sister*". The 11" *Suzette* (molded hair) was also sold separately in trunk with extra clothes, but was called "*Bea*". 1940 John Plain catalog shows 17½" *Patsy Ann* with music box, 21" and 17½" *Portrait* dolls (*American Children*) 15" *Ann Shirley* that does not have Dewees Cochran designed hands. *Dydee* in 9¾", 11¾", 13¾", sleep eyes, 14" with sleep eyes/lashes and both are all rubber and called Dy-Dee's cousin, "The Wonder Doll", full joints, nurser.

1941: Mollye Goldman designed the 1941 line of doll clothes for Effanbee. *Little Lady* with key wound music box that plays Happy Birthday. *Tousle Tot Twins.* 8" (*Patsy Babyette*). All composition, sleep eyes and caracul wig. Continuation of several of the 1940 dolls.

1942: Most factories were making items for the war effort, and many materials could not be gotten for making dolls. When the supply of wigs ran out, Effanbee used yarn for the hair, and when they could no longer use composition for bodies or limbs, they made cloth bodies. *Brother And Sister.* Yarn hair, painted eyes. The Baby Bright Eyes and Sweetie pie molds were used. The dolls had cloth bodies and rest composition. *Bright Eyes* came in boy and girl sets. *Miss Glamour Girl. Babyette.* Sleeping and awake babies (also marked:*Baby-Et).* Cloth and composition heads and hands to the wrists. Painted eyes, open and closed eyes. *Little Lady* in many outfits including blue cotton with red lined cape military outfit. Some with yarn hair and some with mohair wigs. *Heartbeat Baby* 17" cloth and full composition arms and legs. The arms are bent at the elbow. Has clock work mechanism that is key wound to achieve "heartbeat". Came boxed with stethoscope. Open mouth and molded hair. It was November 2, 1940 when Hugo Baum passed away and after that B. E. Fleischaker moved to California to begin a business: "Fleischaker Novelties" that made some of the most collectable dolls of that period. The Effanbee Company was left in the capable hands of the two men's sons, Bernard Baum and Walter Fleischaker, along with the well trained and knowledgeable, Al Kirchof, Perry Epstein and Morris Lutz. 1942 Ward's catalog has two sewing kit dolls-5½" *Wee Patsy* and 9½" *"Susie"* with pre-cut wardrobes to be sewn. The 9½" *Susie's* included a Nurses Uniform.

1943: The little 8" *Button Nose* was heavily marketed this year mainly because of her size, and because she adapted to molded hair. All composition with eyes painted to the sides. *Today's Girl* 18" (Little Lady Doll) with yarn hair, painted eyes and pink cloth body. *Baby Button Nose. Centerpiece Bride.* (Little Lady). *Black Little Lady,* and a *Black Touslehead* were made this year. *Skippy* in military uniforms. Contest run by *"Everywomen's Magazine"* gave a *Little Lady Doll* as a grand prize. Ward's carried a Little Lady Jig Saw Puzzle of 16 dolls. 18", 19", 24" *Sweetie Pie (Tousle-Tot).* Flirty eyes and in white or black. 14" *Mickey* as twins (boy and girl cloth bodies, composition heads and limbs - dressed in 2-piece snow suits and bonnets and with trunk and clothes. *Black Little Lady/Ann Shirley. Bride Little Lady* in white satin, seed pearls on head piece.

1944: A new addition this year in new materials was *Beautee-Skin Baby* that came in 14", 17" and 19" sizes. Composition head on a latex jointed body and limbs. Sleep eyes and molded hair. 12" *Babyette* eyes molded closed. Sold in basket.

1945: Nothing new was added this year, the war had taken a toll on the majority of the doll industry.

1946: Re-issue of the 18" musical girl (Happy Birthday). *Candy Kid.* 13"-14", all composition with blue or brown sleep eyes. Molded hair and came in many different outfits and packs with clothes. There was a special Easter Promotion for 1947 with the *Candy kid* dressed in yellow, and same dress in pink was shown in the 1946 catalogs. *Little Lady* was a popular doll again this year. Re-issue *Patsy.* 13"-13½", all composition with painted eyes and sleep eyes. (to 1949). Also came black *Patsy Joan,* 17" re-issue. All composition with sleep eyes of brown or blue, molded hair or wig. Also made black *Baby Bright Eyes* re-issue of cloth and composition, glassene sleep eyes, molded hair. During 1946, Effanbee as well as many other companies, found they were in financial difficulty, and in 1947 the company was sold. The metal wrist bracelet with heart was discontinued.

1947: Noma Electric bought the Effanbee business and were to keep the ownership into 1953. Produced this year, along with models from earlier years were: *Howdy Doody. Lil' Darlin.* Cloth and early vinyl with open/closed mouth,

painted eyes, molded hair. Re-issue *Patsy Babyettes.* All composition, wigs over molded hair and sleep eyes.

1948: *Honey,* composition that came in 20"-21" to 27" sizes and used the Dewees designed hands and arms (*Little Lady).* The *Honey* this year came with flirty, as well as regular sleep eyes. *Little Lady* came in several different outfits which included a majorette. *Sweetie Pie,* cloth body, composition head, arms and legs. Flirty eyes, and caracul wig (also called *Tousle-Tot).* Came in 19" and 24" sizes. *Dy-Dee* came in 11" and 15" rubber body and hard rubber head. Caracul wig and sleep eyes. Also available in suitcase with wardrobe. Marionettes: *Macawful The Scot.*

1949: *Honey* and *Little Lady* were still in composition. (MCD-2). *Babykin,* 9", 12". Hard plastic head, latex body. Caracul wig or molded hair. 25" to 30" *Noma Talker's* were made with both molded hair and glued on wigs. 27"-28" *Mommy's Baby* hard plastic/cloth/early vinyl.

1950: A few of the dolls were available in composition during this time of changing from one material to another. *Babyette* with hard plastic head came with molded hair or glued on wig, sleep eyes and as boy and girl twins. *Honey-Walker,* all hard plastic, closed mouth (there were several copies with open mouths, by other companies). Came in many outfits with various wigs, also as a boy. 16", 18", 21", 24" and 28" sizes this year. The 16" and 18" was used for a Majorette and one 21" size with flirty eyes was made in composition. A 19" size came in trunk with a wardrobe. *Little Lady* in hard plastic with a vinyl head. *Dy-Dee* with rubber body and limbs and hard plastic head. Molded hair or wig. 11", 15" and 20" *Howdy Doody.* Cloth and hard plastic with sleep eyes. *Mommy's Baby,* hard plastic and latex. Came with sleep eyes, molded hair or caracul wig and as a boy or a girl. 16", 19", 22" and 25" sizes. *Noma's Electronic Talking Doll* 28" with cloth body, hard plastic head, vinyl arms. Open mouth and molded hair. Push button, battery operated.

1951: *Mommy's Baby* in sizes 17", 21", and 28". *Tintair,* all hard plastic. Came with dynel wig and in rayon taffeta dress, 14", 16", and 18". *Dy-Dee* in 11", 15", and 20" same as 1950. *Lil' Darlin,* available as twins and quads, or separately, 13" and 16". Cloth with vinyl head and limbs. Molded hair, painted eyes, open/closed mouth and cryer box. (MCD-1&2). *Sweetie Pie,* 27" with cloth body, hard plastic head and vinyl arms. This was the *Noma Electronic Talker* without the talker mechanism and with caracul wig over molded hair (some came with molded hair also). The *Noma Talker* was also available this year, and could come in English, French, or Spanish. A line of Elsa Schiaparelli dolls (18") were sold through Neiman-Marcus.

1952: By 1952 the use of hard plastics had become extensive and the quality of this era would not be repeated. During this time span of less than ten years, not only the quality of the dolls themselves are important to the collector, but also the quality of the clothing was the best ever. This year Effanbee followed their pattern of excellence and had on the market a set of hard plastic doll house dolls. *Patsy Babyette,* hard plastic with sleep eyes, with molded hair or caracul wig in the 9" and 11" sizes. Also came as twins. *Mommy's Baby,* 27" cloth with early vinyl arms and legs, hard plastic shoulder plate and head. Open mouth with two upper teeth. Came as boy or girl. *Baby Twinkie. Dy-Dee.* Same as 1951. *Baby-Kins,* hard plastic with sleep eyes and molded hair, 9" and 11". *Honey Girl,* all hard plastic with sleep eyes, closed mouth (ran from 1949 to 1955). Came in five school outfits, majorette, traveler, Prince Charming, Cinderella, Bride formals, cheerleader, as Lucinda from the book "Roller Skates" by Ruth Sawyer. This outfit was an old fashioned dress, special wig, high button boots and skates tied to the wrist. *Re-Issue Ann Shirley*, hard plastic and dressed in formals. *Honey Ann*, 24″ hard plastic walker with sleep eyes and dressed in formals. *Mickey*, cloth with vinyl limbs and hard plastic head. Sleep eyes, closed mouth with molded hair or caracul wig. Boys outfits. *Howdy Doody* in two sizes. *Lil' Darlin'*, new born baby that also came as twins or quads. *Portraits*, 12″ hard plastic in picture boxes. *Bo Peep*, *Bride* and *Groom*, *Majorette*, *Gibson Girl* and *Southern Belle*. *Tv Puppets. Jambo* (Black), *Kilroy*, *Toonga* (Black) and *Pimbo* (Clown). FAO Schwarz offered 11″ *Dydee-Ette* in standing wicker basket with wardrobe. *Dydee* also came in 11″ and 15″ with layette with caracul wig. 15″ *Tintair* (Honey) with trousseau case, and regular *Tintair* in 15″ and 19″ sizes.

1953: *Honey*, 18″ in fourteen different Schiaparelli outfits. (Heart. MCD-1). *Honey Walker*, 15″, 18″, 21″ and 25″. With jointed knees and ankles, hard plastic with vinyl arms. Came dressed as skater and ballerina. *Melodie*, 30″ with vinyl head, sleep eyes and hard plastic body and legs. Jointed knees. Talking mechanism in body. Cost in 1953 was $29.95. Battery operated. *Cuddle Up*, 20″, 23″, and 27″ with vinyl head and legs, vinyl coated cloth body and sleep eyes. Open mouth with two teeth and came with molded hair as well as rooted. *Noma Talker* available. *Dy-Dee* one piece stuffed body and legs with disc jointed stuffed vinyl arms. Vinyl head with open/closed mouth. Sleep eyes.

1954: *Patricia Walker*, 15″, 19″, 21″, and 25″. Hard plastic with vinyl head, rooted hair and sleep eyes. All sizes came in formals this year. (*Cissy* look-a-like). *Fluffy*, 8″, 12″, all vinyl with rooted hair and sleep eyes. Had many outfits, including Girl Scouts, etc. 8″ came also as Campfire and Bluebird. *Candy Walker*, 12″ plastic with vinyl head and rooted hair, inset glassene eyes. (*Candy Kid* on straight leg plastic body). *Candy kid*, all vinyl with sleep eyes, molded hair and came as boy, girl or twins. *Candy Ann*, 20″, 24″, 29″, vinyl coated body, vinyl head and legs, sleep eyes and rooted hair. *Little Lady*, all vinyl with sleep eyes and rooted hair with center bangs and rest of hair pulled back into finger curls (sausage curls). Packed with Little Lady Toiletries designed by Helene Pessl, Inc. Old fashioned outfit with pantaloons. *Katy*, 13″ vinyl coated body, vinyl head and limbs. Inset glassene eyes. *Rootie Kazootie* and *Polka Dottie*, 21″ vinyl head and limbs vinyl coated body. Boy has spray painted hair with molded on hat, hers is molded too. Large painted eyes, open/closed mouths. Both also came in the 11″ size with vinyl heads and latex bodies and limbs. *Honeykins*, 12″ all hard plastic with sleep eyes and glued on wig. *Christening Baby*, 20″ all vinyl with molded hair, sleep eyes and open/closed mouth. *Cuddle-Up* girl or boy, same as in 1953, but different clothes. *Howdy Doody Still Available. Dy-Dee* came in 11″, 15″ and 20″ sizes. *Honey Walker* in 15″, 19″, 21″, and 25″. All hard plastic. The 15″ size came in a suitcase/trunk and the 15″ and 19″ came with a rain set and dog on a leash.

1955: *Tiny Tubber*, 10″ all vinyl with spray painted hair and available with layettes. *Mary Jane*, 32″ vinyl and rigid vinyl, with flirty sleep eyes and a walker. *Lil' Darlin'*, 16″ all vinyl with sleep eyes and rooted hair. *Christening Baby*, 14″ and 20″. All vinyl, sleep eyes and spray painted hair. *Rusty and Sherry*, from the *Make Room For Daddy* A.B.C. Television show. He has deeply molded hair, sleep eyes and has a vinyl head. She has pigtail hairdo, an open/closed mouth and her body may be hard plastic. *Patricia Walker*, 22″ all hard plastic and head turns. *Howdy Doody* still

available. *Cuddle Up* in 23″ size. Names for *Dydee* in *F.A.O. Schwarz* Catalogs are: 9″ *Dydee Wee*, 11″ Dydee Ellen, 15″ Dydee Jane and 20″ as *Dydee-Lu, Lou and Louise*.

1956: *Dy-Dee Baby* in 11″, 15″ and 20″ sizes. Vinyl body and limbs with hard plastic head. Sleep eyes, molded hair or caracul wig. Available in layettes and cases. *Mickey*, The All American Boy. All vinyl with painted eyes and molded hair/hats & caps. Available in 12 different outfits, and in 20 different by 1958. Rarest of the Mickey's apparently is the painted face clown. *Baby Twinkie*, *Candy Walker*, 24″ hard plastic, pin through hips walker, head turns and arms are strung. Vinyl head with sleep eyes and rooted hair. *Babykin*, 10″ with hard plastic head, vinyl body and limbs. Was a special Birthday doll throughout 1956. Organdy and lace over pink taffeta and bonnet. *Melodie*, 30″ same as 1953, but shown in Montgomery Ward's as "new".

1957: *Tiny Fluffy*, 8½″ all vinyl with sleep eyes and rooted hair. *Katie*, 8½″ all vinyl and same as *Tiny Fluffy* with molded hair. *Most Happy Family*. Mother, 19″ and 21″ lady doll of rigid vinyl, vinyl head, sleep eyes and rooted hair. *Mother, Fluffy* 8½″ & 10″, *Mickey* 8″ & 10″, and *Tiny Tubber* 8″ came packaged in a family group. *Dy-Dee* came in three sizes and was called: *Dy Dee Ellen, Dy Dee Jane, Dy Dee Lu. Lawrence Welk's Champagne Lady*. Rigid vinyl body, hard plastic legs jointed at knees and ankles, vinyl arms and head. Sleep blue eyes and rooted hair.

1958: *My Fair Baby*, 14″, 18″, and 22″. The 22″ size does not look like the other My Fair Babies, but used the Bubbles head. All vinyl with sleep eyes and either molded hair or rooted. Open mouth/nurser. *My Precious Baby*, 20″ all vinyl with extra joints at knee and elbows. Rooted, or molded hair, sleep eyes and open mouth/nurser. *Bubbles*, 23″ vinyl coated cloth body, vinyl head and limbs, sleep eyes, molded or rooted hair. *Toddle Tot*, 13″, 19″, 22″, all vinyl toddler, sleep eyes, rooted hair and open mouth/nurser. Also came with molded hair. *Little Lady* 19″, all vinyl, sleep eyes and rooted hair. *Alice* 15″, 19″, all vinyl, sleep eyes and rooted hair. *Junior Miss* (Alice in 15″ and 21″) with rigid vinyl body and vinyl arms and head. Ballerina, walker with jointed ankles. Came as a Bride and Bridesmaid in the 21″ size with jointed ankles and knees. *Happy Family*, sets came in two sizes: 21″, 8″ and 10″, and 19″, 8″ and 8″. *Alyssia*, 19½″ with hard plastic body and limbs. Walker and head turns. Vinyl head with closed mouth smile, rooted hair. *Dy-Dee*, 12″, 17″ and 21″ sizes with vinyl body and limbs and hard plastic head. Came with molded hair or wig. *Dy-Dee Baby* in 12″, 17″ and 21″ sizes. All vinyl with hard plastic head. and rubber ears.

1959: *Patsy*, 11″ all vinyl with sleep eyes and rooted hair. *Toddler* using the Twinkie style face, not a Patsy type face. *Patsy Ann*, 15″ vinyl head on rigid vinyl body and legs. Sleep eyes and rooted hair. Came in many outfits and packed with a wardrobe. Some had jointed waists. *Patsy Ann* was the official Girl Scout doll and also used for the Brownie doll, with both these available with wardrobe in a box. During 1959 *Patsy Ann* was promoted as the *July 4th Holiday Doll* in tam and bodice of red, white pleated skirt and red shoes. *Twinkie*, 15″-16″ all vinyl baby with molded or rooted hair, bent legs and open mouth/nurser. *Sugar Baby*, 18″ and same as *My Fair Baby*, but tiltable head. Came with both molded and rooted hair, and also sold in a bassinette. *Sugar Pie*, 18″ same as *Sugar Baby*, but in fleece coat and hood. This version also came in a 22″ size. *Suzette*, 15″ all vinyl with tiltable head, sleep eyes and rooted hair. Open/closed mouth with painted teeth and came dressed as Bride, BoPeep and in five other dresses.

Alyssa, 23" rigid vinyl and vinyl with jointed elbows, tiltable head, rooted hair and sleep eyes. Came in two different outfits. *Boudoir Doll*, 28" with vinyl head, sleep eyes and rooted hair. *Toddle Tot*, same, but called *Nap Time Gal*, in Sears catalog. *Fluffy* in Sears catalog was 11" and came with four outfits, and six other outfits are shown in the Effanbee catalog. *Mary Jane*, 32" flirty eye walker of plastic and vinyl. Came in three outfits, including a nurse. *Lil Darlin'*, 13" and 16" all vinyl with sleep eyes and either rooted or molded hair. *Babykin*, 8" all vinyl with sleep eyes and molded hair. Open mouth/nurser. *Tiny Tubber*, 10½" all vinyl sleep eyes, molded or rooted hair and open mouth/nurser. *Dydee*, 17" hard plastic head with vinyl body and limbs. Came with wig or molded hair and in a suitcase with layette. *Happy Boy*, 11" all vinyl with painted features (eyes closed) and in three outfits. *My Fair Baby*, 14" all vinyl with sleep eyes, open mouth/nurser. Had a squeeze body cryer and ID bracelet. *Little Lady*, 20" all vinyl with sleep eyes and rooted hair. One outfit was a Bride. *Suzie Sunshine*, 18" plastic and vinyl with sleep eyes and rooted hair, also available in nine different outfits. *My Precious Baby*, 22" cloth and vinyl, open mouth/nurser and had cryer. Sleep eyes and ID bracelet. Available in six different outfits, also in basket on tall legs. *Mickey* was available in twenty different outfits: Baseball, football, policeman, soldier, sailor, fireman, Boy Scout, Air Cadet, Marine, Boxer (with and without robe), Cub Scout, cowboy, hunter, bellboy, jockey, clown, sport outfit, Johnny Reb, Yankee Boy. Some have molded hats. *Sweetie Pie*, 22" in 3 outfits, molded or rooted hair. All vinyl nurser.

1960: *Alyssa and Bud*, 24" rigid vinyl with vinyl heads, sleep eyes, she has rooted hair and he has very deeply molded hair. *Bettina*, 16" all vinyl toddler, sleep eyes and closed mouth with dimples. This same doll was also sold as *Susie Sunshine*. *Happy Boy*, same as 1959. *Bubbles*, 23" with vinyl coated cloth body, vinyl head and limbs. Rooted hair, cryer, and open/closed mouth. *My Fair Baby*, 20" and 22" cloth and vinyl with sleep eyes, rooted hair and open/closed mouth. *My Precious Baby*, same as 1959, but different outfits. *Mickey*, same as 1959. *Mary Jane*, same as 1959 in different outfits. *Most Happy Family*, same as 1959 in different clothes. *Fluffy*, same as 1959 with change of outfits.

1961: *Suzie Sunshine*, 17"-18" all vinyl toddler. Rooted hair, sleep eyes and freckles. Came in black and white. This doll is being made still and the marks will be the same year. The use of a plastic body and legs started in 1962. *Most Happy Family* this year came in sizes: 19", two 8½" and 8". *Twinkie*, 16" all vinyl with jointed knees, squeeze cryer, ID bracelet, sleep eyes and molded hair.

1962: *Gumdrop*, 16" all vinyl with sleep eyes and rooted hair. Closed mouth smile. This doll has been used continuously through the years. *Precious Baby*, 24"-25" cloth and vinyl with rooted hair and sleep eyes, and open/closed mouth. *Belle Telle*, Registered #140,248 on March 20, 1962. Came with telephone on stand (battery operated that held a record player. Hand is molded to hold the telephone. Has Suzie Sunshine body, but different head. *Precious New Born*, 14" rooted hair, painted eyes and deeply molded open/closed mouth. *Mary Jane*, 32" plastic and vinyl with flirty eyes and freckles. *Susie Sunshine*, 18" with white rooted hair and came with cradle and white haired 14" baby that had a cloth body and vinyl head and limbs. Painted eyes on baby. Came in matching pajamas. She also came in a sailor suit. *Alyssa*, 15" as: Blue Bird, Campfire Girl, Girl Scout & Brownie. Plastic and vinyl with sleep eyes and

rooted hair. *Fluffy*, 11" all vinyl and in four outfits. *Alyssa* in the 24" size available as was the 11" *Mickey*.
1963: *Baby Winkie* 10" all vinyl with sleep eyes and molded hair. *Sweetie Pie*, 12" & 14" all vinyl, open mouth/nurser, cryer, rooted hair and sleep eyes. *Baby Butterball*, 12" all vinyl, bent legs, sleep eyes and rooted hair. *Baby Cupcake*, 12" all vinyl toddler with deep dimples, open mouth with no wetting hole. Sold in 1964 through Sears catalog. 1963 started a tradition of elegantly dressed dolls from Effanbee and included: *My Baby*, 23" cloth and vinyl with sleep eyes and dressed in red velveteen. *Susie Sunshine*, 18" freckles, dressed in red velveteen jumper. *Twinkie*, 15" in red cotton velveteen dress, also in dotted Swiss dress with red velveteen bodice and came on pillow. *Mary Jane Toddler*, 13" (small *Suzie Sunshine*) with red velveteen bodice and white skirt. Sears carried the "Sugar Plum" collection this year (see 1963 this book) and The Suzie Sunshine as "Schoolgirl Writing Doll".
1964: *Babykin*, 8½" all vinyl with bent legs, molded hair and sleep eyes. Open mouth/nurser. *My Fair Baby*, 12" & 22" all vinyl with bent baby legs, sleep eyes, open mouth/nurser, molded hair. *Sugar Plum*, 18" cloth and vinyl with sleep eyes, closed mouth dressed in pink and white. *Bettina*, plastic and vinyl with same body as *Susie Sunshine* and marketed the same. The special dressed dolls for this year are listed by name and are dressed in bright kelly green and white. *Gumdrop*, 16" which was also offered by S & H Green Stamps dressed in red and white. *Sweetie Pie*, 16" came with pillow and in all white dress of eyelet. *Baby Cupcake* also came dressed in pink and white. *Candy Kid*, 11" also dressed in pink and white. *Sugar Pie*, 24" also sold in pink coat and bonnet with muff. *Honey* (*Susie Sunshine*) with freckles and red-orange rooted hair. Green dress, bloomers and head band.
1965: *Miss Chips*, 18" all vinyl and in several different outfits. *Chipper*, 14"-15" plastic with vinyl arms, legs, and head. *Thum'Kin*, 24" cloth and vinyl with rooted hair, sleep eyes and wide/open/closed mouth. *Peaches*, 15" cloth and vinyl, rooted hair, sleep eyes and dimples. *Twinkie*, 16" with rooted hair and sleep eyes in two outfits. 16" all vinyl with sleep eyes and molded hair, I.D. bracelet in two different outfits, plus was available in box with layette. 18" cloth and vinyl, rooted hair, sleep eyes and closed mouth. *Peaches and Cream Group: Baby Peaches* sold on pillow, all vinyl and in white with peach ribbons. *Dydee Baby* sold in sacque and blanket that was white with peach trim. *Sweetie Pie*, 18" cloth and vinyl and dressed in white dress with peach coat and bonnet. *Gumdrop*, 16" white hair and dress with peach coat and hat. *Gumdrop*, 18" auburn hair, white velveteen dress with organdy ruffle at hem and peach ribbons. *My Baby*, 14" cloth and vinyl, hand painted eyes, rooted hair and cryer. (looks close to Vogue's *Baby Dear*). Left hand has 2nd and 3rd finger curled into palm. Right hand 1st finger extended away from others. Came in polka dot flannel sleep saque in ruffle trimmed flannel pillow with pocket for baby, organdy Christening gown with lace trim and matching bonnet, and in lace ruffle trimmed polished cotton romper. *My Baby*, 18" cloth and vinyl with sleep eyes and in seven outfits, 24" in five outfits. *Tiny Tubber*, rooted hair and molded hair. All vinyl and in four outfits. *Susie Sunshine*, 18" in six outfits: Gingham check, striped polished cotton with "Stop, Look and Listen" printed on front. Striped cotton with wide stripes and rick-rack trim. Gingham check apron with embroidered apron. Wide stripe cotton and lace apron. Nautical print cotton with solid color coat and straw hat. *Gumdrop*, 16" in five outfits: Polka dot

polished short play dress with solid color romper panties. Two piece nautical cotton slack set with nautical motif, sandles and head scarf. Gingham check romper with solid color pinafore trimmed in gingham check and sandles. Organdy party dress with rosette on bodice, ribbon bow in hair. Print cotton dress with coat and hat with matching print trim. *Suzette,* 15″ all vinyl with sleep eyes and all fingers of right hand spread open and 2nd and 3rd fingers of left hand molded together. She is a teen style doll and came in gingham check dress with ribbon in hair, plaid dress with side part hair with ribbon, taffeta party dress with nylon overskirt, full bangs and long hair rolled up shoulder length and nylon hose. Bride with skirt in three tiers, short nylon veil. She also came as offical Blue Bird, Campfire, Brownie and Girl Scout. *Fluffy,* 11″ all vinyl with sleep eyes and in six outfits. *Baby-Kin,* 8″ all vinyl, sleep eyes and molded hair in five outfits. 10½″ *Mickey* came in these outfits this year: Baseball, football, sailor, fireman, Boy Scout, fighter (without robe). Cub Scout, Cowboy, Johnny Reb and Yankee Boy, 10½″ *Happy Boy,* all vinyl came in overalls, nightshirt & cap, and as boxer without a robe. *Sweetie Pie,* sizes 14″, 18″ and 19″. Cloth and vinyl with rooted or molded hair, sleep eyes and all fingers on right hand curled with thumb molded between first finger. Left hand has 2nd and 3rd fingers deeply curled. Came in six different outfits. *Susie Sunshine,* 18″ and 14″ *My Baby.* Cloth and vinyl with painted eyes in print flannel pajamas. *Susie* in matching pajamas. Also available was a wood, swinging type bassinette. FAO Schwarz shows this size in blue or pink long gown housecoat with hem ruffle and 8″ baby in matching material. *Love And Learn Set,* with 18″ *Sweetie Pie.* All vinyl with rooted hair, sleep eyes open mouth/nurser. In fleece pajamas and layette. Came boxed with record explaining the "How and Why" of a Mother's love and tenderness.

1966: *Charlee,* 13″ toddler, all vinyl, freckles and dressed in different outfits. *Peaches,* 16″: *Half Pint,* 11″: All tagged: *Baby ½ Pint.* All vinyl. *Pum'Kin,* 11″ all vinyl. Came in black or white, and as a boy or girl. The boy has freckles. *Miss Chips,* 17″ came in ball gown, as a Bride and four other outfits. *Chipper,* 14″-15″ plastic and vinyl. *Baby Winkie,* 12″ all vinyl, open mouth/nurser sold on blanket or pillow. *Gumdrop,* 15″ with matching 8″ *Baby-Kin,* also used the 17″ *Gumdrop.* The *Baby-Kin* was also available in five other outfits. *Gumdrop* was also used with the 14″ *My Fair Baby* in the S & H Green Stamp catalog dressed in white eyelette skirt with red bodice, and was available in the Effanbee catalog in four outfits. *Precious Baby,* 24″ cloth and vinyl and came in five different dresses, plus a three piece knit pants and bonnet set. *Lil Darlin',* 18″ cloth and vinyl. Came in Christening gown and a dress with coat and bonnet. *Thumkin,* this year came in five dresses, a dress with sweater and a fleece bunting. *Twinkie,* 16″ came in five dresses, or a sacque and diaper and was available in black or white. *Mickey,* 11″ was sold as baseball, football, sailor, and a fighter. *Tiny Tubber,* 11″ all vinyl, sleep eyes and came with rooted or molded hair. *Susie Sunshine* in matching outfit as 8″ *Baby-Kin.*

1967: *Honey Bun,* cloth and vinyl sleep eyes, rooted hair and open/closed mouth. 18″ and came black or white. All fingers separate on both hands with 1st on left extended higher than others. *Dy Dee Darlin'.* (Lil' Sweetie). *Lil' Sweetie.* (Also called Dy Dee Darlin'). In F.A.O. Schwarz catalog in three different outfits. 16″ all vinyl, open mouth/nurser, no lashes or eyebrows painted on. Same doll also sold through Ward's in four different outfits. *Baby*

Cuddles, cloth and vinyl with sleep eyes and rooted hair. The 16″ size is in the Effanbee catalog in six outfits. The left small finger and 4th fingers are joined together, and the lower lip is protruding. The left hand has the 2nd and 3rd fingers together and curled. This baby was also sold through Ward's in two dresses, a dress and coat/bonnet and in pajama and robe. *Baby Face,* 15″ plastic and vinyl, rooted hair and sleep eyes. The eyes are to the side. She came in two-piece pajamas, organdy dress with pleated collar, print dress, embroidered organdy dress, pleated nylon dress with wide pleated collar, velvet coat/hat/muff with maribou trim and cotton dress. *New Dy Dee Baby,* all vinyl with sleep eyes, rooted hair, open mouth/nurser. *Precious Baby,* 26″ cloth and vinyl with open/closed mouth, rooted hair and sleep eyes. 24″ came in six outfits. Doll's left hand has all fingers curled with middle one deeply curled and thumb molded into 1st finger. Right hand has all fingers separate, but 2nd and 3rd are curled. A 17″ doll was made for Ward's and came in four outfits. *Bettina,* 21″ open/closed mouth, sleep eyes and rooted hair. *Half Pint,* 11″ all vinyl. Boy or girl and black or white this year. Boy came in short velveteen pants and strap top with white shirt and girl in velveteen dress with lace trim, print cotton dress, two piece pajamas, or pink nylon formal. *Twinkie,* 16″ all vinyl dressed in pink and white. Open/mouth-nurser and came with molded hair. Was in the Effanbee catalog this year in seven outfits, plus available in suitcase with a layette. *Celeste,* (Miss Chips) 18″ exclusive for Marshall Field's and sold with wardrobe and trunk. She also sold as "Miss Chips" at Marshall Field's in trunk with wardrobe. In the Effanbee catalog she is shown as a Bride with rose and embossed lace gown, and available in black or white, formal, mini-dress and vinyl raincoat with polka-dot trimmed boots, scarf and on coat. This version was also available in black or white (in rain outfit). *Lil' Darlin,* cloth and vinyl, rooted hair and sleep eyes. Left hand the first finger is extended and others are only slightly curled. Right hand has 1st and 2nd fingers extended. Came in two outfits. *My Fair Baby,* 14″ cloth and vinyl, molded or rooted hair and all fingers on right hand curled with thumb under first finger. Came in one outfit only, and that was a zippered fleece bunting and hood. *Baby Winkie,* 12″ all vinyl with molded hair, open mouth/nurser and came in two outfits. *Little Gum Drop,* 14″ in velveteen jumper and cotton blouse. Full bangs and long straight hair. 16″ *Gumdrop* came in black in a velveteen and eyelette lace dress. *Charlee,* 13″ all vinyl with rooted hair. All fingers of right hand curled and holds thumb between 2nd and 3rd fingers, but is also shown in catalog with right hand that has all fingers extended . Left hand has 2nd and 3rd fingers curled. Shows sleep eyes to side as well as to the front. Came in three outfits. *Chipper,* 15″ Bride with three tiers of lace and short veil. Printed flannel night gown and matching night cap, short dress with dropped waist.

Babykin, 8″ all vinyl, open mouth/nurser, with rooted or molded hair and in six outfits. The 11″ *Mickey* this year was available as a baseball player, football, sailor and a fighter with no robe. *Tiny Tubber,* 11″ all vinyl, open mouth/nurser, rooted or molded hair and in four outfits. *Pun'Kin,* 11″ came in a velveteen dress, flannel nightie, and nylon pleated dress. *Susie Sunshine,* 18″ all are shown with full bangs and long straight hair. Print flannel nightgown and holds an 8″ *Babykin* in matching sleeper bag, striped jersy dress with horizontal stripes. Knit dress with wide open lace hem, and long velveteen gown with lace bodice. Same doll was offered through F.A.O. Schwarz with the

8″ *Babykin* in housecoat-nightgown with wide ruffle hem and she has the left hand deeply curled to hold a bottle. The baby was in a sleeper bag. *Honeybun*, 18″ called *Susan*. Cloth and vinyl with rooted hair, sleep eyes and came in two piece pink brushed snowsuit and matching bonnet.

1968: *Dy Dee Darlin'*, (Lil' Sweetie) 18″ all vinyl, open mouth/nurser with no painted brows or lashes. Came in Black or White. Was offered through Sears in a white two tier dress. *Cookie*, 16″ cloth and vinyl with sleep eyes and rooted hair, open mouth/nurser and was available in black or white. Came in four outfits, also in a suitcase with wardrobe. *Tiny Tubber*, 8″-10″ all vinyl, sleep eyes, rooted hair, and open mouth/nurser. Came in four different outfits and either black or white. *Sweetie Pie*, 18″ either black or white. *ToddleTot*, all vinyl toddler with molded hair, sleep eyes and open mouth/nurser. Came in three outfits. *Button Nose*, 16″-17″-18″ cloth and vinyl with sleep eyes, molded or rooted hair and available in five outfits. *My Fair Baby*, 12″-14″, 16″, also in 18″. All vinyl, open mouth/nurser, sleep eyes, and came either black or white. Doll was available as twins or singles and was offered through Sears in four outfits made for them. The 18″ size (*Precious Baby*) sold at J.C. Penny's in five different outfits. *DyDee Baby*. All vinyl with molded hair. Came as twins or singles and in the 14″ & 16″ sizes. *Baby Winkie* in the 12″ size was all vinyl with molded hair, sleep eyes and open mouth/nurser and came in two outfits with one being on a checked cotton pillow. The 16″ came in a pink party dress for J.C. Penney's. *Twinkie* and *Lil' Darlin*. Still available. *Babykin 8″*. All vinyl, molded hair, sleep eyes, pen mouth/nurser, and offered as singles or twins. Came in four outfits. *Precious Baby*, 24″ cloth and vinyl, sleep eyes and rooted hair in six different outfits. *Baby Cuddles*, 16″ cloth and vinyl with sleep eyes and rooted hair. Protruding lower lip. Came in six outfits, and available in black or white. *Half Pint* was offered as a boy or girl in back or white and had four outfits for the girl and two for the boy.

Baby Face, 16″ all vinyl with sleep eyes to the side, came in black or white. Available in five outfits: two piece printed flannel pajamas, two color silk broadcloth dress with pom-pom and embroidered clown (black or white), long nightgown with four rows of lace at hem (black or white), dotted organdy dress with wide ruffle at hem, and an embroidered organdy party dress with scalloped hem line. *Susie Sunshine*, 18″ came in long dotted cotton granny gown with ruffle hem and matching head band. White eyelet lace trimmed pinafore. Gingham check skirt, lace trimmed organdy blouse (attached) and two hair bows that match the skirt. Floral print flannel gown with matching 8″ *Babykin* in sacque. *Miss Chips*, 17″ black or white in five different outfits. *Chipper*, 15″ in four outfits. *Pun'Kin*. 11″ in four outfits. One was a plaid cotton dress and bonnet with doll (*Pun'Kin*) having **molded hair**. *Mickey* was offered in black or white and in same five outfits offered in 1968. *HoneyBun*, 18″ cloth and vinyl, sleep eyes, rooted hair with two models offered in black, and came in eight outfits. F.A.O. Schwarz offered the 18″ *Susie Sunshine* in two outfits. Polkadot gown, ruffle at waist and long sleeves and with white pinafore and matching head band. Also in flowered long housecoat and carries 8″ baby with left hand molded to carry bottle. *My Fair Baby*, 13″ was offered as twins in pink or blue. They came in flannel buntings style jacket, and bunting holder has a flower on each flap. The babies wear a peaked bonnet. *Baby Face* 16″ in floral organdy dress with scalloped edges around hem. "New" version of *DyDee Darlin' Baby*, 18″ and has no painted lashes or

brows. A 16″ *Baby Face* was offered at the J.C. Penneys stores (not in catalog) and she was dressed in red flannel skirted gown with ruffle hem, bodice is white organdy with lace and trim of red, with red hair ribbon. She holds an 8″ *Babykin* in white flannel and red trim.

1969: *Baby Face*, 16″ also as 19″ through Penneys catalog in two piece pink snow suit, muff and bonnet, but doll actually has a *Precious Baby* head. *Baby Button Nose*, 12″ all cloth stuffed with vinyl head. Body is covered with printed cloth, sleep eyes, rooted hair, and came in black or white. *Sugar Plum*, 20″ cloth and vinyl with sleep eyes, rooted hair, and was available either black or white. One shown in the Effanbee catalog dressed in Christening gown with rose embossed wide lace border trim and with knit sweater, bonnet, plus being on a pillow with same lace trim is actually a *Sweetie Pie Head*. The doll came in seven outfits, and one outfit was called the Pioneer Collection. *Gum Drop* was also included in the Pioneer Collection. *Tiny Tubber*, 11″ all vinyl, as twins or as singles, in black or white and available in three different outfits. *Pun'Kin*, 11″ all vinyl, rooted hair, sleep eyes and in black or white came in three outfits. *Baby Butterball*, 11½″-12″ all vinyl, sleep eyes, molded hair and open mouth nurser. A *Baby Cuddles* sold through J.C. Penneys in a pink party dress was actually a *Precious Baby*. *Babykin*, 8″ all vinyl with molded hair, sleep eyes and open mouth/nurser came in six outfits. *Half Pint*, 11″ came in black or white, as boy or girl and in six different outfits including one as a ballerina. There was one special made this year for a few customers and it was dressed in short white dress with straw hat, pink ribbon and sash, had white leotards, black shoes and white two button spats. *Tottletot*, 13″ all vinyl, as boy or girl. *Button Nose*, 16″ all cloth with vinyl head and hands. Came with rooted or molded hair and as black or white. *Fair Baby*, 14″ all vinyl, open mouth/nurser, sleep eyes, rooted or molded hair, and came in black or white, and in five outfits, plus a suitcase with wardrobe. *Mickey*, available in five different outfits that were the same as 1968, and either black or white. *DyDee baby*, 18″ all vinyl and in three outfits. *Susie Sunshine* in two granny style gowns, with one holding 8″ *Babykin*, and one in snowsuit on a Susie body, but with a *Precious Baby* head. *Butterball*, 13″ all vinyl, molded or rooted hair, black or white, and two outfits, plus in a suitcase with a wardrobe. *Precious Baby*, 25″ cloth and vinyl in five different outfits. *Miss Chips*, 17″ available either black or white and in two outfits. *Chipper*, 15″ in two outfits. *Tiny Tubber*, 11″ all vinyl, as singles or twins. *Baby Winkie*, 12″ all vinyl with rooted or molded hair and in two outfits. Sear's carried a 14″ version in pink and white bunting and suitcase with layette. *Sweetie Pie*, 17″ cloth and vinyl with all having rooted hair. black or white in five different outfits. Sold in Sear's catalog in four different outfits than shown in Effanbee catalog. J.C. Penneys had a *Button Nose* called *Twinkie* in white Christening gown on a pink pillow. Sear's carried an 18″ *DyDee* in pink fleece coat and bonnet in a bunting, and a *Button Nose* called *Susie Sunshine* that was dressed in two piece blue fleece snowsuit with muff and bonnet. F.A.O. Schwarz offered 18″ *Susie Sunshine* in two outfits, plus one holding an 8″ *Babykin*. They also carried *My Fair Baby* as twins. *Sunny*, (Button nose) plastic and vinyl, sleep eyes and in four crochet outfits. Marshall Field's sold 18″ *Susie Sunshine* in deep pink check Granny style gown and white pinafore with ruffles over the shoulders and eyelette around the hem. *Lynn*, toddler in pink snowsuit. *Brother and Sister* dressed in blue. 18″ *Miss Chips* was called *Chris*, and was dressed in yellow with wide cape collar and ruffle at hem of collar. *Chris* was sold in a blue flowered trunk and additional wardrobe.

1970: 15" *Chipper*. Blue nightgown and matching cap, both with lace trim. Bride with three tier lace gown with roses embossed, full veil with flowers across head. This same Chipper Bride was called *Miss Chips* in one wholesale catalog. *Miss Chips*, bride same as the *Chipper* bride but with side part in hair and was available in black or white. She also came in colored cotton long dress with lace eyelette trim, straw bonnet and has full bangs. Printed long gown with velvet cumberband and white cotton bodice, felt hat, eyelette ribbon trim near hem and full bangs. Long dress in stripes and "dust cap" trimmed with flowers, full bangs and twin pony tails. This model came either black or white. Striped cotton bell bottom pants, long sleeve blouse, braid trimmed cotton vest, and full bangs with twin pony tails. Midi length dress and coat, coat has velvet "V" collar, cuffs, velvet boots and felt hat center part long hair. Pink nightgown and matching cap, both lace trimmed. *Gumdrop*. 16" white cotton nightgown with deep ruffle around hem and flower applique near hem. Came in black or white. Dotted cotton skirt dress with "A" line blouse with puffy, full sleeves, eyelette ruffle near hem and pleated dotted material at hem. Dotted cotton, midi length granny dress with "dust cap", eyelette ruffle at hem and Peter Pan collar. This model came either black or white. *Susie Sunshine*, 18" printed flannel nightgown ruffle hem and matching 8" *Babykin* in sleeping bag. Long eyelette cotton robe over solid color nitie. Long solid color granny gown with three rows lace trimmed organdy pinafore, plus eyelette row with ribbon running through near hem, large bows in twin pony tails. *Baby Button Nose*, 12" came in two styles: gingham cotton check body and limbs and printed cotton covered body and limbs. Both with vinyl heads. Came with molded or rooted hair. *Luv*, 18" all vinyl toddler (Button Nose style face). Came in jumpsuit with "A.B.C.'s" and giraffe on leg. Eyelette embroidered cotton dress. Coat, hat, legging set with matching muff. *Button Nose*, 16" cloth and vinyl in knit sacque with ribbon draw string at bottom, molded hair and either black or white. The Effanbee catalog also shows a non-Button nose faced doll with either rooted or molded hair, and eyes to the side with cotton covered body and limbs with vinyl head and hands. *Baby Winkie*, 12" in three outfits, open mouth/nurser. *Fair Baby*, 14" all vinyl, open mouth/nurser in two outfits. With molded or rooted hair and in black or white, and has right thumb under first finger. *DyDee*, 18" all vinyl, rooted hair and uses the same body as the Fair Baby. Sear's carried the *DyDee* on a pink blanket. *Toddletot*, 13" all vinyl with molded hair, boy or girl, open mouth/nurser and dressed in check gingham. *Butterball*, 13" all vinyl, open mouth/nurser, rooted or molded hair, and either black or white. One in lace trim fleece blanket and other on lace trimmed organdy pillow. Also available in suitcase with wardrobe and Johnson Baby Products. *Babykin*, 8" in windowbox with a wardrobe and Johnson Baby Products. *Tiny Tubber*, 10" in windowbox with wardrobe and Johnson Baby Products. *Half Pint*, 11" in windowbox with wardrobe and Johnson Baby products. *Twinkie*, 16" in four outfits, black or white, with molded or rooted hair, open mouth/nurser and all vinyl. Sold through J.C. Penneys in pink party dress on pillow and in pink coat, bonnet and cotton dress. *Sweetie Pie*, 17" cloth and vinyl in nine different outfits, with two available in black or white, all have rooted hair, and one as a boy in short pants. Sold through other than company catalogs in

crocheted white and pink bonnet, sweater, leggings and booties. *Little Luv*. 14" cloth and vinyl. Rooted or molded hair, dimples, black or white and in three outfits. *Sugar Plum*, 20" cloth and vinyl with rooted or molded hair, two available in black and came in four outfits. One in long christening gown with rose lace hem, knit sweater and bonnet, on pillow with rose lace ruffle and this one has a Button Nose face. *Precious Baby*, 25" cloth and vinyl, all rooted hair. Came in five outfits with one two piece pajamas and holding 8" *Babykin* in matching sacque. *Pun'Kin*, 11" all vinyl toddler in three outfits with two available in black. *Half Pint*, 11" all vinyl, as Bride boy, and five other outfits, with two available in black. *Tiny Tubber*, 11" all vinyl with rooted or molded hair, twins, ad in black or white, open mouth/nurser. *Babykin*, 8" all vinyl in four outfits. *Mickey*, 11" in same five outfits as last three years. The S & H Stamp stores offered 11" *Tiny Tubber* as twins. F.A.O. Schwarz once again carried the *My Fair Baby* twins and *Susie Sunshine* with matching 8" *Babykin*, dressed in green gown with patch quilt pinafore. Marshall Field's offered *Susie Sunshine* dressed in long yellow gown with white pinafore, and also *Sweetie Pie* and *Twinkie*.

1971: *Frontier Series* included: *Pun'Kin, Little Luv, Chipper, Gumdrop, Miss Chips, Susie Sunshine, Sugar Plum* and *Precious Baby*. F.A.O. Schwarz carried *Susie Sunshine* and 8" *Babykin* in pink check gown and white pinafore (the Marshall Field's Company carried this same doll.) Also this year, they carried *Little Luv* and *Sweetie Pie*. Marshall Fields also had *Half Pint* in pink check dress and two button spats over shoes. They too had the *Sweetie Pie. Baby Winkie*, 12" came in three outfits. *Butterball*, 13" had seven outfits and was also sold in suitcase with layette. *Fair Baby*, 14" had three outfits, and was available either in black or white. *Twinkie*, 16" came in four outfits and black or white. *DyDee Darlin'* came in three different outfits. *Baby Button Nose*, 12" came with molded or rooted hair, and both had all cloth bodies and limbs and vinyl heads. One body was check gingham and the other was flesh colored cotton fabric. The doll came in three outfits this year. *Button Nose*, 16" came with rooted or molded hair, either black or white and in two outfits. *Little Luv*, 14" came in either black or white and in four different outfits. *Little Luv* was also available in black or white. *Susie Sunshine*, 18" and in three outfits. *Sweetie Pie*, 17" molded or rooted hair. Black or white and in eight outfits. *Gumdrop*, 16" in one outfit and either black or white. *Sugar Plum*, 20" in seven outfits, black or white and with molded or rooted hair. *Butterball* in suitcase. *Pun'Kin*, 13" came in long pink flowered striped flannel nitie, and the black version of this doll had blue flower printed flannel nitie. Green dotted short cotton dress with attached organdy apron with hemed sleeves and neck lace trimmed. This same doll was available in black. Pleated pink nylon short party dress, pink ribbon sash and lace at sleeves and neck. *Precious Baby*, 25" with rooted hair and two outfits. *Half Pint*, 11" boy came in red short suit with shoulder straps and one across front, also two buttons. White shirt with the black version having an Afro-hairdo and the white version with full bang, short hairstyle. Matching girl had red velveteen jumper dress with two buttons on front, and white cotton blouse. The girl was also available in black or white. Blue eyelette lace cotton nitie with lace at neck and arm holes. Printed cotton short dress, black leotards, white straw hat with black ribbon tie, black shoes, white spats with two black buttons. Pink gingham check short dress, white trim at hem with pink ribbon running through it. White leotards, black shoes and white spats. This model also came in black. *Miss Chips.* 17″ and in four outfits. *Babykin,* 8″ in three outfits. *Chipper,* 15″ either black or white and in six outfits. *Tiny Tubber,* 11″ either black or white and in five outfits. *Mickey* in black or white and in same five outfits as previous years. *Educational Doll,* 20″ available either black or white.

1972: 20″ *Educational Doll* same as 1971. *Party Time Collection* of *Ten* dolls. Brides, Bridesmaids and Flowergirls, although two do not look like it. 18″ *Miss Chips* in pink gingham gown with organdy hat and wide lace band skirt over ruffled hem. Matching 15″ *Chipper.* Both have side part with long bangs and both hold fans. 18″ *Miss Chips* in yellow gown with red/yellow embroidered flowers around hem, organdy hat with yellow ribbon. Matching 15″ *Chipper* (see photos for 1971 as Chipper on market first). Both have center part hair, and this year Chipper holds a white fan. *Chipper,* 15″ and *Miss Chips,* 18″ in matching pleated pink nylon gown with ruffled net head piece. Both hold flowers. *Pun'Kin,* 11″ flowergirl in yellow pleated nylon gown and head piece. Holds flowers. 18″ *Miss Chips* with white organdy Brides gown with wide eyelette lace and large flowers at hem and just below the waist. Matching 15″ *Chipper* in either black or white. *Daffy Dots Collection* of nine dolls. *Miss Chips,* 18″ and 16″ *Gumdrop* both with patchwork long gown and red polka-dot aprons with rows of black, yellow and white rick rack, and lace trim. matching poke bonnets. 20″ *Sugar Plum,* 18″ *Miss Chips,* 16″ *Twinkie,* all have multi-colored patchwork and white skirts or aprons with red, black and yellow rick rack trim. The *Twinkie* came with patchwork pillow. *Precious Baby* 25″, 11″ *Pun'Kin* are in matching red/white dotted dress/gown with patch-work aprons and bonnets. *Butterball,* 13″ came on round patchwork pillow and has red, yellow and black rick rack and wide lace at hem of dress. *Sugar Plum,* 20″ is in patchwork dress and bonnet but white eyelette apron. *Pajama Kids Collection* of six dolls. *Susie Sunshine,* 18″ (holds 8″ *Babykin).* 11″ *Pun'Kin,* 10″ *Tiny Tubber,* 17″ *Sweetie Pie,* and 8″ *Babykin* all in gown or two piece pajamas with red rose flowers on off white back-grounds. The 11″ *Pun'Kin* and 17″ *Sweetie Pie* came in black or white. *Strawberry Patch Collection* of six dolls. *Gumdrop,* 16″ in long gown of pink check with wide ruffle at hem, striped flowered pinafore and straw hat. *Sweetie Pie,* 17″ in pink check one piece romper, straw hat. *Pun'Kin* 11″ in long gown of pink check with white apron and appliqued strawberry on the apron. *Susie Sunshine,* 18″ in pink check long gown, white organdy pinafore with appliqued strawberry on bodice, and three rows of lace at hem of pinafore. There is white eyelette and a black ribbon running through it near hem. *Butterball,* 13″ in black or white dressed in white diaper set and on white pillow with pink check ruffle and ties, plus the strawberry applique. *Twinkie,* 16″ in pink check dress on pink check pillow with wide organdy ruffle. *Baby Classics* of thirty-nine dolls: plus four *Mickeys. Sugar Plum,* 20″ in pink fleece snowsuit and bonnet. Linen pink dress, with tucked white organdy bodice (this one available in black or white). Dotted Swiss pink dimity dress, bonnet. Pique pink coat, hat with cotton dress. All have rooted hair, except one with molded hair, lace trimmed dotted Swiss Christening dress. 25″ *Precious Baby.* Cotton shag pink coat, bonnet with organdy dress. Pink organdy dress with embroidered yoke and bonnet. 16″ *Twinkie* in floral pink flocked Chistening gown on pillow (came in black or white), rooted hair. Diaper set with hand crocheted yellow blanket and has molded hair. Diaper set with fleece blanket and molded hair (this one came either

black or white). Red/yellow flowered nylon gown with yellow pillow and rooted hair (gown matches *Party Time* dolls except the background of gown is white). 17″ *Sweetie Pie* in floral flocked, lace trimmed bunting in pink, rooted hair. White organdy and check gingham dress, rooted hair. Organdy dress and hand crocheted sweater and bonnet and booties. 18″ *DyDee* in three piece hand crocheted pink legging set, organdy dress, both have rooted hair. 14″ *Little Luv.* Pink and white linen dress with tucked yoke. Pink hand crocheted dress and booties. Two piece white and blue fleece snowsuit and hood. Embroidered pink organdy dress (this one either in black or white). All rooted hair. 14″ *Fair Baby.* Lace trimmed pink bunting of flannel with molded hair and available in black or white. Lace trimmed pink bunting with rooted hair. 16″ *Gumdrop,* pink floral flocked dress and either black or white. 13″ *Butterball.* In pink floral flocked dress, rooted hair. Short embroidered dress on pillow with rooted hair and in black or white. Embroidered Christening gown on pillow, with rooted hair. Two piece hand crocheted outfit with booties. 11″ *Half Pint.* Boy and girl. Red velveteen jumper dress, white top and boy in red short jumper pants with white top. Both available in black or white. Floral pink flocked dress and straw hat. 12″ *Baby Button Nose.* Cloth body and limbs in blue or pink fleece pajamas, with molded hair. 8″ *Babykin* in blue/white check gingham infant gown and blanket. Blue or pink fleece bunting and hood. Both have molded hair. blue or pink check gingham dress with rooted hair. 12″ *Baby Winkie.* In diaper set and blanket with molded hair. 10″ *Tiny Tubber.* In hand crocheted dress and booties. Check gingham dress in blue or pink and this one came in black or white. Floral flocked dress that is pink. All with rooted hair. Diaper set and blanket in black or white and with molded hair. *Bedtime Story Collection* of six dolls. 14″ *Little Luv.* Red one piece pajamas and rooted hair. 14″ *Sissy (Gumdrop).* Red dotted and white stripe with red flowers nightgown and cap. 12″ *Baby Button Nose.* Molded hair in red dotted, white striped and red flowered sleeping bag. 18″ *Suzie Sunshine.* Nightgown with red dotted "apron" look and vertical stripes with red flowers. 11″ *Pun'Kin* in two piece pajamas with red dotted and two white stripes on bodice with red flowers. 13″ *Butterball.* Shortie nitie and booties that are red dotted. Rooted hair. *Anchors Aweigh Collection,* 18″ *Miss Chips.* Long red/white gown with wide ruffle hem, organdy pinafore with navy and red trim. Wide red/white bow in her hair. 20″ *Sugar Plum.* Striped red/white dress, white bodice with "V" red trim and anchor, sailor style hat with red and blue trim. 25″ *Precious Baby.* White fleece snowsuit with sailor collar, red and blue stripe. Red anchor applique and matching bonnet. 12″ *Baby Button Nose.* All red cloth body and limbs, red/white stripe dress with red collar and white trim, matching hat. 15″ *Chipper.* Long red/white stripe gown with large ruffle around hem and two rows blue trim at top of ruffle. White bodice with red pinafore look over the shoulder straps with two rows of white trim. *Butterball,* 13″ rooted hair and available in wicker basket with layette. Also the 16″ *Twinkie* with rooted hair came in same set. 13″ *Butterball* in pink check suitcase with layette and has rooted hair. Also available this year without a doll: Yellow hand crocheted blanket with fringe, and an organdy pillow with wide ruffle. 14″ *Happy Little Sister,* for Montgomery Wards. (was part of the *Bedtime Story Collection).* 15″ *Chipper* in four special outfits for J.C. Penneys (see 1972).

1973: *Bridal Suite Collection. Pun'Kin,* 11″ ring boy with long blue satin pants and lace trimmed shirt. *Pun'Kin,* 11″

flowergirl in pale pink multi color flower wreaths on organdy gown. Holds pink rose and has two pink ribbons in hair, and sash tie. *Pun'Kin*, 11″ bride in organdy with two rows scolloped lace trim at hem and carries roses (came either black or white). *Chipper*, bridesmaid in multi color embroidered nylon gown, wide pink band on the underslip that shows and pink bodice and ribbon in hair. Holds rose. Matching 18″ *Miss Chips*. Both available in black or white. *Chipper*, 15″ and *Miss Chips*, 18″ Brides. Organdy and lace gown veil. Has ring wreaths within rings at scolloped hems and "V" lace on bodice. Only the 18″ one came in black. Montgomery Ward's had a different Bridal party. (See 1973 in this book). *Over The Rainbow Collection*. All in check of purple, blue and pink. *Pun'Kin*, 11″ in gingham long gown with pink and purple ruffles at hem. Pink apron with blue ruffles and blue bodice with pink sleeves. *Susie Sunshine*, 19″ in long gown of gingham that is purple and pink with white organdy pinafore and black ribbon binding at ruffled hem. Came either black or white. *Baby Face*, 16″ in long gingham gown with blue pinafore-look top over white organdy and blue, purple and pink ruffles at hem. Came in either black or white. *Baby Winkie*. 12″ in long pink gingham gown and organdy over dress with embroidery. Came on check pillow with wide lace organdy ruffle. *Butterball*, 13″ in blue check dress with wide lace ruffle at hem, or pink check on round pillow with matching lace trim. *Lil' Darlin*, 13″ cloth and vinyl in pink with blue ruffle at hem and white organdy sleeves. *Sweetie Pie*, 18″ cloth and vinyl in pink dress and purple with organdy apron. *Highland Fling Collection* of seven dolls, with none offered in black. All have Scotch plaid dress, ruffles or trim. 11″ *Pun'Kin*, 18″ *Miss Chips*, 19″ *Susie Sunshine*, 16″ *Baby Face* 13″ *Butterball*, 15″ *Little Luv*, 20″ *Sugar Plum*. *Crochet Classics. Tiny Tubber*. 11″ in pink dress and booties. *Sunny*, 19″ in pink dress. *Fair Baby*, 13″ in pale green bunting and white fleece gown and hood. This model came either black or white. *DyDee*. 18″ in pink sweater, cap and legging set. *Half Pint*, 11″ in blue dress. *Butterball*, 13″ in blue sweater, hood, soaker and booties. *Little Luv*, 15″ in blue dress, white booties. *Sweetie Pie*, 18″ in organdy white dress, pink sweater, cap and booties. This doll was available in black or white. *Sweet Nostalgia Collection. Pun'Kin*. 11″, *Susie Sunshine*. 19″, *Twinkie*. 17″, *Baby Face*. 16″, *Little Luv*. 15″. All in multi colored, flowered dress or long gowns with matching material and lavender ruffles. 15″ *Little Luv* and 16″ *Baby face* had pink/multi color/flowered bonnets and *Susie Sunshine* had lavender and multi color cap. 17″ *Twinkie* was only one with a pink ruffle on a pink, lace trimmed pillow. *Baby Classics Collection* of 19 Dolls in 41 outfits. The 18″ *Sweetie Pie* came in red and white striped patchwork dress with rick rack trim, and was available in black or white. In a blue and beige plaid dress with wide lace trim just above the hem. 20″ *Sugar Plum*. In pink and white stripe long gown and with molded hair. Also in embroidered band trim down the front, and came either black or white. In a multi color gingham dress in pink, yellow, green and lavendar, black or white and with rooted hair. This same doll was dressed in an organdy dress with gingham pink ruffle at bodice and rick rack and multi color embroidery trim near hem and around ruffle at bodice. Rooted hair. She also came in white knit coat and hat with inside of the hat being pink, white stripe, which matches the dress. Rooted hair. 25″ *Precious Baby* in red and white stripe pants with white cotton blouse with inset red and white stripe front and lace trim. In blue and pink plaid dress with white "apron" effect that has

multi color embroidery trim at bodice. 13″ *Butterball*. In white diaper set with blue trim on fleece blanket with blue and pink ruffle. Molded hair and either black or white. Pink and blue plaid baby dress and rooted hair. Pink and yellow plaid dress on pink pillow with lace trim. Rooted hair and either black or white. 15″ *Little Luv*. Multi color, lace trimmed gingham dress. Rooted hair and either black or white. Pink fleece snowsuit and hood. Rooted hair. White fleece bunting and bonnet. Blue and pink plaid ruffle trim. Pink and white check gingham dress with multi color flower embroidered around hem and lace. White knit coat and hat with pink and white striped dress. Rooted hair. 17″ *Twinkie*. In pink one piece diaper set tied to white fleece blanket. Molded hair and either black or white. Pink and white stripe gown with lace trim. Molded hair. Embroidered crepe Christening gown and cap with eyelette scalloped near hem. Bonnet and rooted hair. On pillow 13″ *Little Darlin'*. Molded hair and in cotton Christening gown of white with embroidery on nylon ribbon used as trim. Patchwork red and white check dress with two rows rick rack trim on bodice, rooted hair. In Pink and white stripe dress with white band and lace at hem. Rooted hair and either black or white. In blue and pink plaid dress with wide ruffle at hem and white organdy sleeves. 15″ Chipper. In patchwork check red and white dress and white cotton bodice, long sleeves. 19″ *Susie Sunshine*. Same outfit as the *Chipper*, but came either black or white. 16″ *Baby Face*. Knit coat with cape collar, pink and white stripe dress, straw hat and either black or white. 19″ *Sunny*. In red and white stripe long pants, white blouse with red rick rack trim, white bonnet with red and white stripe inside. 13″ *Fair Baby*. White Christening gown with pink and green embroidery on pink pillow. Rooted hair and either in black or white. 12″ *Baby Winkie*. Pink fleece outfit and bonnet in pink fleece bunting. Molded hair and either black or white. Same outfit with rooted hair and in white only. Pleated Christening gown of nylon on matching pillow and with rooted hair. In long knit white coat, pink and white stripe dress and pillow. 13″ *Buttercup*. In knit white coat and bonnet and pink and white stripe dress and panties. Rooted hair. 11″ *Pun'Kin*. In long gown of patchwork that is red and white check with wide eyelette hem. Came in either black or white. 9″ *Babykin*. In pink and white check gingham infant gown and white blanket with pink and white check edging. Molded hair. Fleece pink bunting outfit and hood with molded hair. In blue and white check gingham short dress with wide lace hem. Rooted hair. 11″ *Tiny Tubber*. In pink diaper set and white knit blanket with pink edging. Molded hair and either black or white. In flower printed infant gown and bonnet on white pillow with flower print trim. Molded hair and either black or white. In lace trimmed white bunting with flannel diaper set of pink. Molded hair and either black or white. In a pink and white stripe short dress with wide lace at hem. Rooted hair and either black or white. 11″ *Half Pint*. In multi color plaid dress and panties, either black or white. In blue and pink plaid dress with lace hem and matching bonnet. 14″ *Baby Button Nose*. All cloth body and limbs in pink fleece pajamas and with molded hair. *The DyDee Educational Doll* was available in black or white. *Candy Land Collection*. 11″ *Pun'kin*. In long red and white stripe gown, velveteen red jacket and straw hat. 15″ *Chipper*. Long red and white stripe gown with wide ruffle at hem and has long white organdy sleeves with white organdy pinafore with red trim. 18″ *Miss Chips*. Long red and white gown with wide ruffle at hem, red on white embroidered (three leaf clovers) cotton apron and wide white collar. 13" *Butterball* in red cotton dress with wide band with red dots above hem, red and white stripe band at waist and rooted hair. Also in short dress with red embroidered three leaf clovers and molded hair. 15" *Little Luv*. In red and white stripe cotton dress with white apron that is embroidered with red three leaf clovers, rooted hair. *Pajama Kids Collection*. All are in white materials. 11" *Pun'kin*. White with pink flower and green leaf print nightgown with wide ruffle at hem, and available in black or white. 9" *Babykin*. Two piece pajamas. Rooted hair. 16" *Baby Face*. Nightgown with wide ruffle at hem and holds a 9" *Babykin* in pink sleeping sacque. 18" *DyDee* with rooted hair and in a one piece pajamas, holds a 9" *Babykin* in pink sleeping sacque. 13" *Buttercup* in one piece pajamas and has rooted hair. 15" *Little Luv* in one piece pajamas and has rooted hair. *Travel Time Collection*, 17" *Twinkie* with rooted hair in wicker hamper and has layette. 12" *Baby Winkie* in suitcase that is pink and white stripe, and layette. Rooted hair. 13" *Butterball* in wicker hamper, rooted hair and layette. Also available was a green crocheted blanket with fringe edge and white organdy pillow (no dolls). Marshall Fields carried the 16" *Baby Face* in white knit coat and hat with stripe dress. 11" *Pun'kin* in pastel pink and blue check gingham, ruffled at hem and with matching apron, straw hat. 18" *Suzie Sunshine* in plaid *Highland Fling* long gown and matching 15" *Little Luv Baby*. 11" *Pun'kin* in white organdy with two ruffles at hem and sash in matching plaid. *Effanbee Fan Club Mascot* in 1973 was an 11" *Half Pint* from the *Crochet Classics Collection*, has tag with identification (written) as official and first Club doll. See club address in front of this book. Sear's carried *Baby Beauties*, (see 1973 of this book). J.C. Penneys sold the *Country Look* (see 1973 of this book). Montgomery Ward as one of their anniversary dolls carried the DyDee Baby (see 1973 of this book).

1974: *Bridal Suite Collection*. 11" *Pun'Kin* in red velveteen short pants and white ruffle shirt, red tie and holds lace pillow. Has orange-red hair. The 11" *Pun'Kin Flowergirl* has organdy pink, lace embroidered gown, pink bows in hair and holds pink rose with pink ribbon streamers. 15" *Chipper*, same as the *Pun'Kin Flowergirl*, also the 18" *Miss Chips* is the same. 15" *Chipper* and 18" *Miss Chips* in organdy and lace Bridal gowns with eyelette "V'ed" around the hems, short double veil. Only the *Miss Chips* was available in black. *Enchanted Garden Collection* of seven dolls. 11" *Pun'Kin* in pale multi pastel print long gown with three rows of lace ruffles at hem, organdy cap. 15" *Chipper* in lace trim long pinafore style gown with large ruffle around hem, and straw hat. Gown in pale pastel multi color print. 19" *Suzie Sunshine*. Same print with wide white organdy ruffle around hem and organdy cap. 17" *Twinkie*. All white organdy, long sleeve dress with scolloped hem and four rows of embroidered lace, large pink bow and tied to pastel pale multi colored print pillow with wide organdy ruffle around edge. 13" *Butterball* in sleeveless dress with three rows lace at hem on white pillow with matching trim and lace around edges. 13" *Lil' Darlin'*. Same dress as *Butterball*, but with sleeves and no pillow. 18" *Sweetie Pie*. Pale pastel multi print bodice and top part of skirt, rest is organdy. Also available was a 12" x 12" child's pillow with the pale pastel multi color print in center and wide organdy ruffle with lace edge. *Carousel Collection* of six dolls. 11" *Pun'kin*, 16" *Baby Face*, 15" *Little Luv*, 18" *Miss Chips*, 19" *Susie Sunshine*, and 20" *Sugar Plum*. All in white with multi color stripe trim. *Charming Checks Collection* of six dolls. 11" *Pun'Kin* in pink check gown with

multi color embroidery apron look. 19" *Suzie Sunshine* in blue check gown and multi color embroidery on pinafore, and came in either black or white. 16" *Baby Face* in pink gingham with multi color embroidery apron. Came either black or white. 12" *Baby Winkie*. Long white infant gown with embroidery down front and came on pink check pillow. 13" *Butterball* in blue gingham dress with multi color embroidery inset. 18" *Sweetie Pie* in pink gingham dress with multi color embroidery trimmed apron. Also available was a 12" x 12" child's pillow of blue with wide ruffle. *Country Cousins Collection* of seven dolls. 11" *Pun'Kin*, 16" *Miss Chips*, 19" *Suzie Sunshine*, 16" *Baby Face*, 13" *Butterball*, 15" *Little Luv*, and 20" *Sugar Plum*. All were in red check and black printed with white figured aprons, bodice, sleeves or pockets. *Suzie Sunshine* and *Pun'Kin* had head scarf or bonnet. *Baby Classics Collection*. Twenty-two dolls. 17" *Twinkie* in pink diaper set tied to pink blanket and came in black or white. In long infant gown with pink lace embroidery down front. Both have molded hair. In eyelette embroidery batiste infant gown on pink pillow with ruffle eyelette ruffle, rooted hair, and also available in black or white. 20" *Sugar Plum* in organdy pink dress with pink lace, came in black also. In eyelette batiste pink dress and bonnet. 12" *Baby Winkie* in lace trimmed pink fleece bunting, which also came in either black or white, with molded or rooted hair. 13" *Butterball* in white diaper set and tied to white blanket, also available in black. 15" *Little Luv* came in red check dress with patches printed on dress, rick rack trim and was available in black also. 18" *Sweetie Pie*. In pink dimity infant gown with wide lace at edge of sleeves and two rows around hem, molded hair and also came in black. In pink, blue and yellow multi stripe check dress with blue rick rack trim, rooted hair and also in black. In pink lace trim dimity dress and bonnet, rooted hair. 11" *Pun'Kin* in long lace trimmed white and multi colors on skirt at angles, also available in black. In plaid pleated short dress and straw hat. 19" *Suzie Sunshine* in long lace gown with multi color angled stripe sections and wide ruffle at hem, also came in black. 16" *Baby Face* in same long style gown as *Suzie Sunshine*, and in either black or white. In plaid coat, straw hat. 11" *Half Pint* in lace trim red check dress with multi color patches, also came in black. In pink ballerina outfit. 13" *Butterball* in plaid coat, straw hat. 14" *Baby Button Nose* with all cloth multi color body and limbs with matching removable dress. Vinyl head with molded hair. 15" *Little Luv* in lace trimmed multi color dress and also in plaid coat and straw hat. 9" *Babykin* in pink baby gown and tied to white blanket. Molded hair. In blue, lace trimmed bunting and hood, molded hair. Rooted hair version in short pink dress and pink bow in hair. 11" *Tiny Tubber* in pink diaper set tied to fleece blanket and has molded hair, also came in black. In lace trimmed on blue dimity infant gown, bonnet, on pillow, and also came in black, and with molded hair. In lace trimmed fleece bunting in pink with hood, molded hair and also available in black. The rooted hair version was in blue dimity short dress with two rows of lace at hem. The black version was in blue dimity short dress with two rows of lace at hem. The black version of rooted hair was in pink short dress with two rows of lace at hem, both have rosettes on front. 14" *Baby Button Nose*. Has removable fleece pajamas that cover the hands and feet. White version is in pink and the black version in blue. Both have molded hair. 13" *Lil' Darlin'* in long infant gown of white with pink lace embroidery insert down front, also available in black. Molded hair. The rooted version is in dress of white with red and white checked sleeves and hem, with multi color patches and flowers embroidered on front. *Pajama Kids Collection* of six dolls. 11˝ Pun'kin in nightgown of long red skirt, white bodice and floral trim at neck and waist. Also came in black. 15˝ *Chipper* in nightgown same as the Pun'kin, only wide ruffle at hem. 11˝ *Tiny Tubber* in two piece pajamas with red bottoms and white top with lace at hems and red trim and ribbons. Rooted hair. 16˝ *Baby Face* in gown with red skirt, ruffle at hem, white bodice and sleeves, and red trim around neck with two rows down the front of top. Carries 9˝ Babykin in sleeping bag with red trim around neck and arms. 12˝ *Baby Winkie* in red pajamas tied to white blanket and has molded hair. 13˝ *Lil' Darlin'* in one piece red bottom and white topped pajamas. The sleeves are white also and she has floral trim at waist and red trim at neck and sleeves. The hair is rooted. *Crochet Classics Collection.* Six dolls. 11˝ *Tiny Tubber* in pink, booties and rooted hair. 18˝ *DyDee* in pink sweater, cap and legging set. 11˝ *Half Pint* in blue short dress, pink rosettes on front and white around neck and hem. 13˝ *Butterball* in blue sweater, hood soaker and booties, rooted or molded hair, but rooted hair came in pink bunting with white fleece hood and was also available in black. 18˝ *Sweetie Pie* in organdy dress, sweater, cap and booties. *Travel Time Collection.* 17˝ *Twinkie* in wicker basket with tray and layette. Rooted hair, also on pink pillow and in organdy infant gown. 12˝ *Baby Winkie* in red and white check suitcase with rooted hair and in pink bunting lined in multi color plaid. 13˝ *Butterball* with rooted hair, in wicker basket with tray and layette in pinks. Also available was a hand crocheted carriage blanket with fringe edge, and an organdy pillow with ruffle (no dolls with these last two items). Montgomery Ward's carried *Suzie* at five doll ages from baby to Bride: Newborn, Christening, Little Girl, Schoolgirl and Bride. It should be noted that all Effanbee designs are made exclusively by their designer Eugenia Dukas.

1975: *Lovums Collection* (new this year). 18˝ and all have molded hair, but one with cloth legs, vinyl arms and head and all cloth parts are pink and white check. In white short dress with inset pink check heart shaped bodice. In long white infant gown with pink ribbon and lace trim down front. This model came either black or white. In white sleeper with pink pom-poms on feet and tied to pink, lace trimmed blanket. This one came either black or white. In white outfits with bonnet and two pink pom-poms in pink bunting. In woven pink dimity infant gown and bonnet with lace trim and either black or white. Also came in this same outfit with pink pillow. *Granny's Corner Collection* of eight dolls. All in paisley print with off white circles with flowers inside circles among the print. 11˝ *Pun'kin Boy* has above ankles red velveteen pants and lace trimmed shirt, red velveteen cap. 11˝ *Pun'kin* in full length gown with wide ruffle and off white cap. 15˝ *Chipper.* Two rows of off white ruffles at and near hem. 18˝ *Miss Chips,* same as *Chipper.* 19˝ *Suzie Sunshine.* Wide ruffle at hem and red velveteen long sleeve vest like jacket and bonnet. 17˝ *Twinkie.* Long gown and bonnet on red and lace trimmed velveteen square pillow. 13˝ *Butterball.* Lace trim dress and bonnet, with molded hair and on a red and lace velveteen round pillow. 15˝ *Little Luv.* Lace trim dress with white insert in bodice with two red buttons. 20˝ *Sugar Plum,* same as *Little Luv. Crochet Classics Collection* of 8 dolls. 11˝ *Pun'kin,* pink gored dress. 11˝ *Tiny Tubber,* blue gored dress and booties, rooted hair and either black or white. 17˝ *Twinkie.* Blue sweater, cap and legging outfit, molded hair and either black or white. There is white trim on cap. 11˝ *Half Pint.*

Pink dress, bonnet with white trim on bonnet and has white muff. Came either black or white. 13˝ *Butterball.* Sweater and hood, soaker and boots, all in pink. Rooted hair and either black or white. In a pink bunting, white fleece outfit and bonnet with molded hair. 13˝ *Lil' Darlin'.* White fleece sleeping pants, pink jacket and hood, white trim on hood and has white muff. 15˝ *Little Luv,* blue gored dress and booties. 18˝ *Sweetie Pie.* Organdy dress that is white and pink sweater, cap and booties. *Bridal Suite Collection.* 11˝ *Pun'kin* Ringbearer boy in long red velveteen pants, lace trimmed pink taffeta shirt, red tie and pillow. 11˝ *Pun'kin* Flowergirl in lace trimmed pink taffeta gown with wide ruffle at hem, velveteen backed bouquet. 15˝ *Chipper* in lace trimmed pink taffeta gown with wide ruffle at hem, pink bonnet, and either in black or white. Also in white organdy and lace bridal gown with scalloped edges with white daisy, also down front and ending in white bow. Came in either black or white. 18˝ *Miss Chips.* Flowergirl is same as *Chipper* in pink and Bride same as the *Chipper* Bride. Came either in black or white. *Baby Classics.* 15 dolls and 39 outfits. 15˝ *Little Luv.* Organdy sleeves and dimity print dress with tiny red roses. Rooted hair and either black or white. 18˝ *Sweetie Pie* with rooted hair and 20˝ *Sugar Plum* both in the same outfit as *Little Luv.* The 15˝ *Little Luv* also came in lace trimmed blue and white stripe dress and bonnet with rooted hair and either black or white. 20˝ *Sugar Plum* in white only, and 18˝ *Sweetie Pie* with molded hair and either in black or white came in this same outfit. 15˝ *Little Luv* also came in pink batiste stress with wide band above hem, and bonnet and white sleeves. 20˝ *Sugar Plum* and 18˝ *Sweetie Pie* came in same outfit and all had rooted hair. 17˝ *Twinkie* in pink diaper and white blanket with molded hair and either in black or white. In a pink diaper, white fleece blanket with dimity print tiny rose ruffle and has molded hair, and came either black or white. Also in pink infant dress with lace and ribbon trim up the front, molded hair and either black or white. Matching 13˝ *Lil' Darlin'* with molded hair and in black or white. 17˝ *Twinkie* in pink fleece, lace trimmed bunting, and white outfit and hood. Rooted hair. Also in organdy infant gown with two rows lace and pink ribbon down the front and double ruffle at hem, bonnet and on pink pillow with wide lace ruffle. Rooted hair. 13˝ *Lil' Darlin'* in gingham pink check body and legs, white short dress with insert of pink check heart shape that is lace trimmed and on bodice. Molded hair. Matching 15˝ *Little Luv* with molded hair. 11˝ *Pun'kin* in long, lace trimmed gown of white dimity, tiny rose print, wide ruffle at hem and short sleeves. 15˝ *Chipper,* either black or white and 18˝ *Suzie Sunshine,* either black or white in matching gowns only theirs have long sleeves. 18˝ *Baby Face,* either black or white and 18˝*Miss Chips* and 13˝ *Butterball,* all in same outfit only with blue roses on blue dresses and white long sleeves, except the *Butterball.* 13˝ *Butterball* in pink fleece diaper set and pink blanket, molded hair and either black or white. Also in pink diaper set and white fleece blanket with red rose print ruffle. 9˝ *Babykin.* In red rose print infant gown with white fleece blanket, molded hair. Also in all pink outfit and hood, plus bunting and molded hair. In a blue rose print on blue dress with wide white lace ruffle. Rooted hair. 11˝ *Tiny Tubber* in red rose print dimity gown and bonnet on white pillow with molded hair. Also in pink diaper set, white fleece blanket with molded hair and either black or white. In white fleece outfit and hood in white fleece bunting with red rose print inside. Molded hair. In blue rose print on blue dress. Rooted hair and either black or white. 12˝ *Baby Winkie* in white outfit and hood in pink bunting with molded hair and either black or white. Same, but with rooted hair. 11" *Half Pint* in red rose dimity dress, either in black or white. Also in pink ballerina outfit. *DyDee Educational Doll*, same as 1974, 20" tall. *Half Pint Collection*. All 11", in white eyelette dress, long sleeves, straw hat, white leotards and cranberry ribbons, black shoes and white spats. In pink and white check gingham dress with eyelette white ruffle at hem, cap, leotards, white spats. Also in blue jersey dress, blue leotards, white spats and straw hat and in pink crocheted jacket and hat with white trim and muff. White leotards and spats. Came in either black or white. *Pajama Kids Collection* of six dolls. 11" *Pun'kin* in pink with embroidered lace trim on bodice nightgown, white lace trim at hem. Either black or white. 16" *Baby Face* in same outfit and either black or white. 11" *Tiny Tubber* in pink leggings and white dress type top, pink bows and rooted hair. 19" *Suzie Sunshine* in one piece pink footed sleeper with Teddy Bear. 13" *Butterball* in two piece pink legging and dress type top, molded hair. 15" *Little Luv* in long pink infant gown with embroidery trim and lace down front, long sleeves, molded hair and either black or white. *Americana Collection* of seven dolls. 11" *Pun'kin* in blue and white gingham with wide ruffle at hem, white bodice and apron with pink bow. Either black or white. 15" *Chipper* in long blue and white check gingham gown with bonnet and white sleeves and apron with multi color embroidery hem. 19" *Suzie Sunshine* in long blue and white check gown with ruffle at hem, white cap and pinafore with multi color embroidery above ruffle. Came either black or white. 16" *Baby Face* in pink and white long gown with wide ruffle at hem, white apron with multi color embroidery trim on white apron. 13" *Butterball* in pink and white check dress with white insert front and multi color embroidery trim. Rooted hair and either black or white. 15" *Little Luv* in blue and white check dress, white hem and inset apron look with multi color trim. 20" *Sugar Plum* in pink and white check, white short sleeves, white apron with eyelette and scalloped edging. Came either black or white. *Travel Time Collection*. 11" *Tiny Tubber* in wicker basket with layette and pink pillow. 17" *Twinkie* in wicker basket, and in eyelette gown, on pink pillow and with layette. 12" *Baby Winkie* in pink and white check suitcase with layette. In red rose print gown and pillow. Rooted hair. 13" *Butterball* in wicker basket with layette and pink pillow. Rooted hair. *Duck Duck Goose Collection* of seven dolls. All have white short sleeves except the *Butterball*, which is sleeveless. 11" *Pun'kin*, 17" *Twinkie*, 19" *Suzie Sunshine* are all in blue with the *Twinkie* on a blue pillow. The 16" *Baby Face* in yellow was available either black or white. 13" *Butterball* in yellow with round yellow pillow. 15" *Little Luv* in yellow with rooted hair and either black or white. 18" *Sweetie Pie* came in blue and with rooted hair. All have embroidered ducks and geese on front of dresses. *Ragamuffin Collection* of three dolls in nine outfits. All have full cloth body and limbs. 14" *Baby Button Nose* in all blue fleece pajamas and bonnet, with rooted hair and either in black or white. In red and white stripe body with white dress, rooted hair and either black or white. In pink and white check body, dress and bonnet with molded hair and came either black or white. 14" *Pint Size* in all pink and white check body and dress, white cap and "V" trim on bodice with black ribbon. In red with white dots body, white pinafore with three red buttons and straw hat. In paisley print body, off white dress and cap with lace trim. 21" *Floppy* in all pink body and dress with white cap, multi color trim across bodice, white two snap high top shoes.

In red and white check body and dress and bonnet, white pantaloons, sleeves and apron look with eyelette. Black two snap button high top shoes. With paisley body and dress, off white cap, sleeves and pantaloons, black two button snap high top shoes. Marshall Field's carried the *Baby Winkie, Chipper Bride* and *Suzie Sunshine* of the *Americana Collection*. F.A.O. Schwarz had the *Twinkie* with Layette of the *Travel Time Collection*. Effanbee Fan Club Mascot this year was a 11" *Boy Pun'Kin* in maroon short pants and beige shirt, maroon cap.

1976: *Four Seasons Collection.* This set introduced the *Carloine* face to the Effanbee line and that face continues and is one of the prettiest they have produced. It was 1976 **only** that the *Spring* from this set was dressed in yellow. See this set in the 1976 section of this book. *Baby Face Collection.* She came dressed three ways: All have black shoes, white spats and bonnets that match the materials of the dresses. Blue velveteen pinafore dress with white long sleeves, lace slip shows under the scalloped skirt. Pink rose on cap and long white, lace trimmed pantaloons. In all white dress with two tiers to shirt, long sleeves, cap with pink rose and rosettes down front of dress, pink sash. The tiers of the skirt have eyelette cutouts. In pale colored floral print dress with long sleeves. White pinafore with scolloped edge and lace around face part of bonnet. *Americana Collection* that included the 11" *Pun'Kin* boy and girl as *Spirit Of '76.* (see 1976 section). *Granny's Corner Collection*, see 1976 section of this book. *Travel Time Collection.* 11" *Tiny Tubber* in wicker basket with layette and dressed in long, lace trimmed dress with bonnet, and on pillow. 17" *Twinkie* in wicker basket with layette. Dressed in long, cutout embroidery dress with bonnet and on pillow with matching ruffle. All in pink. 13" *Butterball.* In wicker basket with layette in long gown with cut out embroidery and a band near hem. *Grand Dames Collection.* Although the *Four Seasons* are listed in the catalog as part of this collection, they are considered to be their own collection by collectors. This collection also included: *Peaches And Cream, Southern Belle, Ma Chere, Victorian Lady, Mint Julep And Mam'selle.* See all these dolls in the 1976 section of this book. *Regal Heirloom Collection.* The 1976 set included: The *Crown Princess, The Baroness, The Princess, The Countess, The Duchess And Her Royal Highness.* See the 1976 section of this book. *The Ragamuffins Collection* included: *Baby Button Nose* which was only one available in black, *Pint Size*, with one being also a part of the *Granny's Corner Collection.* See the 1976 section of this book. *Pajama Kids Collection.* 11" *Pun'kin*, which was available in black or white, 19" *Suzie Sunshine*, and 18" *DyDee.* All are dressed in one piece pink sleepers, and all hairdos are pulled to the sides and tied with ribbons. Pun'kin is holding a white vinyl Teddy Bear and the other two carry brown plush Teddy Bears. *Prairie Nights Collection.* Included five dolls: 11" *Pun'kin* in pale beige long nightgown and sleep cap. Gown is lace trimmed around hem, and has two rows of lace down the front, the bonnet is tied with blue ribbon. 19" *Suzie Sunshine* is in pale beige long gown with wide ruffle at hem, lace down front of bodice and the shoulders at the sleeve holes, and the neck are lace edged. She wears a sleep cap and has blue ribbon on cap and at waist. 13" *Butterball* is in pale beige short dress with lace hem, cap with blue ribbon and blue ribbon at neck line, also a blue rosette near hem. This is only model that came in black. 11" *Tiny Tubber* and 15" *Chipper* are dressed in blue with lace trim and sleep caps. *Crochet Classics Collection* of seven dolls. 11" *Pun'kin* in pink short dress with two rosettes on front. 11" *Tiny Tubber* in blue short dress and booties, available in black. 18" *Dydee* in blue sweater, leggings and bonnet. The bonnet has white edge. Also available in black. 11" *Half Pint* in pink jacket dress, hood and muff, with white edging and muff, as well as, white leotards and spats with black shoes, available in black. 13" *Butterball* in pink sweater and hood, soaker and booties. Rooted hair. Also in white fleece outfit, blue trimmed and crocheted bunting-blanket. White version is in blue and black is in pink. Molded hair. 15" *Little Luv* in pink weave dress and booties. Available also in black with both having rooted hair. 18" *Sweetie Pie* in long sweater, bonnet and booties and wears soft floral print dress. Came in black, also and both have rooted hair. *Lovums Collection.* All have molded hair. In long infant pale pink gown with wide lace trim down front, and this one was available in black. In pink dimity full infant gown with lace at hem and sleeve edges, also wears bonnet that is lace trimmed. In this same outfit, but with a pink pillow with lace edged organdy ruffle. In lace trimmed pink fleece bunting and dressed in white fleece outfit and bonnet. 20" *Educational Doll* same as 1975. *Half Pint Collection.* In white eyelette short dress, straw hat, leotards and spats. Has black shoes and cranberry ribbons in hair, on hat and at front waist. In pink check gingham, long white sleeves, lace at hems, and matching bonnet with cranberry tie and sash. White leotards and spats with black shoes. In blue velveteen, white long sleeves and lace trim at hem. Blue cap with pink rose, white leotards and spats with black shoes. In pink crocheted sweater dress, bonnet and muff, white spats and leotards. *Bridal Suite Collection.* 11" *Caroline* in lace trimmed organdy bridal gown with wide lace collar and wide lace band above hem line. Pink flowers across head attached to veil. 15" *Chipper* in matching bridal gown, but has two wide bands of lace above hem, and available in black, too. 18" *Miss Chips* is in same bridal gown, except her skirt has three wide lace bands above the hem. 11" *Pun'Kin* Ring Boy is in short white pants with shoulder strap top and long sleeve pink shirt with lace edging at wrists, pink slipper shoes and carries white pillow. 11" *Pun'Kin* Flowergirl is in long gown with flocked white flowers and has long pink slip that shows through gown, carries pink rose that is lace backed, pink ribbons in hair, and at waist. Eyelette lace at hem and a row above hem. 15" *Chipper* in same material gown and slip, but has puff sleeves and lace trim at hem. She wears pink roses tied over top of head. Available in black. 18" *Miss Chips* in same outfit as the *Chipper.* *Internationals* included this first year: *France, Germany, Holland, Ireland, Italy, Poland, Scotland, Spain, (Girl) And United States* (see chapter that follows this one for complete discription). *Historical Collection.* Included: *Paul Revere, Betsy Ross* and *Martha Washington* (see chapter that follows this one for complete description). *Baby Classics* of 13 dolls. 27 outfits and 15 black dolls. 15" *Little Luv.* In pale pink soft floral dress with organdy sleeves, lace at neck and pink ribbon bow at waist. Rooted hair, and available in black. In pink organdy dress with lace at neck and pink ribbon bow at waist. 18" *Sweetie Pie* is in matching outfits as the *Little Luv*, rooted hair and the one in floral print being made in black also. 20" *Sugar Plum.* Matches the *Little Luv* and *Sweetie Pie* with the one in floral print available in black. Rooted hair. 17" *Twinkie* in pink diaper set and tied to white fleece blanket. Also made in black and has molded hair. In pale pink diaper set and tied to deeper pink blanket with floral print ruffle and sash tie of floral material. Molded hair. In pale pink gown with wide

lace trim down front and pink ribbon tie at neck. Molded hair and available in black. 12" *Baby Winkie* in pink, lace trimmed bunting and white fleece outfit with peaked hood, molded hair and also came in black. Same outfit, but in fleece bunting with floral print inside and lace edging. Rooted hair. 13" *Lil' Darlin'* in matching long infant gown as 17" *Twinkie.* Molded hair. The 17" *Twinkie* was available on a pink pillow with organdy ruffle dressed in an organdy dress and bonnet. Rooted hair. 11" *Pun'Kin* in long flocked-floral print gown with wide ruffle at hem and dark pink sash and ribbon in hair. Sleeveless, but with lace at arm holes and at neck. 15" *Chipper* in same outfit, but with puff sleeves and available in black. 18" *Miss Chips* in matching outfit as the Chipper. 19" *Suzie Sunshine* in matching outfit as others only the sleeves are long and she is available in black. 13" *Butterball* in pink diaper set with molded hair, tied to pink blanket with pink ribbon, and also came in black. In a pale pink diaper set, tied to darker pink blanket with floral ruffle and tied with floral ribbon. Molded hair. In floral print short dress and bonnet that is tied with blue ribbon, came with round blue pillow with floral ruffle around edge. 9" *Babykin* came in floral print long infant gown, molded hair and tied to a pink fleece blanket. In a pink bunting, lace trimmed and matching outfit with hood. In lace trimmed sleeveless short floral print dress and with rooted hair. 11" *Tiny Tubber* came in pink diaper set and tied to pink blanket and had molded hair, plus being available in black. In lace trimmed long infant gown of floral print, bonnet and came with blue lace trimmed pillow. Molded hair and in black also. In a pink fleece bunting with floral print on the inside and lace trimmed. Wears a white long sleeve outfit with hood. Molded hair and available in black. In short floral print dress that matches the 9" *Babykin* has rooted hair and made in white and black. The *Limited Edition Club* doll for 1976 was the 16½" *Patsy* made of vinyl and has molded hair.

1977: *Country Bumpkin Collection* of eight dolls with two being offered in black. See 1977 section of this book. *Sweet Dreams Collection* of seven dolls. 11" *Pun'Kin* in long gown of pale pink flowered print with long sleeves and has wide ruffle at hem, she wears a matching bonnet with pink ribbon tie and came either black or white. 15" *Chipper* in same outfit as the *Pun'Kin* except she wears a sleep cap. 19" *Suzie Sunshine* in plain white gown and floral print peignoir tied in front with pink ribbon, and a sleep cap. Came either in black or white. 18" *DyDee* lace trimmed floral one piece sleeper and carries a plush Teddy Bear. Rooted hair, and either black or white. 13" *Butterball* in floral print diaper set with pink blanket that has a floral ruffle and tied with floral ribbon. Molded hair and came either black or white. 14" *Baby Button Nose.* In long sleeve, enclosed feet floral print, one piece pajamas with lace trimmed collar. Molded hair and either black or white. 15" *Little Lovums* in long floral print infant gown with eyelette lace around hem and pink bow at neck. Molded hair and either black or white. *Regal Heirloom Collection.* See the 1977 section of this book. *Passing Parade Collection.* Set included *Colonial Lady, Frontier Women, Civil War Lady, Gibson Girl, Flapper* and *70's Women.* See 1977 section of this book. *Yesterday's Collection* that includes: *Pun'Kin, Chipper, Miss Chips, Suzie Sunshine, Floppy, Twinkie, Pint Size, Little Luv, Sweetie Pie And Sugar Plum.* See 1977 section of this book. *Vanilla Fudge Collection.* Set includes *Pun'Kin, Suzie Sunshine, Floppy, Butterball, Little Luv And Sugar Plum.* See 1977 section of this book. *Travel Time Collection.* The International doll *Miss Holland* was offered in a green trunk with wardrobe that are national costumes. 11" *Tiny Tubber* offered in green trunk with layette. 17" *Twinkie* in wicker basket and layette. Dresses in long pink gown with flower embroidery down front and on pink pillow with organdy and lace ruffle. 13" *Butterball* in wicker basket with layette, came with pink pillow and organdy ruffle. *Grand Dames Collection* included: *Coquette, Madame DuBerry, Lady Ashley, Violette, Champagne Lady, Mam'selle, Victorian Lady, Fluerette.* See 1977 section of this book. A *Touch Of Velvet Collection.* Dolls included are: *Pun'Kin, Chipper, Suzie Sunshine, Little Lovums, Sweetie Pie* and *Sugar Pie.* All are dressed in deep burgandy and white pinafores/apron-look. All have rooted hair, except the 15" *Little Lovums*, who has molded hair and came with burgandy pillow with white ruffle. *Blue Heaven Collection* of 15" *Little Lovums*, 18" *Lovums*, 20" *Sugar Plum.* There are two 18" *Lovums*, one with rooted hair and a short dress and one with molded hair and a long infant gown. The others have rooted hair. All are dressed in white organdy over blue batiste slips. *Baby Face Collection* of three dolls. All have black shoes and white spats. One is in all white dress with two tier skirt and rosettes on bodice, long sleeves and cap with burgandy ribbon. She has a burgandy sash around waist. One is dressed in burgandy dress with lace slip that shows under the scalloped edge of dress, white straw hat and burgandy ribbon. White pantaloon with burgandy ties on sides and long white sleeves. The other one is in a dark floral print dress with white pinafore. Her bonnet is dark floral with white lace around front and burgandy tie. *Four Seasons Collection.* 11" *Spring* is in green, she was yellow only in 1976. The 1977 *Limited Edition Club Doll* for 1977 was the 16½" *Dewees Cochran* as a young girl. In 1977 and 1978 only, Effanbee made four very unusual dolls for *Disneyland* and *Disneyworld, Cinderella, Snow White, Alice In Wonderland* and *Sleeping Beauty. Bridal Suite Collection.* 11" *Carloine* in white organdy with embroidery at hem, and hem line is scalloped. Matching cap and veil, carries rose with pink streamers. Same doll also available in black. 15" *Chipper* Bridesmaid wears the same gown as the Bride except she has a blue slip, sash and head band. 11" *Pun'Kin* Ring boy wears short white pants with shoulder straps, blue long sleeve shirt with lace down front and carries a white pillow. 11" *Pun'Kin* Flowergirl in lace trimmed white taffeta gown with multi color embroidery trim at waist and across white bonnet, carries rose backed with lace. The 15" *Chipper Bride*, and the 18" *Miss Chips Bride* wear same gown of white embroidered organdy that looks open down the front from the waist with inset of same material. Matching cap and veil. *Baby Classics Collection* are the same as 1976 and include: 11" *Tiny Tubber*, 17" *Twinkie*, 12" *Baby Winkie*, 13" *Butterball* and 18" *Lovums.* The 1977 *Internationals* are: *Black America, France, Germany, Holland, Ireland, Italy, Poland, Scotland, Sweden, Switzerland, Spain* and *U.S.A.* The *Historical Collection* included: *Betsy Ross, Davy Crockett, Florence Nightengale, Martha Washington, Pavlova* and *Pocahantas.* The *Storybook Collection: Alice In Wonderland, Cinderella, Little Bo Peep, Little Red Riding Hood, Mary, Mary,* and *Snow White.* See chapter following this one for full description. *Crochet Classics Collection.* 11" *Tiny Tubber* in pink dress and booties, with pink ribbon in hair (rooted). In pink blanket tied with pink ribbon and in white fleece outfit and hood. Has molded hair, and came either black or white. 18" *DyDee* in pink sweater, cap and legging set, molded hair. 12" *Baby Winkie* in long white infant gown with lace at hem and down front. Multi

color embroidey also down front. long pink sweater and bonnet. White pillow with lace trim. 13" *Butterball* in pink creeper set and beanie, rooted hair. In pink bunting like blanket and dressed in pink fleece outfit with hood. Molded hair and came either black or white. 15" *Little Lovums* in pink sweater and cap in lace trimmed white dress with multi color embroidery down front of skirt. Molded hair and either black or white. 18" *Sweetie Pie* in long sweater and bonnet with white dress with lace trim and multi color embroidery down front of skirt.

1978: In 1978 the *Passing Parade Collection* included eight dolls: *Gay Nineties, Civil War, Frontier Woman, Colonial Lady, Hourglass Look, Gibson Girl, Flapper* and *70's Women.* See the 1978 section of this book. *The Regal Heirloom Collection* included: *Crown Princess, Prince, Princess, Duchess, Her Royal Highness, Queen Mother,* and *Countess.* See the 1978 section of this book. *Sweet Dreams Collection.* All are floral print with little heart-shaped pink buds, and the name Effanbee in pale pink. 11" *Pun'Kin* in long sleeping gown with four rows of lace around hem and matching sleep bonnet with lace. Pink ribbon on bonnet and tie. long sleeves. Came either in black or white. 16" *Lil' Suzie Sunshine.* In same outfit as the Pun'kin. 18" *DyDee* with rooted hair and in one piece sleeper with feet enclosed and carries a plush Teddy Bear. Available in black or white. 14" *Baby Button Nose.* In one piece sleeper with enclosed feet, and has wide collar that is lace trimmed. Molded hair and either black or white. 13" *Butterball* in fleece diaper set tied to pink blanket with floral print ruffle and tie. Molded hair. 15" *Lovums* in long infant gown with eyelette lace at hem and pink bow at neck. Molded hair. *Innocence Collection.* 11" *Caroline*, 15" *Chipper* and the 18" *Miss Chips* all have matching outfits. Long white gowns with three tiers on skirt, puff sleeves above the elbow, eyelette ruffle on bodice. Black ribbon at neck with cameo, and black ribbon running through sash. All have natural straw hats with flowers and tied with net material. The 16" *Lil' Suzie Sunshine*, 19" *Suzie Sunshine*, and the 11" *Half Pint* are in matching white dresses, white leotards and spats with black shoes. Half pint has a one piece skirt where the others have two tiers and pink waist sash. The 15" *Lovums* and 18" *Sweetie Pie*, both with rooted hair have the same dress of white with elbow length puff sleeves and lace at neck, pink ribbon in hair and at waist. 17" *Twinkie* with rooted hair is in white long infant gown, matching pillow and has pink ribbon in hair, on waist and trim on the pillow. Available in black were: *Caroline, Suzie Sunshine*, and *Sweetie Pie. Currier And Ives Collection.* Included Girl and Boy Skater, *Life In The Country, Wayside Inn, Central Park*, and *Night On The Hudson.* See 1978 section of this book. *Grand Dames Collection:* 15" *Madame DuBerry*, 15" *Lady Grey*, 18" *Champagne Lady*, 18" *Nicole*, 15" *Coquette*, 15" *Downing Square*, 18" *Fleurette* and 18" *Blue Danube.* See the 1978 section of this book. *Four Seasons Collection.* Same as 1977. *Travel Time Collection.* 11" *Caroline* in blue trunk with old fashioned wardrobe. *Tiny Tubber* in blue trunk with layette. *Chipper* in trunk and with old fashioned wardrobe. *Twinkie* in wicker basket with layette and on pink pillow with wide organdy ruffle. *Butterball* in wicker basket with layette and on pink pillow with organdy ruffle. *Blue Heaven Collection.* All are dressd in white organdy with deep blue slips have lace trim and all but one (18" *Lovums*) have rooted hair. This set includes: 11" *Pun'Kin*, 16" *Lil' Suzie Sunshine*, 13" *Butterball* (9" with bonnet), 15" *Little Lovums*, 18" *Lovums* (with bonnet), 18" *Sweetie Pie* and 20" *Sugar Plum. Touch Of Velvet*

Collection is same as 1977 and included: 11" *Pun'Kin*, 15" *Chipper*, 16" *L'il Suzie Sunshine*, 19" *Suzie Sunshine* and 20" *Sugar Plum*. The Pun'kin, Chipper, Suzie Sunshine and Sweetie Pie were available in black. The *Internationals* for 1978 were: *Black America, Canada, China, France, Germany, Holland, Ireland, Italy, Poland, Russia, Scotland, Spain, Sweden, Switzerland,* and *United States*. See chapter following this one for complete description. *Historical: Betsy Ross, Cleopatra, Davy Crockett, Florence Nightengale, Pavlova* and *Pochantas. Storybook Collection: Alice In Wonderland, Cinderella, Little Bo Peep, Little Red Riding Hood, Maid Marion, Mary Mary, Robin Hood, Snow White, Tinkerbell.* See chapter that follows this one for a complete description. *Crochet Classics Collection.* All were the same as 1977 except a 13" *Butterball*, which was in a pink creeper with shoulder straps and wears the same beanie. *Baby Classics Collection.* All are the same as the 1977 series except one 11" *Tiny Tubber* who wears a floral print long infant gown on the same print fleece blanket that is lace trimmed. *Bridal Suite Collection.* 11" *Nicole* faced Bride that was available either black or white. The gown has scalloped eyelette around the hem and three scalloped rows of eyelette mid skirt, plus embroidered roses above and a row of embroidered flowers. Below. Matching cap and veil. The black version of the Bride used the Caroline face. The 15" *Chipper* and 18" *Miss Chips* brides wore the same gown, and both were available in black. 11" *Pun'Kin* ring boy wears red organdy velveteen short pants with lace down front beige shirt, red burgandy long sleeve jacket with lace at wrists. Carried matching, lace trimmed pillow. 11" *Pun'Kin* flowergirl has red-burgandy bonnet with elbow length sleeves, lace at neck and around inside of bonnet. Wears embroidered long skirt. The 15" *Bridesmaid* (Chipper) wears same as the 11" flowergirl except the beige skirt is made like the brides. *Memories Collection.* The "Memories" colors are burgandy flowers, on deep tan, beige and a burgandy/tan striped material. 11" *Pun'Kin Boy* is ankle length burgandy pants, collar and billed cap. The bodice-shirt is burgandy/tan stripe, white socks and burgandy slippers. The 11" *Pun'Kin* girl has burgandy flowered print long gown with beige puff sleeves and ruffle at hem. 15" *Chipper* and 18" *Miss Chips* are dressed alike in "Memories" print long gown with one ruffle of burgandy and one of beige at hem, with a burgandy band at upper edge of ruffles, sash and bow at waist and in back of hair. Pinafore style top with beige bodice and sleeves that are long. 16" and 19" *Suzie Sunshine* are dressed alike in organdy (beige) "pinafore" dress with "Memories" print at the top with lace trim, and a band around the ruffled hem that is lace trimmed. Burgandy bow at waist. 11" *Half Pint* is in "Memories" print short dress with lace at hem, long lace trimmed organdy sleeves and matching bonnet. White leotards, black shoes and white spats. 13" *Butterball* in all beige long sleeve short dress with "Memories" band above hem and matching bonnet. 15" *Lovums*, 18" *Sweetie Pie* and 20" *Sugar Plum* are dressed alike in organdy beige dress with long sleeves and "Memories" print on bodice and with band above hem line, as well as a lace edge, lace at wrists and a burgandy bow at waist, in hair. All in this collection have rooted hair except the 13" *Butterball*. The *Limited Edition Club Doll* for 1978 is in all gold gown and called *Crowning Glory*.

1979: *Grande Dames Collection* included: 15" *Blue Bayou*, 15" *Magnolia*, 18" *Lady Snow* and 18" *Cherries Jubilee* both have the *Nicole* face. 15" *Emerald Isle.* 15" *Downing Square.* 18" *Crystal* has the *Nicole* face. 18" *Nicole.* See 1979

section of this book. *Soft 'N Sweet Collection.* All are dressed in wide stripe materials with different colors and flowers to each stripe, all have flowers in the stripes and all have tan velveteen bows in hair and/or bow at waist. The main colors are: blue with beige flowers and beige with blue flowers. Set includes: 11" *Pun'kin*, 15" *Chipper*, 16" *L'il Suzie Sunshine.* 19" *Suzie Sunshine.* 18" *Miss Chips*, 11" *Half Pint*, 13" *Butterball*, 15" *Buttercup*, 18" *Sweetie Pie*, 20" *Sugar Plum. Keepsake Collection* of Antique Brides, Old Fashioned boy and girl and baby. See 1979 section of this book. *Faith Wick's Anchors Aweigh,* and *Party Time* boy and girl. See 1979 section of this book. *American Beauty Collection.* All are dressed in ruby red gowns (babies in dresses) with line tucked organdy apron edged with heavy lace and American Beauty rose (embroidered) on white apron. Ruby red bows in hair and at waist. Dolls include 15" *Buttercup*, 18" *Sweetie Pie*, 20" *Sugar Plum.* 16" *L'il Suzie Sunshine*, 19" *Suzie Sunshine*, 15" *Chipper* and 11" *Pun'kin. Rainbow Parfait.* These dolls are dressed like the *Blue Heaven* collections, in pastels: 11" *Pun'kin* yellow under organdy. 16" *L'il Suzie Sunshine* in pink under organdy. Only one that came in black is the *Pun'kin. Crochet Classics,* same as 1978. *Passing Parade,* all use the Caroline face: *Colonial Lady, Frontier Women, The Hour Glass Look, Gibson Girl, Civil War Lady, Gay Nineties, Flapper* and *The 70's Women.* See 1979 section of this book. *Through The Years With Gigi,* all are Caroline face, and 11". *Papa's Pet, School Girl, Ingenue, Femme Fatale, Mama, Grand-Mere.* All are shown in this book in the color section. *Internationals: Ancient Egypt, Black America, Canada, China, France, Germany, Holland, India, Ireland, Italy, Mexico, Poland, Russia, Spain Boy, Spain Girl, Scotland, Sweden, Switzerland, United States. Storybook Collection: Alice in Wonderland, Cinderella, Goldilocks, Jack, Jill, Little Bo-Peep, Little Red Riding Hood, Mary Mary, Pavlova, Snow White.* See chapter following this one for complete information on Internationals and Storybook dolls. *Bridal Suite Collection* see 1979 for dolls. *Baby Classics Collection,* same as 1978. *Currier and Ives Collection: Boy and Girl Skater, Life in the Country, Wayside Inn, Castle Garden* and *Plymouth Landing.* See 1979 for the dolls. *Four Seasons,* same as 1978. *Innocence Collection,* same as 1978. *Sweet Dreams Collection,* same as 1978. *Travel Time Collection,* 11" *Caroline* in blue trunk with old fashioned wardrobe, also the 15" *Chipper Doll.* 12" *Tiny Tubber* in trunk with layette. Has molded hair. 17" *Twinkie* in wicker basket and layette, 16" *Butterball* in wicker basket with layette. 15" *Little Lovums* in Christening gown and in a wicker bed on wheels and with handle, see 1979 section of this book. The *Effanbee Club Doll* in 1979 was the *Skippy.*

1980: *Grand Dames: Hyde Park, Magnolia, Jezebel* and *Ruby* are all the 15" *Carolina* faced dolls, and *Night At The Opera, La Vie En Rose, Coco* and *Carnegie Hall* are 18" and use the *Nicole* face, see in 1980 section of this book. *Petite Filles Collection: Monique, Madelaine, Babette, Gabrielle, Lili, Brigitte, Mimi* and *Giselle* are all 16" and 11" dolls, see in the 1980 section of this book. *Cotton Candy Collection:* All are in pink and white check with white pinafores and multi color flower trim: 20" *Sugar Plum,* rooted hair and pink bow. *Half Pint Boy* has white suspender short pants, check shirt and cap. *Half Pint Girl* in short check dress and apron that is white with flowered band at waist. 15" *Chipper,* black or white, 16" *L'il Suzie Sunshine* and 20" *Floppy* are all in long gown with ruffles at hem, white pinafores. The *Floppy* has a pink/white check body and limbs. 18" *Sweetie Pie,* either in white or black has same dress as *Sugar Plum* and has rooted hair. 15" *Buttercup* is in same dress as *Sugar Plum* and *Sweetie Pie*, and has rooted hair. 13" *Butterball* is in pink and white check short dress with white ruffle around hem, molded hair and bonnet that matches the dress. *Rhapsody in Blue Collection*, see the 1980 section of this book. *Sweet Dreams Collection*, same as 1978 & 1979. *Travel Time Collection*, 11" *Caroline* in white trunk with blue trim and old fashioned wardrobe. 16" *L'il Suzie Sunshine* in white trunk with blue trim and came with floral print nightgown, crocheted sweater, leggings and cap and is dressed in blue short dress with white pinafore (looks like an *Alice In Wonderland*). 11" *Tiny Tubber* in white trunk with blue trim and layette. 11" *Tiny Tubber* as twins in wicker basket with layette. The twins are in a white fleece bunting that is half pink/white and half blue/white check on the inside and lace trimmed. 17" *Twinkie* in wicker basket and with layette. 12" *Baby Winkie* in white wicker cradle on pink pillow with eyelette lace ruffle. 15" *Little Lovums* in same wicker bed with handle and wheels as shown in the 1979 section. *Through The Years With Gigi*, same as 1979. *Faith Wick Originals: Party Time Boy* and *Girl* and *Anchors Aweigh Boy* and *Girl*, same as 1979. Added this year *Boy* and *Girl Clown*, see 1980 section of this book. *Keepsake Collection*, same as 1979. *W.C. Fields Centennial* doll 1880-1980. 15" and produced only during the year of 1980. *Craftsmen's Corner*. *Baby Lisa* by Astry Campbell, with model made in porcelain for the Smithsonian Institution. Molded hair and painted eyes, 11" long. Excellent quality and design. Came on pillow, tied to blanket and in wicker basket with layette. *Crochet Classics Collection*, same as 1979. *Four Seasons Collection*, same as 1979. *Heart to Heart Collection*: All have tiny blue heart shaped rose bud print with the name Effanbee printed among the buds. The name is very pale. 20" *Sugar Plum*, 14" *Baby Button Nose*, 15" *Buttercup*, 18" *Sweetie Pie* are all in same dress with all having rooted hair except the *Baby Buttercup*, who has molded hair and wears a bonnet. The *Baby Buttercup* does not have a white collar, as the others do. 11" *Pun'kin* and 16" *L'il Suzie Sunshine* wear short dresses with white collars and the *Pun'kin* was available in black, as the *Baby Button Nose* was, also. 17" *Twinkie* came either black or white with long infant gown and lace at hem, molded hair. 18" *Lovums* came in long infant gown of white with the heart to heart print in a ruffle down the front and had molded hair. 11" *Tiny Tubber* came in white fleece hooded outfit in white fleece bunting with the heart to heart print on the inside and is lace trimmed. Was also available in black or white. Also came tied to heart to heart print blanket that is lace trimmed, either black or white. The 11" *Tiny Tubber* also came in short dress and bonnet. All in this collection, except the *Tiny Tubber* tied to the blanket came with a blue ribbon tied at neck. *Currier and Ives Collection*, see 1979 and 1980 section of this book. *Cream Puff Collection*. All have organdy dresses with different colored slips. 18" *Sweetie Pie*, 15" *Buttercup* and 20" *Sugar Plum* have blue slips and rooted hair. 17" *Twinkie*, 14" *Baby Button Nose* and 18" *Butterball*, who comes on blue pillow have molded hair. The 17" *Twinkie* came with a pink pillow. *Bridal Suite Collection*. 18" *Bride* with the *Nicole* face, pleated center to gown with overskirt of organdy lace, and she wears a pill box style hat-veil. 15" *Bride* with the *Caroline* face came either black or white and has a full lace organdy gown with tiara style head piece with veil. 15" *Bridesmaid* with the *Caroline* face is in soft floral print organdy gown with wide ruffle at hem, wears hat with large bow of the same material

and carries a rose. *Internationals: Brazil, Canada, China, France, Germany, Greece, Soldier, Holland, India, Ireland, Israel, Italy, Mexico, Poland, Russia, Scotland, Spain Boy, Spain Girl, Sweden, Switzerland, United States. Storybook: Alice In Wonderland, Cinderella, Goldilocks, Heidi, Jack and Jill, Little Bo Peep, Little Red Riding Hood, Mary, Mary, Mother Hubbard, Snow White, Sleeping Beauty* and *Prince Charming*. See chapter following this one for complete description. The Effanbee Limited Edition Club Doll for 1980 was *Susan B. Anthony*.

1981: *Grand Dames Collection*, see 1981 section of this book. They included: 15" *Shauna, Chantilly, Gramercy Park, Covent Garden*. 11" *Saratoga, Lady Ascot, Francoise, Peaches* and *Cream*. 18" *Topaz, Turquoise, Daphne, Opal*. A special limited edition of the set of four 11" black dolls from this collection was made in 1981 for Treasure Trove of New York. *Over The Rainbow Collection*, all are dressed with large bows on skirts, or bands across bodices of check in green, yellow, blue and pink. The boy has blue check suspender short pants and white shirt, and only the 11" *Half Pint Boy* and *Girl* wear straw bonnet hats. All dolls have rooted hair, except the 13" *Butterball*, who wears a baby bonnet and has molded hair. This set included: 20" *Floppy* with pink check body and limbs, 18" *Miss Chips*, 11" *Half Pint Boy* and *Girl*, 20" *Sugar Plum*, 13" *Butterball*, 15" *Buttercup*, 15" *Chipper*, 11" *Punkin*, 18" *Sweetie Pie*. The only black dolls available in this group were: *Chipper, Sweetie Pie* and *Pun'kin*. *Petite Filles Collection*, see 1981 section of this book. Dolls included were: *Denise, Bebe Denise, Marianne, Bebe Mariann, Nanette, Bebe Nanette, Genevieve, Bebe Genevieve. Heart To Heart Collection*, same as 1980. *Pride Of The South Collection*, see 1981 section of this book. Dolls were: *Mobile, Charleston, Natchez, Savannah, New Orleans, Riverboat Gambler. Crochet Classic Collection*, same as 1980, except that the 15" *Little Lovums* in white dress, pink sweater and bonnet was dropped. Changed 11" *Tiny Tubber* from a blanket bunting tied with wide pink ribbon to a square pocket style bunting with fringe edging. New was 18" *Cookie* (using the *Lovums* head), made on a toddler body (*Suzie Sunshine's*) in short pink dress, sweater and bonnet and has molded hair. 15" *Buttercup* in long suspender leggings, pink cloth long sleeved shirt and pink bonnet with ruffle around edge. She has rooted hair. Others were: 18" *DyDee*, 11" *Pun'kin*, 12" *Baby Winkie*, 11" *Tiny Tubber*, 13" *Butterball*, 18" *Sweetie Pie. Send In The Clowns Collection*. 11", 15", and 18" have plastic bodies, and a 15" and 18" have cloth bodies. All have white painted faces, black painted hair and white two piece clown suits with red pom poms. See 1981 section of this book. *Sweet Dreams Collection*, same as 1980. Has the pink heart shaped flower print and the Effanbee name is lightly printed on the material. *Travel Time Collection*: 16" *L'il Suzie Sunshine*, 11" *Tiny Tubber* in white/blue trunks are the same as 1980. *Tiny Tubber Twins* and 17" *Twinkie* in the wicker baskets are the same as 1980. 15" *Little Lovums* and 12" *Baby Twinkie* in the white wicker cradle and bed are same as 1980. The 11" *Caroline* is still in the white and blue trunk, and has two old fashioned outfits, but the doll is dressed in a sailor dress with below waist pleats, two red bands, white collar with red trim, and has red trim at wrists. The basic dress is navy blue. Matching cap with red pom, pom. *Hattie Holiday*. 16" *L'il Suzie Sunshine* in four season outfits, see 1981 section of this book. The *Four Season Collection* was re-introduced in 1981 using a "new" face and clothes, see 1981 section of this book. The 15" young girl style dolls use the heads like the

Day By Day Collection, which were the same in 1981 as in 1980. The *John Wayne* doll was the limited production of one year doll for 1981, see 1981 section of this book. The Treasure Trove of New York offered a solid bronze medal, like one issued by Congress as a tribute to John Wayne. The medal has the bust of Mr. Wayne on one side, the other side has Mr. Wayne on a horse. *Huggables Collection.* All are 14" tall, have pink cloth bodies and limbs. *Little Bo Peep* is dressed in the pink heart shaped flowered dress with the Effanbee name lightly printed on it and has a pink velveteen shoulder straps/band attached to side panniers, and blue ribbon at waist. "Poke" bonnet of printed material with ruffle at edge and ruffle at hem. Center part long blonde hair. Black shoes and white spats. *Alice In Wonderland* has blue dress, white pinafore with blue ribbon and trim, blue ribbon around long blonde center part hair. Black shoes with lacing tied around legs. Little Red Riding Hood is in red and white check dress, white shoulder strap apron and wears red velveteen hood cape. Black shoes with white spats. *Craftsmen Corner* featuring Faith Wick Dolls with the boy and girl clowns the same as 1980. In 1981 were: 16" *Peddler Women*, see 1981 section of this book, and *Hearth Witch* and the *Wicket Witch*, see 1981 section of this book. Also the *Baby Lisa* by Astry Campbell, same as 1980. The Effanbee Limited Edition Club doll for 1981 was the *Girl With The Watering Can*, see 1981 section. Also the Amway Corporation has an exclusive doll made by Effanbee called *Miss Amanda*, see the 1981 section of this book. *Les Enfants Collection.* 18" *Lovums* in long infant gown with wide lace to form a collar look/pink ribbon bow and matching bonnet. Molded hair and has two rows of pink rick rack trim above hem. 15" *Little Lovums* is in same outfit as the 18" *Lovums*. 15" *Buttercup* and 20" *Sugar Plum* are in same dress. Only theirs are pink and short, both have rooted hair. The 18" *Sweetie Pie* and 14" *Baby Button Nose* are in same short dresses, but the color is blue. All these short dresses have one row of rick rack trim. The *Baby Button Nose* has molded hair and a bonnet. 17" *Twinkie* is in same short dress of white, but has two rows of pink rick rack above the hem and is sold with a pink pillow with wide lace trim. 13" *Butterball* is in pale pink short dress with wide lace at hem and one row of rick rack above the hem, rooted hair with matching bonnet, and sold on pink pillow with wide lace trim ruffle. *Internationals: Brazil, Canada, China, Czechoslovakia, Denmark, France, Germany, Holland, Israel, India, Ireland, Italy, Mexico, Norway, Poland, Russia, Scotland, Spain Girl, Switzerland, Sweden, United States. Storybook Collection: Alice In Wonderland, Cinderella, Gretel, Goldilocks, Hansel, Heidi, Jack, Jill, Little Bo Peep, Little Red Riding Hood, Mary Had A Little Lamb, Mary Mary, Mother Goose, Mother Hubbard, Pinocchio, Prince Charming, Sleeping Beauty, Snow White.* See chapter following this one for complete description. *Lady in Velvet Hat* made for the Smithsonian Institute (see 1981 section).

1982: Clothes change: *Canada, China, Russia, Israel, Cinderella, Mary Mary, Jack and Jill, Prince Charming* and *Sleeping Beauty. Les Enfants Collection, All Grand Dames, Bridal Suite.* Discontinued: *Riverboat Gambler,* four from the Crochet classics, *Over the Rainbow, Petite Filles,* and there will be a new different *John Wayne.*

Internationals,
Historical, Storybook
and Specials - 1976 to 1981

The following is a list of dolls and the year they were discontinued follows this section.

Miss Ancient Egypt: 1979 (#1116). Made this year only, but is very like the *Cleopatra* of the Historical Collection (made in 1978 only) with the same clothes and sandles, but entirely different head gear. *Ancient Egypt's* head gear is gold with crown cut top and folds behind the ears so the hair is inside the head piece. A black band encircles it with gold and eyelette trim.

Miss Black America: 1977-1979 (#1110). All are same costume of long plain cut gown with long sleeves, high collar and wound head piece. The print for 1977 and 1978 are actually the same, but most will look different from each other due to the cut of the material. All are brown and white with upside down, and right side up hearts in one band, square brown blocks with floral design and mixed geometric designs. In 1979 the print is grey and gold on rust with the flowers being large grey ones outlined in the gold. In 1979 a metal "tiara" tab was added to front of wound head piece.

Miss Brazil: 1980-1982 (#1120). Has red and yellow head band, and in 1981 she has gold earrings sewn onto same head band.

Miss Canada: 1978-1982 (#1113). Has white slippers in 1978, and black all other years. 1978-1980. Embroidered trim braid on pinafore apron has a red flower, and two white flowers pattern repeated. 1981 has a red flower, smaller yellow flower and two white flowers pattern repeated. 1982 has costume change.

Miss China: 1978 (#1114) has a large yellowish flower and no ribbon in hair. 1979-1980 has a "puffy" yellow flower and head band ribbon. 1981 has the puffy yellow flower, but no ribbon. Made in 1982 also.

Miss Czechoslovakia: New in 1981 (#1123). 1982 costume change.

Miss Denmark: New in 1981 (#1124).

Miss France: 1976-1978 is the same. 1979 bonnet changed from a "Dutch" look to a provincial style that is like an upside down bowl with band of embroidered flowers and with lace lower trim. This hat continues into 1982. The 1979 dress was the same as those back to 1976. The 1980-1981 is a complete change to deep blue bodice, white long sleeves, red, yellow, and blue flower braid and lace up front of bodice. Black skirt with one red band above hem. Attached apron has scalloped lace hem and red, black band trim mid way up, plus red bow at waist. (#1102).

Miss Germany: 1976 has wide stripe vertical pattern on skirt with different floral patterns within each stripe, and bodice with white sleeves. White apron with red and green embroidered band above the hem. Red velveteen vest with cut out and black bow. Her blonde hair is in braids that loop up and are tied with red bows. The head band matches the band on the apron. In 1977 she is changed to a solid red floral print of gold and black on red, with white sleeves and apron. The band on the apron matches the dress, and there is eyelette lace at hem. The vest is now black and the hair braids are interwoven with red, black ribbons and she has no head band. 1978 is the same as 1977, as is 1979. All have black stockings and shoes. In 1980 there was a wide ruffle added at the hem that makes the

dress stand out and the band across the apron was dropped. The hair has been left long, with full bangs, and she wears a flat brim white straw hat with red band and three red pom poms in front (Black Forest Provincial item). All have lace at the neck. 1981 is same. (#1103).

Greece: (Soldier). Made in 1980 only (#1121). Has mustache, red, gold, and white short Greek outfit. An excellent doll.

Miss Holland: 1976-1979 the embroidered braid trim covers about three-fourths of the bodice, but print changes. 1976 and 1977 has heart shaped with red and yellow flowers. 1978 has wider spaced figures and gold leaves with small black flower. 1979 has two white flowers close together with black leaf and stems, small gold flowers. In 1980 and 1981 the trim covers only about one third of the bodice, with both using blue flowers with gold centers, along with red flowers. (#1104).

Miss India: In 1979 the long chiffon blue scarf with gold braid edging is wrapped around waist and tied in front. In 1980 and 1981, it is caught up at the side of the neck with a small ring. (#1119).

Miss Ireland: 1976-1977 has the green dress to just below the knees. In 1978 to 1981 the dress is almost to shins, otherwise all years are the same. (#1105).

Miss Israel: 1980-1981 are the same. Change in 1982.

Miss Italy: 1976 has red stripes on white head scarf tied in back under the hair. Plain white long sleeves, white and red flowers with tiny green leaves on embroidery band that is midway down on white apron, and it has eyelette trim at hem. 1977 has green with white stitching all around the edges head scarf, tied in back under the hair. Apron band has just red flowers, green leaves and tiny specks of white, but same eyelette at hem. 1978 has all red bodice and sleeves with white lace bands above the elbows, eyelette hem on apron replaced by wide lace edging that matches the arm bands. Head scarf is red and tied around the head in front. 1979 is same with head scarf being narrower, but still tied under the chin. 1980-1981 now has wide lace band down the front of the bodice, lace scarf tied under chin, and wider embroidered band on the apron, with red, white and green flowers. (#1106).

Miss Mexico: 1979-1981 only difference is red rick rack on hat. In 1979 it is right at the very edge of the straw hat, and others have the rick rack lower down. (#1118).

Miss Norway: New in 1981. (#1125).

Miss Poland: 1976 and 1977 have the same red scarf with white stitch edging and tied under the chin, white boots. 1978 has red scarf with eyelette lace edging made into a shoulder shawl. A red band has been added to the black skirt above the hem, and the red band trim on the bodice and apron of the 1976 and 1977 has been changed to black trim. The all white sleeves have been changed to sleeves with same matching floral material as apron, and lace edging has been replaced with eyelette that matches the shawl. She wears a black head bonnet with floral print inside, plus lace ruffle next to hair. The bonnet has a white chin tie. Still has white boots. 1979 still has the same shawl, boots and black trim, but apron and sleeves and bonnet have been changed to yellow with red and black floral print. A black band edges the yellow floral bonnet, which has a white bow near top and chin tie. 1980-1981 have same basic outfit from waist down, but boots are now black slippers. She now has full white bodice and sleeves with no lace at wrists, and a red velveteen cutout vest with black ribbon bow in front. The red head piece stands up in back and has yellow and black bands, and a white band next to face, also has short yellow, black and white streamers at each side of the head piece. (#1107).

Miss Russia: 1978 to 1980 has gold, blue, green and red on black paisley print on crown hat with gold and red bands on each edge. 1981 this crown hat head band has been changed to embroidered floral print of white, green and red on black with white edges. (#1115). 1982 costume change.

Miss Scotland: 1976 has a large plaid print, a red jacket with scarf over the shoulder and it ends at the hips. Her black knee high hose are held up with red ribbon tied near the top. The pom pom on the tam is red. She has plaid band at wrists of sleeves. 1977 to 1980 have dark green and red small lined plaid, black jacket with red bands just above the wrists, and a black pom pom on tam. The shoulder scarf ends near hem of skirt. 1981 is same except plaid has white stripes, as well as green and red. (#1109).

Miss Spain: 1976-1981. No changes. (#1109).

Spain Boy (Toreador): 1979 has gold sleeves and wide brimmed hat. 1980 had black sleeves and almost a round hat. (#1117).

Miss Sweden: 1977 to 1979 has black skirt, fringe on shawl and heat bonnet with red chin tie, plus curly hair. White blouse top, red apron. 1980 has red bonnet and tie, red apron with green skirt, shawl and black fringe. All have white bodices and sleeves. 1981 complete new outfit with green skirt and bodice, white sleeves and apron. Has wide floral print on black band on skirt, third of bodice and head gear. Lace at hem of apron, scalloped across the bodice, and lower edge of skirt's black floral band and at neck. Yellow band at top of black floral one on skirt, and yellow bow on front, at waist. Long straight hair. (#1111).

Miss Switzerland: 1977 to 1979 has green tam brimless style hat with yellow feather. 1980-1981 brimmed green hat and yellow feather. (#1112).

Miss United States: 1976 to 1980 are the same. 1981 changes include no fringe and red band on skirt, which is replaced with red and white check that is much smaller than earlier ones, and there is a hem ruffle with white stitching above the ruffle. Has black cuffs and red bands on sleeves that are replaced with white stitching above wrists. White stitching around all of the vest and hat is red with white ties. (#1101).

1982 International Collection (21 dolls)

Austria: (New-1982). Brown/white stripe short skirt, brown bodice and sleeves with brown backed, lace apron attached. Row of lace above the elbows and at wrists. White kerchief at neck. Brown with lace over half, head scarf, white leotards and brown slippers.

Argentina: (New-1982). In long black gown with white lace at hem, across bodice, and at cuffs. Gold, blue and red bands of trim above hem line. Black with gold trim at edges, shawl and white lace with gold trim long head piece.

Brazil: Same as 1981.

Canada: Completely re-dressed for 1982. Now in dark green flowered calf length dress with deep ruffle, white attached apron with wide lace hem, dark green flowered bodice with lace inset, white full length sleeves. Straw

brimmed hat pulled down at sides with dark green tie and has large puffy bow on top of hat that matches the dress material.

China: Redressed for 1982. With one piece gown that has flowers printed on blue material. Wide pink band at hem and at wrists. Pink ribbon across head with pink "roses" at sides.

Czechoslovakia: Same as 1981.

Denmark: Same as 1981, except bands across bib apron are different colors.

France: Same as 1981, except basic dress is now royal blue with lace trim at edges now regular lace, and not eyelette lace. Flowers down front of bodice (on embroidery inset), and on hat are different now being just pink and yellow.

Germany: Same as 1981.

Holland: Same as 1981, except band of embroidery trim above waist goes higher onto bodice, and has different flowers (smaller red ones).

India: Same as 1981.

Ireland: Same as 1981.

Israel: Complete change for 1982: Royal blue dress with white lower sleeves and wide hem. White eyelette ruffle at mid-bodice, white lower sleeves and wide hem, band at neck and around hair. Both head band and near hem has dark blue design trim. White leotards and black slippers.

Italy: Same as 1981.

Mexico: Same as 1981.

Norway: Same as 1981, except apron is a little shorter.

Poland: Same as 1981, except bands on stand up cap are (face to back of head) yellow, red, black, and green.

Russia: Complete change in 1982. All burgundy coat dress with white "fur" cuff, at neck and stand up hat. White embroidered trim at waist.

Scotland: Same as 1981.

Spain: Same as 1981.

Sweden: Same as 1981.

Switzerland: Same as 1981.

Turkey: (New-1982). This boy doll is dressed in royal blue, just below the knees, one piece pant outfit in a puffy style. Burgandy sleeveless ¾ length coat jacket. Black lace around edges of jacket and around burgandy hat. Gold trim also around hat along with a black tassel. Burgandy slippers.

United States: Same as 1981.

Historical Dolls

Betsy Ross: 1976 to 1978. 1976 has small foral print and 1977, 1978 have larger even spaced flowers in the print. (#1152).

Cleopatra: 1978 only. Plain round gold and black head gear with shoulder length "flap" that does not enclose the hair as it does when this doll was changed to Miss Ancient Egypt in 1979 as part of the International series. (#1158).

Davy Crockett: 1977, carries tan "purse" bag next to pouch and in 1978 this purse bag is same color as the pouch, jacket and boots (dark brown). (#1154).

Florence Nightengale: 1977 and 1978 are the same. (#1155).

Martha Washington: 1976-1977. Same. (#1153).

Paul Revere: 1976 only. (#1151).

Pavlova: 1977 and 1978 are the same. (#1156). Became part of the Storybooks for 1979 only.

Pocahontas: 1977 and 1978 only. The 1978 has shorter

turned fringe top to boots and thinner fringe at hem of skirt. (#1157).

Storybook Dolls

Alice In Wonderland: No changes. (#1175).

Cinderella: 1977 has two tiers of soft pink nylon chiffon over pink satin skirt on long gown. Pink sleeveless bodice with same soft nylon chiffon folded in four tiers, stole style around the shoulders. Silver crown with four front parts cut taller than rest and goes under hair in back. Pink bows and streamers and rose at waist. Very pale blonde, with rest of the years being a tosca blonde. 1978 has all pink gown with lace at hem and pink overskirt caught up at sides with pink bows. Nylon chiffon piece used as stole. Gold mesh crown around the head and fits down onto the forehead. 1979 is same as 1978, except gold bows tie up overskirt. 1980 and 1981 the gown is white with silver dots and silver band above the hem. Same material overskirt with sides caught up with silver bows. Stole now of same material as the gown with silver bow in front, plus silver collar necklace. Mesh silver crown encircles the head. Costume change in 1982. (#1176).

Gretel: New in 1981. (#1195).

Goldilocks: 1979 has long yellow gown skirt with ruffle at hem, multi color on blue floral apron with ruffle at hem. White bodice with puffy sleeves above the elbows and tight below the elbows, with lace at wrists. Royal blue velveteen cut out vest with inverted "v" at bottom. Two blue bows in hair, white sandles. 1980 the gown is shorter to show white pantaloons with same lace trim as on the sleeves wrists. The vest is green and not cut out. The apron is green floral print and she wears one green bow at top, near the back of her head, white sandles. 1981 is same as 1980 except the lace around the hem of the pantaloons are eyelette. Changed in 1982. (#1184).

Hansel: New in 1981. (#1194).

Heidi: 1979-1980. No change. (#1191).

Jack and Jill: 1979-1981. No changes, except the embroidery trim on Jills apron. It has blue and pink hearts in 1979. 1980 has blue and red flowers with interwoven green leaves. 1981 has narrow embroidered multi color band with white border bands. Change in 1982 for both dolls. (#1186 & 1187).

Little Bo Peep: 1977-1981. No changes. (#1177).

Little Red Riding Hood: 1977-1981. No changes, except in 1977 the cover for her basket has a criss-cross open weave with black dots and the rest of the years have the same material as her dress, which is red and white check. (#1178).

Maid Marion: 1978 only. (#1182).

Mary Had A Little Lamb: New in 1981. (#1196).

Mary, Mary: 1977 has red and white flower pattern on dark background and carries a white basket with green felt cover tied to wrist. Square ruffle lace trim comes three-fourth way down on bodice. 1978 is same except lace ruffle on bodice now forms a yoke and print has much more red flowers in it with background deep green. 1979 is same as 1978 except the hem ruffle is deeper and she carries a white watering can tied to her wrist. 1980 same as 1979. 1981 has very tiny yellow and red floral print on green. Rest is same as 1979-1980. Change in 1982. (#1179).

Mother Goose: New in 1981. (#1193).

Mother Hubbard: 1980 and 1981 same except 1981 carries a wood handle mop tied to wrist. (#1188)

Pavlova: 1979 only and carried over from the Historical set (1977-1978) was #1156 in Historicals and #1185 in Storybook set.

Pinocchio: New in 1981. (#1192).

Prince Charming: 1980 and 1981, no change. Change in 1982. (#1189).

Robin Hood: 1978 only. (#1183).

Sleeping Beauty: 1980-1981. No change. (#1190). Change in 1982.

Tinkerbell: 1978 only. (#1183).

Snow White: 1977-1981. No change. (#1180).

Storybook Dolls For 1982 (23 dolls)

Alice In Wonderland: Same as 1981.

Cinderella: Re-dressed in pink satin with white lace rowed net overskirt and floor length cape. Two pink bows on front of skirt front and silver crown.

Gretel: Same as 1981, except lace around apron is ruffled.

Goldilocks: Completely changed for 1982 to green dotted skirt with wide ruffle, white bodice, long sleeves and organdy apron with lace ruffle hem and rose applique. White bow at waist. Green dotted sleeveless vest top, straw hat with white bows and ties, and lace trimmed pantaloons with white slippers.

Hans Brinker: (New-1982). Navy blue knee, long sleeve outfit with red trim to form jacket look and four gold buttons. Red flowered kerchief, red leotards, wooden shoes and carries old fashioned skates. Navy billed cap with red trim.

Hansel: Same as 1981.

Heidi: Changed to dark blue skirt with wide ruffle that has white circles printed on. Shorter apron with hem lace more ruffled.

Jack and Jill: Completely changed for 1982. Jack has blue with white dots, one piece overalls that have long pants and shoulder straps with two buttons. Same long sleeve white shirt and black tie at neck. Rolled brim straw hat with black bow in back. Jill: White dotted on blue, long sleeve dress and white pinafore with eyelette ruffle around shoulders and at hem. Red flowered embroidered band above eyelette lace at hem and same straw hat as Jack.

Little Bo Peep: Same as 1981.

Little Red Riding Hood: Same as 1981.

Mary Had A Little Lamb: Same as 1981.

Mary, Mary: Complete change to one piece green with white and gold flower print pinafore dress with wide ruffles over shoulders and wide pink ruffle at hem under ruffled pinafore. Long pink sleeves and pink trim just above green ruffle of skirt. Full brim straw hat with pink ties, and carries white basket with flowers.

Mary Poppins: (New-1982). Navy blue coat dress with wide light blue band around hem and small light blue band above hem band and around sleeves at wrists. Dark navy hat with flowered pattern material band around it and carries same flowered print purse. High button spats over black slippers. Yellow neck scarf around neck.

Mother Goose: Same as 1981, except two rows of trim and shoulder fringe shawl is now navy blue.

Mother Hubbard: Same as 1981, except lace band at hem of apron is wider.

Peter Pan: (New-1982). Forest green leotards and brown roll top slippers. Forest green short jacket with cut edges and elbow length sleeves. Blue long sleeve, high neck shirt, green felt hat with yellow feather.

Pinocchio: Same as 1981.

Prince Charming: Complete change. White leotards, black slippers and forest green short jacket with gold long sleeves and gold belt. White pleated wide lace trimmed collar with small buckle in front. Forest green cap with white feather.

Sleeping Beauty: Complete change. Long gold skirt, white long sleeve bodice and forest green bonnet with white lace around inner edge. Cut out waist vest band with gold bow.

Snow White: Same as 1981, except bow and streamers in front are narrower.

Sugar Plum Fairy: (New-1982). Pale pink two layer dotted net, calf length tutu. Scalloped edge hems, lace ruffles at neck and pink sash. Pink ballerina slippers and matching dotted pink cape with pink bow tie. Pink ribbon around hair with three pink embroidered rosettes.

Rapunzil: (New-1982). Burgandy long gown with long white sleeves, white pleated neck collar that is lace trimmed, and white embroidered band around waist. Matching burgandy hat with same trim as waist. Gold trim down front of gown and around edge of hem. Very long, almost to the floor, tosca blonde hair.

Discontinued Dolls 1976 to 1981

Internationals: *Miss Black America* - 1980, *Miss Ancient Egypt* - 1979 only, *Spain Boy* - 1979-1980 only, *Greece Soldier* - 1980 only.

Historicals discontinued: All have been.

Storybook Dolls discontinued: *Maid Marion* 1978. *Pavlova* 1979. *Robin Hood* 1978. *Tinkerbell* 1978.

Others Discontinued From 1976 To 1981.

1976: Americana "76 Collection of ten dolls. Granny's Corner Collection of nine dolls. Prairie Nights Collection of six dolls. Ragamuffins of eight dolls.

1977: Country Bumpkin Collection of nine dolls. Vanilla Fudge Collection of six dolls. Yesterday's Collection of eleven doll.

1978: Memories Collection of eleven dolls. Touch of Velvet of seven dolls.

1979: American Beauty Collection of eight dolls. Blue Heaven Collection of seven dolls. The Heirloom Collection of seven dolls. Rainbow Parfait Collection of seven dolls. Soft and Sweet of ten dolls. 1978 and 1979 used the Nicole face, then they were discontinued except for the Miss Amanda doll made for Amway Corporation, a very few in 1980.

1980-1981 into 1982: Innocence Collection of nine dolls. Keepsake Collection of four dolls. My Friend doll made for the Smithsonian Institute. Petite Filles using the Suzie Sunshine, etc. dolls. Ship Ahoy Collection of six dolls. Through the Years with Gigi of six dolls. Cream Puff Collection of seven dolls. Currier & Ives. Four Seasons using the Caroline face, re-issued in 1981 with little girl face (same as Day by Day set). Cotton Candy Collection of ten dolls. Party Time boy and girl by Faith Wick. W.C. Fields. Rhapsody in Blue. Les Enfants. Heart to Heart with ten dolls. Over the Rainbow. John Wayne. Riverboat Gambler and Savannah from the Pride of the South Collection. From the

Crochet Classics of 1981: Pun'kin, Cookie, DyDee and Tiny Tubber on pillow. From Heart to Heart: Pun'kin, Baby Button Nose. Antique Bride. Clown Boy by Faith Wick. Baby Lisa on pillow. Sweet Dreams the Half Pint. Travel Time Suzie Sunshine in trunk, twin Tiny Tubbers and in wicker cradle. Little Lovums in wicker bed on wheels, with handle.

Clothes are changed each year on the Grand Dames.

Effanbee Limited Club Series.

1975: Precious Baby, **1976:** Patsy, **1977:** Dewees Cochran, **1978:** Crowning Glory, **1979:** Skippy, **1980:** Susan B. Anthony, **1981:** Girl with Watering Can.

Others - 1982

Absolutely Abigail: (New-1982). See photo section of 1982.

Age of Elegance: Collection of 18" exquisitely dressed antique French looking dolls. Cathedral (Bride), Buckingham Palace in deep red, Versailles in blue, Victoria Station in forest green and white. New-1982.

Baby Liza by Astri: Only offered on pillow and in wicker case with layette.

Billy Bum. New in 1982. Boy dressed as Hobo. Designed by Faith Wick.

Bobbsey Twins: (New-1982). See photo section.

Bridal Suite Collection: Same as 1981, except gowns changed. Bridesmaid in beautiful blue gown.

Clown Girl: Same as 1981. Designed by Faith Wick.

Crochet Classics Collection: Same as 1981.

Day By Day Collection: Same as 1981.

Enchanted Garden Collection: Same as 1981 with clothes now white and paisley blue print.

Four Seasons Collection: Same as 1981.

Hatti Holiday Collection: Same as 1981.

Grand Dames Collection: 8 dolls with four 15" and four 11". All larger ones discontinued. 15" Guinevere, Oliva, Claudette, and Hester. 11" Elizabeth, Robyn, Katherine, and Amanda. All new for 1982.

Hearth Witch and Wicket Witch: Same as 1981. Designed by Faith Wick.

Heart To Heart Collection: Same as 1981.

Heaven Sent Collection: Baby Button Nose in pink, Little Lovums in blue, Sugar Plum in pink, Buttercup in blue, Lovums in pink and Butterball with pillow and in blue.

Huggable Collection: Same as 1981, except added is Pinocchio. John Wayne. New 1982. See photo section. Produced during 1982 only.

Just Friends Collection: See photo section.

Nasta Santa: Santa Claus designed by Faith Wick. New for 1982. Cloth and vinyl. Mae West. New in 1982. See photo section. Produced during 1982 only.

Orange Blossom: New in 1982. Designed by Joyce Stoffard. See photo section.

Parade of Wooden Soldiers: New in 1982. 18", 15", & 11" soldiers in red and white.

Peddler: Same as 1981. Designed by Faith Wick.

Pride Of The South Collection: Same as 1981. Clothes change on Savannah. River Boat Gambler dropped.

Sweet Dreams Collection: Same as 1981.

Send In The Clowns: 18", 15", 11" are all vinyl. 15" only with soft body, otherwise same as 1981.

Travel Time Collection: Same as 1981.

1982 Limited Edition Club Doll: Lady Diane in Wedding Gown. To join club write: Effanbee Limited Edition Doll Club, 200 Fifth Avenue, New York City, New York 10010.

15″ "Baby Dainty" marked on shoulder plate in oval: Effanbee/Dolls/Walk, Talk, Sleep. Came with and without a wig. Blue sleep eyes and open mouth with four teeth and felt tongue. "Baby Dainty" was a successful doll for many years beginning in 1912 to 1925. Courtesy Nancy Lucas.

15″ "Baby Dainty" of 1920. Shoulder head and shoulder are one piece and marked: "Effanbee/Baby Dainty". Stuffed cloth body with full composition arms and half composition legs. Molded hair. This doll also came with wig over the molded hair. Painted blue eyes. Believe her outfit was made years ago from an old pattern. Material has tiny blue hearts on white background and blue blouse. The arms are disc jointed. Courtesy June Schultz.

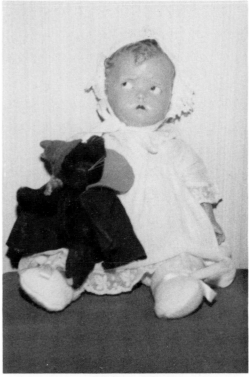

14″ "Grumpy". Original cloth body has disc jointed, bent cloth stuffed legs. Half composition arms. Side glance painted eyes. Composition swivel head on composition shoulder plate. Old clothes, but not original. Doll's head is marked only with a: 176. Deeply molded and painted hair. 1913-1930's. Holds an Austria "Puss 'n Boots". Courtesy June Schultz.

20″ "Grumpy" with cloth body and composition arms, legs and head. Molded hair, painted eyes and very grumpy expression. Small arms in proportion to rest of doll. Marked on shoulder plate: Effanbee/Dolls/Walk, Talk, Sleep, in oval. The 12″ "Grumpy" with composition head, arms and straight legs. Arms are strung through the shoulder plate. Legs are disc jointed. Molded hair and painted eyes. Marks are same as larger doll. 1913. Courtesy Mauldin Collection.

"Baby Blue and Baby Pink". Composition shoulder heads with molded hair and painted eyes. Composition lower arms, and cloth stuffed bodies, upper arms and legs. 1919.

"Teddy Bear and Airman". Cloth bodies with composition lower arms and legs. Composition shoulder head with painted hair and eyes. Knit outfits. Shoes are molded on. 1919.

 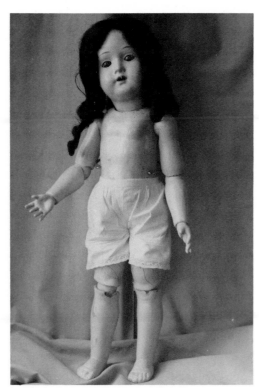

18″ That is marked on head and body: Effanbee. Composition head, blue/green celluloid over tin sleep eyes, dark brown human hair wig. Composition and wood ball jointed body with blushed knees, hands and breasts. Factory made dress. The mouth is open with teeth. 1919. Courtesy Carol Stephens. Photo by Sally Freeman.

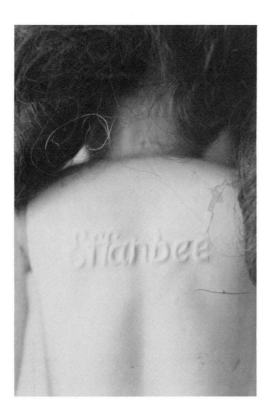

28″ marked in script: Effanbee, on shoulder plate and dress is tagged Effanbee. (Pink organdy). Cloth body with composition head and limbs. Brought from Mandel Bros. Chicago in 1922. The soles of the shoes are marked: Germany. Tin Sleep eyes. The original price on the box is $12.95 and style #2869. Courtesy June Schultz.

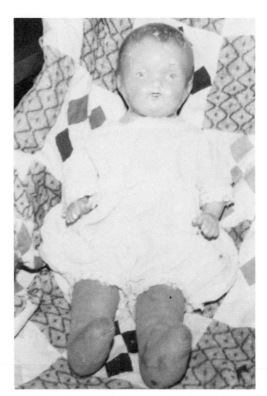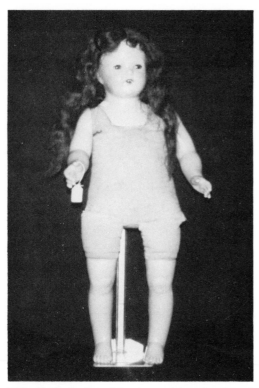

13″ Childhood doll of owner, purchased in 1922. Composition shoulder head, arms and cloth body and legs. Original yellow rompers and bonnet is missing. Old script mark: Effanbee. Courtesy Mary Stolzenberg.

28″ Cloth body with composition head and limbs. Sleep eyes and wig. Open mouth with two upper teeth and tongue. Disc jointed arms and legs. Marked on shoulder plate: Effanbee. Courtesy Mauldin Collection.

 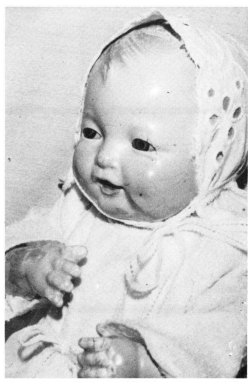

26″ and 12″ "Bubbles". Large one is on cloth body with one piece composition shoulder and head and composition limbs. Molded hair and sleep eyes, open mouth with two upper teeth and molded tongue. Finger or thumb goes in mouth. The 12″ has a composition shoulder plate and head, arms and legs. Arms are bent and strung through the shoulder plate. Straight legs, molded hair, sleep eyes, open mouth with two upper teeth and tongue. Dimples and marked: Effanbee Bubbles/Copyr-1924/Made in U.S.A. Large doll marked the same. Courtesy Mauldin Collection.

13″ and 20″ "Baby Bubbles" by Effanbee Dolls. Composition and cloth and has jointed body with curved legs. Open mouth and sleep eyes. Marks: Effanbee/Bubbles/Copyr.-1924/Made in USA. Smaller doll has been re-painted. Courtesy Mary Sweeney.

The Sears Roebuck catalog of 1924 carried both the 21″ "Betty Lee" and the 29″ "Barbara Lee". Both have cloth bodies and sleep eyes. They both wear the Effanbee heart necklaces.

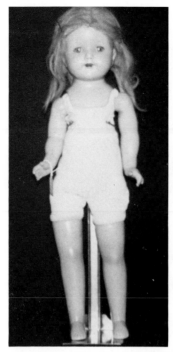

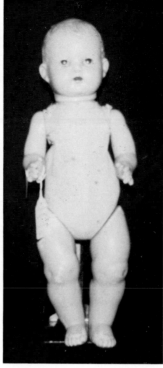

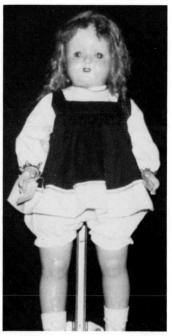

18″ "Rose Mary" with cloth body and composition head, arms and legs. Disc jointed. Wig, sleep eyes, open mouth with four upper teeth. Marks: Effanbee/Rose Mary/Walk, Talk, Sleep, in oval, on shoulder plate. Followed by Made in USA. 1925. Courtesy Mauldin Collection.

17″ "Baby Evelyn" with molded hair, sleep eyes and open mouth with two upper teeth. Cloth body with composition arms, legs and head. Disc jointed. Marks: Effanbee Baby Evelyn, on head. 1925. Courtesy Mauldin Collection.

25″ Cloth body with composition shoulder head and disc jointed composition arms, straight legs. Wig, sleep eyes and open mouth with four upper teeth. Marks: Effanbee/Rosemary/ Walk, Talk, Sleep, in an oval on shoulder. Wears original metal bracelet. 1925. Courtesy Mauldin Collection.

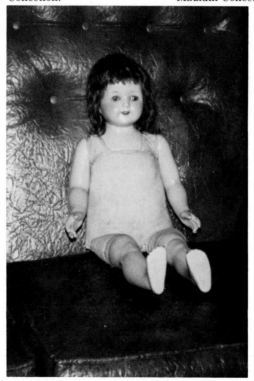

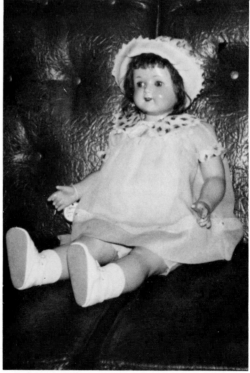

27″ "Rosemary". Composition shoulder plate, head, arms and legs. Disc jointed limbs, sleep blue eyes and open mouth with six teeth and tongue. All original except shoes, undies and socks. Pink organdy dress and bonnet with white lace trim. 1925. Marked in oval on shoulder plate: Effanbee/Rosemary/Walk, Talk, Sleep/Made in U.S.A. Courtesy Jeanne Mauldin.

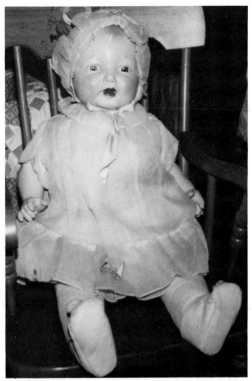

"Baby Effanbee" 13" long and 10" head Effanbee "Bye-Lo-Type" with composition head and hands. Blue tin sleep eyes, closed mouth and painted hair. Cry box in cloth body and has cloth legs and arms to hands. Marks: Effanbee/Made in U.S.A., on head. Original dress marked: Effanbee/Doll/Finest & Best, in oval. Pink and blue crocheted bonnet. 1925. Courtesy Shirley Pascuzzi.

21" "Bubbles" with flange-swivel head that is composition and full composition arms. The body and legs are cloth. Marks: Effanbee Bubbles, on head. Green sleep eyes, painted lashes. All original with tagged dress. Original store tag: Pogue's $3.95. Ca. 1925-1926. Courtesy Mary Stolzenberg.

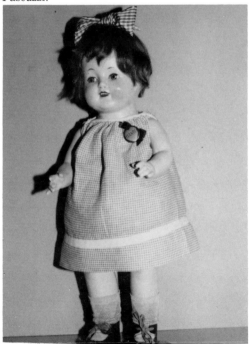

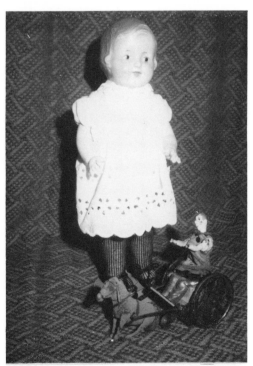

14" "Patsy" and marked: Effanbee/Patsy. Reddish brown mohair wig over molded hair. Blue-grey tin sleep eyes, open mouth with four teeth. Composition shoulder plate, rosy cheeks and dimples. Cloth body with cry box, composition arms and legs with rosy knees and both arms slightly bent. Original blue/white check dress and matching panties, shaded blue silk socks with diamond design. Red imitation leather shoes and celluloid Effanbee button (size of dime), red with gold heart and red silk bow. 1926. Courtesy Glorya Woods.

14" First "Patsy" with molded, well defined hair-do. Unusual in that she has painted eyes to the side and an open-closed mouth. Marks: Effanbee/Patsy. She has been re-dressed. Courtesy Thelma and Joleen Flack.

41

Ihe dolls wil

Take y one

ARE'NT these *adorable dolls?* Which one do you love best? There is Bubbles—just bubbling over with life and laughter, the sweetest, happiest doll-baby that you have ever seen. You almost think the cunning, laughing mite is human, for she has dimpled face and arms just like a real baby. (Indeed she was modeled after a darling little baby.) And she is always so happy that she makes you happy, too!

No little girl can cry or look cross with this darling Bubbles in her arms. Bubbles cheers you up, just as a real playmate would do. And you will be so proud of her. She has the sweetest laughing face in the world: rosy cheeks, beautiful big blue eyes that open wide or go to sleep. She has precious little white teeth in her rosebud mouth, and a tiny little tongue. And you just know she loves you for she will cry for you as plainly as a child. Isn't that darling?

Bubbles is dressed in the sweetest white dress of good quality organdie, with "petties" and a real baby diaper, and little white kidalene shoes. Around her neck she has the golden heart necklace which tells you she is an "Effanbee Doll." Later on I will tell you something more about this golden heart necklace, but now you will want to hear about Lovey Mary, too.

Lovey Mary—every little girl's ideal playmate. You can even teach her to dance the Charleston! She comes in all sizes. Shown here, she is 19 inches tall and costs $5. At all better-class department and toy stores.

Did you see the "Lovey Mary" moving picture? Well here is the Lovey Mary Doll!

DID you see Bessie Love as Lovey Mary in the Metro-Goldwyn-Mayer moving picture? Well, now you can have a Lovey Mary doll.

November 28, 1926, newspapers carried this ad for the "Bubbles" and the "Lovey Mary". This ad asks: "Did you see Bessie Love as Lovey Mary in the Metro-Goldwyn-Mayer moving picture? Well, now you can have a Lovey Mary Doll." Ad states the child can teach the doll the Charleston. Sleep eyes with lashes. Came in organdy dress of purple, pink or blue. This ad also states that Lovey Mary thought of the idea that every little girl should also have a heart necklace and for 6¢ they would be sent one.

The apparent forerunner of the famous Patsy doll came from the Armand Marseille molds of the Just Me dolls. The registration numbers are no help in locating information as to which came first. Courtesy Glorya Woods.

Right is a bisque head "Baby Gloria" by the Armand Marsielle firm of Germany with molded hair, blue sleep eyes and deep dimples. Cloth body and limbs with composition hands. The original white cotton dress is tagged Baby Gloria/RBL(distributor)/New York. The left doll is composition with shoulder plate, sleep blue eyes, open mouth and two upper teeth, as well as deep dimples. The 15″ circumference head is marked: Baby Gloria/Germany and back of head is cut out for talking mechanism. Both courtesy Glorya Woods. The Baby Gloria is either taken from the "Bubbles", or the Effanbee firm bought out the Germany molds when Armand Marseille went out of business.

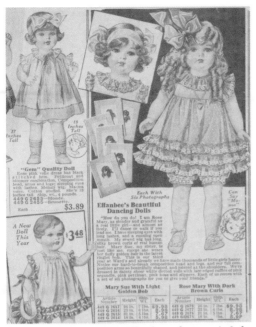

The 1927 Montgomery Ward catalog carried the "Mary Sue" with light golden bob hair style in sizes: 18″, 21″, 23″ and 26″. Also shown is the "Rose Mary" with dark brown long curls in the same sizes. Each doll came with six photos. Also shown (second from left) is a 19″ doll that came as a blonde or brunette. All have cloth bodies with composition heads and limbs.

In 1927 the Montgomery Ward catalog carried "Naughty Eyes" with flirty eyes, open mouth, ¾″ composition legs, full arms and head of composition. She came in sizes: 14½″, 16″, 18″ and 21″.

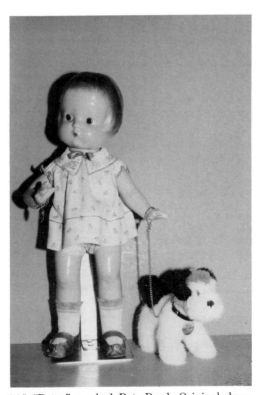

14″ "Patsy" with sleep eyes and marked Effanbee shown with 15″ marked "Patsy" head with sleep eyes on a marked "Patricia" body which has fingers with celluloid cuticles for nailpolish. The head and body apparently are original to each other, as the head fits very naturally. Dress is embroidered with cross stitch, edged in dark green. Cotton panty-skirt combination. Rayon socks with green band at top. Imitation gold leather shoes, gold metal bracelet. Courtesy Glorya Woods.

14″ "Patsy" marked Pat. Pend. Original dress that is light green flowered pique, collar embroidered with cross stitch and edged in dark green. One piece combination slip and panties. Gold side snap shoes, socks with green band at top. The toy is a Steiff "Foxy". Courtesy Glorya Woods.

This McCall pattern shows outfit that could be made for the Patsykins (11½″), and matching one for the Patsy (14″). Courtesy Marge Meisinger.

Almost all the large retail stores, as well as the catalog order firms carried the "Rosemary" dolls with cloth body, straight composition legs, one arm was bent and other straight. Open smile mouth and sleep eyes.

This catalog shows a Patsy and Patsykin lookalikes. Left: 16½″ "Maizie" with sleep eyes, and 12½″ "Bobby Ann". Both are fully jointed, have molded hair and sleep eyes. Note that the second and third fingers are molded together and the bent right arm. Courtesy Montgomery Ward catalog.

This page of the Montgomery Ward catalog of 1928 shows many of the Patsy copies that came on the market after Patsy had become so popular. The upper one 16″ tall and has sleep eyes. Lower left is 12″ tall with sleep eyes, as is the middle one in sailor outfit, except she has painted eyes. The lower right doll is 9¾″ with painted eyes.

Patsy Family. Left to right: 5″ "Wee Patsy", 9″ "Patseyette", 11″ "Patsy Jr.", 14″ "Patsy", marked: Pat. Pend. 17″ "Patsy Joan" with sleep eyes and molded hair. 19″ "Patsy Ann" with sleep eyes and molded hair. Courtesy Glorya Woods.

22½″ Very early "Patsy". Composition shoulder head on cloth body. The shoulder is marked: in oval, Effanbee/Patsy/Copr./Doll. Disc jointed composition arms with half composition legs. Open mouth, four teeth and tongue. Old clothes, but are not original. Courtesy June Schultz.

19″ "Mary Ann" and so marked on her head. All composition with blonde human hair wig, blue sleep eyes and open mouth with four upper teeth. Original light blue organdy party gown with ruffles edged in pink, blue organdy slip with ruffle at hem, panties attached. Original shoes were light blue imitation leather, and former owner went over them with nail polish. Gold heart bracelet. 1928-1937. Courtesy Glorya Woods.

14″ "Patsy", all marked: Effanbee. Left has sleep eyes and other two have painted eyes. Pink organdy dress in center is original, and left is light green, right is light blue and copies by owner. Courtesy Glorya Woods.

13″ Toddler marked: Effanbee with molded hair, Patsy style, with painted blue eyes. Very chubby composition body and limbs. Same body as "Candy Kid" and this doll also comes with sleep eyes and molded curl on forehead. Steiff kitty. Courtesy Glorya Woods.

27″ "Hug Me". Cloth body, sleep eyes, molded hair and cheek dimples. Head and limbs are composition. 2nd & 3rd fingers of both hands are molded together.

14″ "Patsy" all original with red and white rompers with attached white blouse and separate jumper. Brown glass sleep eyes, all composition and marked on back: "Effanbee Patsy Doll". The dress has a tag that is woven: Effanbee Durable Dolls NRA. Original store tag: H & S Pogue $2.95. Courtesy Mary Stolzenberg.

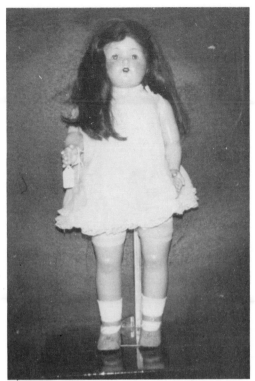

30″ Composition swivel head on composition shoulder plate, cloth body and full composition limbs. Marks on shoulder plate: Effanbee Lovums/Pat. 1283,558. Brown glass sleep eyes. Smiling open mouth with four teeth on top and metal tongue. Brown human hair wig. All original dress with matching bloomer-undies, and matching hair bow. (Note: this same outfit came on a Patsy Lou doll). Dress has original NRA label and is red dots on white. Courtesy Kay Bransky.

29″"Mae Starr" with cloth body and composition head, arms and legs. glued on wig, open mouth with two upper teeth and tongue. Clothes original except socks. 1928. Has opening in back to place wax cylinder discs, and when lever is turned on right side doll talks or sings. Marked on shoulder plate: Mae Starr Doll. Courtesy Mauldin Collection.

Patsy Family: left to right: 5″ "Wee Patsy", painted eyes, molded hair. 9″ "Patseyette" with painted eyes and molded hair. 11″ "Patsy Jr." with molded hair and painted eyes. 17″ "Patsy Joan" with sleep eyes and molded hair. "Patsy Ann" with sleep eyes and wig. 22″ "Patsy Lou" has sleep eyes and wig. Courtesy Glorya Woods.

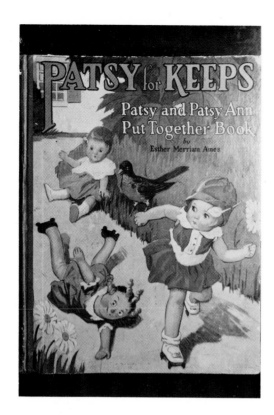

The Fireflies Were Most Polite and Obliging With Their Little Lanterns

"For Goodness Sake, Patsy Ann, Sit Down, Don't Pace the Floor Like That"

"There's Something Really Quite Distinguished About You, Shavings," said Patsy

This is a rare and unusual book called "Patsy for Keeps" with story by Esther Merriam Ames and pictures by Arnold Lorne Hicks. It was published by Sam Gabriel Sons and Company of New York City. There are pages with the figures that are removable, and then they are placed on the vacant spots on other pages (glued on paper doll type). Courtesy Margaret Mandel.

"Can That Be Me?" She Marveled When She Saw Her Reflection

So the New House Was Finished and Furnished

What every young doll mother should know

by

Aunt Patsy

EFFANBEE

This page shows three more pages out of the "Patsy for Keeps" book, and also a booklet called "What Every Young Doll Mother Should Know", written by "Aunt Patsy". "Aunt Patsy" conducted a fan club for the Patsy family dolls with publications, as well as for the "Dy-Dee" baby doll.

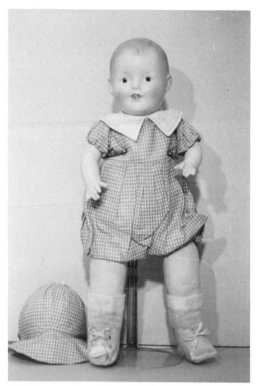

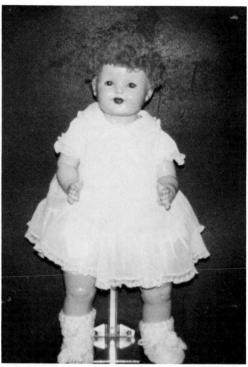

14″ "Lovums" with painted red molded hair, painted blue eyes and open closed mouth with two painted teeth. Composition arms and cloth body and legs. Original red and white checkered romper with matching bonnet. Original shoes and socks. 1928. Courtesy Kay Bransky.

24″ "Lovums" with cloth body, composition shoulder plate head, arms and legs with swivel neck, posable head. Sleep eyes, open mouth with molded tongue, two upper and two lower teeth. Straight fat legs and arms are slightly bent. Marks: Effanbee Lovums/Pat. No. 1283558, on shoulder. 1928. Original dress with tag: Effanbee durable doll. Courtesy Mauldin Collection.

This large "Lovums" has an almost white caracul wig, blue sleep eyes and open mouth with teeth. Composition head and shoulder plate with cloth body and composition limbs. The legs are fat and straight with much detail to the modeling. Courtesy Joleen Flack

14″ "Lovums" with composition flange-swivel composition head, arms and early oilcloth body and legs. Brown glass sleep eyes/lashes. Head marked: Effanbee Lovums. Celluloid pin: Effanbee Durable doll and woven dress tag label. Original store tag: Pogue's $2.25. 1928. Courtesy Mary Stolzenberg.

All "Patsy" with ones in back, left to right: 19″ Patsy Ann, 14″ Patsy, 11″ Patsy Jr. (with wig). Front left to right: 11″ Patsy Jr. with molded hair, 9″ Patsyette and 6″ Wee Patsy. All composition and all are marked. Courtesy Mauldin Collection.

16″ "Patsy look-a-like" that is all original with brown sleep eyes (small eyes). The quality is excellent, but she is not marked. Human hair wig over molded, unpainted hair. All composition and strung. Panties attached to pink organdy dress with white flocks, separate pinafore. Courtesy June Schultz.

Patsy family look-a-likes. Left back: Marked on head: Petite Sally. All original and clothes are also marked: Petite. 19″ all composition, strung and has sleep eyes. Center in blue overalls is 15″ tall and marked: Uneeda, on composition shoulder head, composition pin jointed arms and body and legs are all cloth. Next to her on right: 15″ all composition and original, strung, painted eyes and marked on head: Germany-2. Left front is a 12″ all composition with painted eyes and marked: Sally A Petite Doll. The black one is 10″ and unmarked with painted eyes and very "Patsy" designed arms and legs. She is original. Courtesy June Schultz.

20″ "Mary Ann" composition swivel head on shoulder plate, cloth stuffed body, disc jointed arms and legs. All original including shoes (she may have had a hat). Original human hair wig, sleep blue eyes. Marks: Mary Ann, on head. Effanbee Lovums/Pat. No. 1285-558. 1928-1937. Courtesy June Schultz.

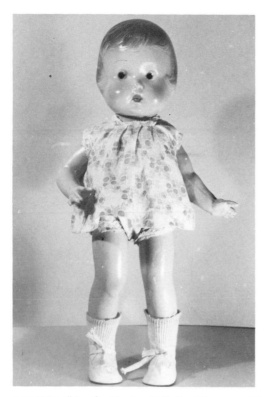

13″ "Mitzi" by the Maxine Doll Co. All composition competition to the Patsy. Molded hair is painted auburn, brown painted eyes and bent right arm. Original cotton dress of blue/green print on white, matching one piece undies. Original socks and shoes. Courtesy Kay Bransky.

Horsman's Patsy-look-a-like was called "Sally" and is shown in this ad. She is shown in the 19″ size, sleep eyes/lashes, ad says the head, arms and legs are composition. She has a bent right arm. 1928.

A company catalog shows the Patsy-look-a-like doll "Judy" that is 18″ tall, has sleep eyes with lashes. She has a cloth body with composition head, full arms and legs. Left arm is bent at elbow. Cry voice. 1928.

Two "Patsy Lou's". Mohair wig over unpainted molded hair, and molded, painted hair. Both have sleep eyes with the one with mohair having brown and one with molded hair, green. Courtesy Bee Johnson.

This "Patsy Ann" has a brown mohair wig over molded, unpainted hair, brown glass sleep eyes and is all original. Pink silk dress, white fur coat and hat. Courtesy Bee Johnson.

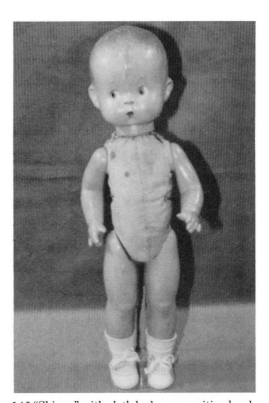

"Patsy Ann" with molded and painted hair, and tin sleep eyes and is shown with her original box, although the doll is not original (clothes). Courtesy Bee Johnson.

14″ "Skippy" with cloth body, composition head, arms and legs that are disc jointed and head is attached with wooden plug. Molded and painted hair, and painted eyes to side. Marks: Effanbee Skippy, on head. Also came with legs painted with brown or black to look like boots. (1940's). Courtesy Bee Johnson.

A 1929 "Patsy Ann" is shown with her furry friend and has molded, painted hair, sleep eyes and is 19″ tall. Courtesy Joleen Flack

19″ "Patsy Ann". All composition and in original clothes. (Socks on left hand doll replaced). Left is dressed in blue and right in pink with red shoes. Green tin sleep eyes and both are marked: "Effanbee/Patsy Ann"/Pat. #1,283,558, on the backs. 1929. Courtesy June Schultz.

20″ "Mary Ann" that is all composition. Her wig is human hair and the dress may be original. She still wears her golden heart bracelet, has sleep eyes and is marked: Mary Ann, on the head and Effanbee/Lovums/Pat. No. 1,283,558, on the back. Courtesy Dorothea Cameron (Cameron Doll Museum).

19″ "Patsy Ann". All composition with molded hair, sleep eyes and closed mouth. Not original. Marks: Effanbee/"Patsy-Ann"/Pat. #1283558. 1929. Courtesy Mary Sweeney.

 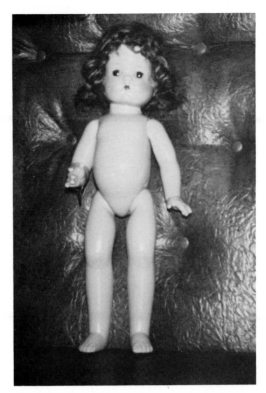

19″ "Patsy Ann" all composition with sleep brown eyes and all original clothes and heart bracelet. The dress and bonnet are green silk. Original wig. Marks: Effanbee Patsy Ann Pat. # 1283558, on back. Courtesy Jeanne Mauldin.

 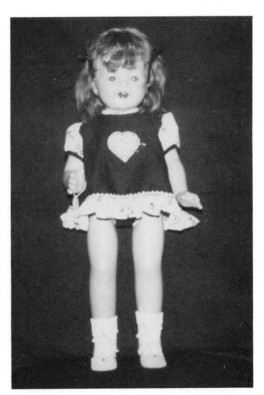

19″ "Patsy Ann". Both are all original and both are marked: "Effanbee/Patsy Ann Pat. #". The right doll is a 1929 one with tin sleep eyes and other is 1940 with green glass sleep eyes. Left: blue with white trim and blue shoes. Right: Roses on pale pink organdy and pink shoes. Courtesy June Schultz.

22″ "Patsy Lou" that is all composition and strung. Bent right arm, wig, sleep eyes and open, smile mouth with tongue and two upper teeth. Marks: Effanbee Patsy Lou, on back. Courtesy Mauldin Collection.

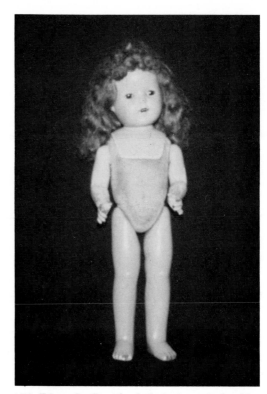

16" "Mary Lee" and so marked on back of head. (very faintly). Body is marked: Effanbee/Patsy Joan. Green sleep eyes and red mohair wig in braids. All original dress with one piece undies, original shoes and socks. 1930 to 1935. Courtesy Kay Bransky.

17" "Mary Lee" with cloth body and shoulder head, legs and arms of composition. Disc jointed. Sleep eyes, open mouth with four upper teeth. Marks: Mary Lee, on head. 1930 to 1935. Courtesy Mauldin Collection.

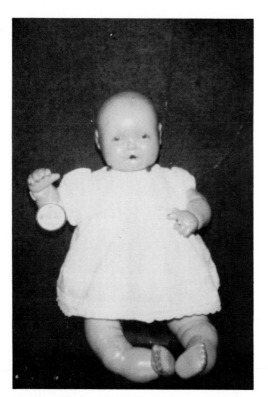

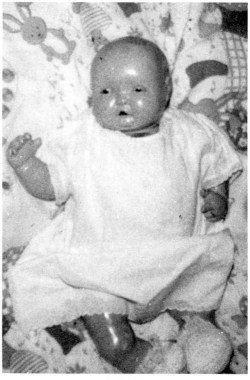

16" "Lamkin" with cloth body, sleep eyes and open "bow" mouth. Composition head, arms and legs. The legs are very bent as are the arms with fingers of right hand into the palm and thumb and index finger pointed on left hand. Has gold ring molded on middle finger. Marks: Lamkin, on neck. 1930. Courtesy Mauldin Collection.

16" Lambkin of 1930. Cloth and composition. Unique finger arrangement with all fingers curled into the palms, and with molded baby ring on left hand. The face of this doll was also a very unique sculpture. Courtesy Mauldin Collection.

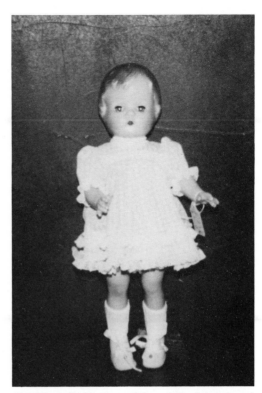

5½″ "Wee Patsy" in original kimono-negligee. All composition with one piece body and head. Molded hair and painted eyes. Marks: "Effanbee Wee Patsy", on back. 1930. Courtesy June Schultz.

17″ "Patsy" all composition, fully jointed and strung. Beautifully molded hair that is more curly than regular Patsy. Sleep green eyes, closed mouth, straight legs and both arms are slightly bent. Ca. early 1930's. Mark: Effanbee. Courtesy Mauldin Collection.

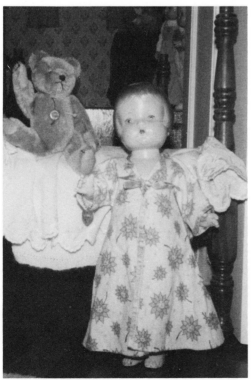

16″ "Patsy Joan". All composition and strung. Wears an original flannel robe trimmed in pink silk ribbon, on floral print. Sleep eyes and molded red hair. Marks: "Effanbee/Patsy Joan", on back. 1930's to 1946. Courtesy June Schultz.

16″ "Patsy Joan". All composition and wearing her original dress and original human hair wig. New shoes and socks. Marks: "Effanbee/Patsy Joan", on back. 1930's-1946. Courtesy June Schultz.

17″ "Patsy Joan" with green sleep eyes and marked Effanbee. 14″ "Patsy" with painted eyes and marked: Effanbee. Original clothes include navy felt coat with embroidery insignia on sleeve, lined in light weight red wool, brass buttons and navy felt tam. The dress is flowered light green with pique collar. Courtesy Glorya Woods.

11½″ "Patsykins" of 1930. Wears original clothes and bonnet. The shoes and socks are replaced. She is all composition, has painted eyes to side and molded, painted hair. Courtesy Joleen Flack

This "Patsyette' is shown with her trunk and wardrobe. There were many combinations of trunks and clothes available for all size dolls in the "Patsy" line. Courtesy Joleen Flack

5″-5¾″ "Wee Patsy". Both arms are bent nearly the same angle and she has molded, painted on "Mary Jane" shoes with white socks. An ad in a national catalog, as well as a national magazine state about this doll: "she lives in the house built for Colleen Moore (doll castle) and is called Fairy Princess." The ads show her dressed in an organdy, with lace at hem, checkered one piece playsuit, short check dress with wide pleated collar and matching panties. There were other packaging for the doll, including a box that looked like a castle. Courtesy Joleen Flack

nnot guarantee to fill all orders after DEC. 20, 19

Sensational! Dolly, Trunk and Cloth

All waterproof composition Doll, 9¾ in. tall, jointed at arms and legs. A red 10½ -in. brass-trimmed fiber trunk, 1 organdie dress, 1 print dress, pajamas, undies, hair bow, 2 hangers. If not part of a $2 order, send 8¢ for postage.
48 T 2459—Complete set .

Onl

34

This shows an ad from the Montgomery Ward catalog and this 9¾″ all composition COPY of a "Patsyette" could be bought, with her trunk for 34¢. Catalog courtesy Marge Meisinger.

9½″ "Patsyette" all composition and all original Dutch Girl, except hat is missing and bucket has been added. Doll is strung. Marks: "Effanbee/Patsyette". 1931. Courtesy June Schultz.

M E   A R T S   *DECEMBER*

rs of

Mary Ann

Who is nothing if not Up-To-Date

Given for Three two-year Subscriptions at 50 cents each

Mary Ann says she knows clothes are not the making of little girls any more than they make the man but she's awfully glad she's got "the bestest clows most any girl ever had." Besides, and Mary Ann admits it, although she is an extremely classy miss she is a mighty good little girl doll, too, all questions of clothes aside. She is right, clothes are not everything with her. She has more attractive qualities than are usually found in one package. To begin with she stands thirteen inches tall with flesh-colored body of break-proof composition throughout. Fully jointed. Which means that head, arms and legs can be moved at will. She can stand alone and sit in almost any position. In fact

Mary Ann's Genius at Posing Is One of Her Greatest Charms

and as you turn her head about, or up and down, you can almost see the change of expression on her face so deliciously sweet are the charming poses she can take. Her hat, with dress to match, is copied from the latest Parisian style. The fact is, the creator of this doll actually bought in Paris the doll clothes used for Mary Ann's patterns. Her suit is made of printed percale trimmed with felt. She wears knitted half hose and real tie-on slippers. Mary Ann is O. K.

Needlecraft Wants Every Little Girl to Have This Doll

no matter how many dolls you already have and so we offer her for only *three* subscriptions which is ridiculously low for a doll of this high quality.
Call on your friends. Show them your copy of Needlecraft. Tell them a two-year subscription costs only fifty cents. Ask them to subscribe through you. Send us the **three** names, addresses and the money collected. We will send each subscriber this magazine two years. We will send you, free and postpaid, this lovely doll. Order by name and by **Gift No. 3944.** Address

NEEDLECRAFT MAGAZINE Augusta, Maine

The December, 1931 Needlecraft Magazine carried this ad of the "Mary Jane" doll that is a Patsy-look-a-like. She is 13″ tall, all composition, fully jointed and has a bent left arm, and the right is slightly bent. "Mary Jane" was offered for three subscriptions to the magazine. Tag states: Gerling Creation. The eyes are painted.

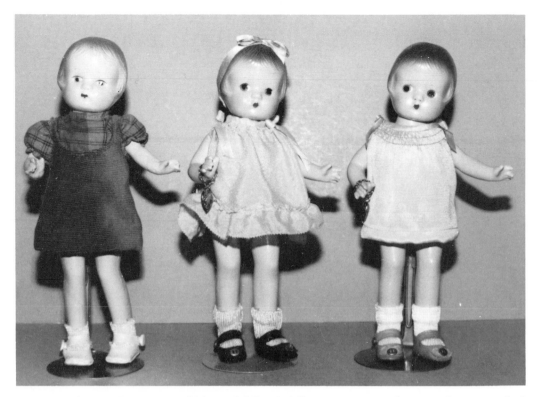

Left to right: 9″ Patsy-type, which is childhood doll of owner and shown with two marked "Patsyette". Courtesy Glorya Woods.

10½″ "Patsy Baby" that has sleep eyes and is all composition. The hair is molded, but unpainted. These babies came with wigs and also in Black. Courtesy Joleen Flack

11½″ "Patsy Baby" that is marked, and all composition with painted eyes to the side and three holes in hair with yarn. See the picture of the Amosandra dolls. Courtesy Joleen Flack

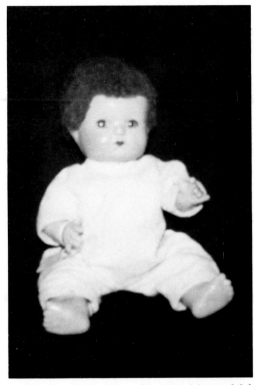

11″ "Patsy Baby" that is all composition and fully jointed. Doll is strung. Caracul wig, sleep eyes and closed mouth. Looks to be original flannel pajamas. Marks: Effanbee Patsy Baby, on head, and back. 1932. Courtesy Mauldin Collection.

12″ "Patsy Baby" Twins that are all original. Pink cloth bodies, legs and arms with composition hands and heads. Sleep eyes, molded hair and closed mouths. Wears diapers, print flannel gowns, buntings and jackets and caps that are part of the bunting. Marked: Effanbee Patsy Baby, on heads. Heads are strung to wooden plugs. 1932. Courtesy Mauldin Collection.

10½″ "Patsy Baby" with composition head and attached to a wooden neck plug. Molded, painted hair, green tin sleep eyes, all cloth body with celluloid hands. Old clothes are not original. Marks: "Effanbee", on head. Steiff "Arco" dog. 1932. Courtesy June Schultz.

This is a Patsy Baby "Tinyette" that measures 7″ tall. All composition with painted eyes to side, and with both arms just slightly bent. These babies were used as twins, triplets and quints. They are marked Effanbee on head and body, with molded hair or wigs. Courtesy Joleen Flack

14½" "Patricia" who is all composition with sleep eyes. All composition with human hair wig in braids, and re-dressed. Courtesy Joleen Flack

Three beautifully mint Effanbees. Two are "Patricia" (1932) and middle one is "Skippy" (1928). All are completely original, including metal wrist heart shaped tags, plus paper tag and pink. The girls have sleep eyes and Skippy has painted eyes to the side, and molded hair. All three are all composition. Courtesy Glorya Woods.

14" "Patricia" of 1932. All composition and the doll is strung. Dark brown human hair wig, brown sleep eyes with small black pupils. Marks: "Effanbee/Patricia". She has been re-dressed. Courtesy June Schultz.

Margaret Mandel is shown holding her childhood doll, a "Patricia" in cowgirl outfit.

9″ "Patsy Babyette". Both have five piece bent leg baby bodies, are all composition and have original clothes. One has molded hair and other has molded hair covered with caracul wig. Marks: Effanbee, on head. Effanbee Patsy Babyette, on backs. Both have sleep eyes. 1932. Courtesy June Schultz.

11″ "Patsy Baby" marked on head and body. 1932. Brown molded, curly hair in ringlets, brown sleep eyes on five piece baby body that is all composition. Original pink organdy dress with lace and ribbon trim, matching bonnet and heart bracelet. The 10″ "Patsy Baby" is marked on head and body and has molded ringlet blonde hair, blue sleep eyes and her blue dress is not original. The other two are 7″ "Baby Tinyette" shown in another photo. Courtesy Glorya Woods.

A "Patsy Baby" is shown with a big "Patsy Mae" who has sleep eyes/lashes, closed mouth and human hair wig. She has been re-dressed and baby has, too. Both courtesy JoLeen Flack.

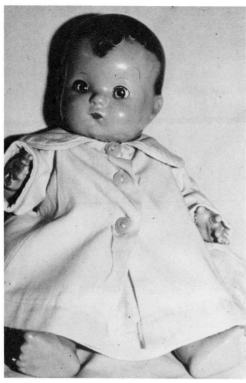

11″ "Patsy Baby". All composition with bent baby legs. Molded hair and sleep eyes. Original clothes. Marks: Effanbee/Patsy Baby. 1932. Courtesy Mary Sweeney.

10″ "Patsy Babykin". Marked on head and back: Effanbee/Patsy Baby, but her bracelet reads: Effanbee Patsy Babykin. Her chiffon organdy outfit is original from a separate boxed set and dress and bonnet have flocked hearts of red. All composition with caracul wig and brown sleep eyes. 1932. Courtesy June Schultz.

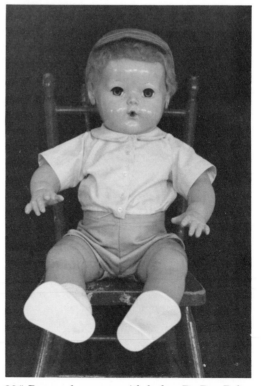

14″ "Dy-Dee". Her back reads like a travelog: Effanbee/Dy-Dee Baby/U.S.Pat. 1-857-485/England 880-060/France 723-980/Germany 5-85-647 /Other Pat. Pending. Body is jointed rubber, the head is hard plastic with inset rubber ears, molded painted hair. Original "mint in box" outfit of coat and hat (Style #51-15). 1933. Courtesy June Schultz.

20″ Brown sleep eyes with lashes Dy-Dee Baby. Inset rubber ears. Hard rubber body with composition head, caracul wig over molded hair. Marks: Effanbee/Dy-Dee Baby. 1933-1940. Courtesy Rilla M. Van Zandt.

9" all original little girl that is all composition on five piece body with woven heart tag on back of dress that is organdy with separate cotton slip and lace trimmed panties. Marks: Effanbee/Made in U.S.A., on back. Courtesy June Schultz.

20" Dy-Dee-Baby. Composition head and rubber body and limbs. Caracul wig over molded hair, applied rubber ears. Marks: Eff-an-bee/Dy-Dee-Baby, on body. 1933. Courtesy Rilla M. Van Zandt.

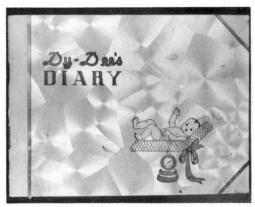

"Dy-Dee's Diary" copyright by Fleischaker & Baum. Inside is like a baby book. Courtesy Margaret Mandel.

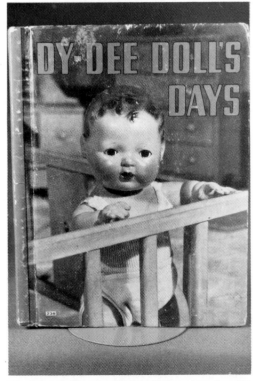

"Dy-Dee Doll's Says" by Peggy Vandegriff. Photos by Lawson Fields. Published by Rand McNally in 1937. Courtesy Margaret Mandel.

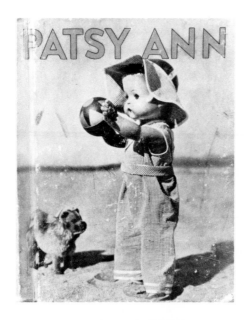 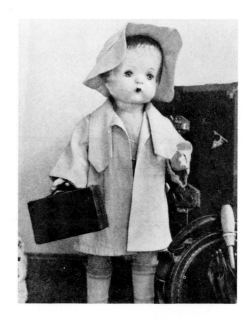

Book "Patsy Ann Her Happy Times" by Mória Reed King. Photographs by G. Allen King. Published by Rand McNally & Company, Chicago. 1935. Shows the cover and four photos from inside the book. Courtesy Margaret Mandel.

Pink on white striped bathrobe for the Patsy doll is shown along with the all metal roller skates for the same doll. Courtesy Pearl Claspy.

Patsy Ann blue/white wool coat and hat with separate belt. Courtesy Ruth Arent.

Green/rose print bloomers, cotton collar, ruffled sleeves and down front with button. Fits Patsy Ann. Courtesy Ruth Arent.

Pink dress with white flower print, double collar and sleeveless. Fits Patsy Ann. Courtesy Ruth Arent.

Cotton play suit with bloomers attached, and blue/white embroidery trim on white cotton. Fits Patsy Ann. Courtesy Ruth Arent.

Patsy Ann's green seersucker pajama top, with no bottoms and an unreadable tag. Courtesy Ruth Arent.

Patsy Ann's print pink flannel robe with figures of boys and girls, three buttons on front. Courtesy Ruth Arent.

Blue/white cotton hat tagged: NIKO and fits Patsy Ann. Courtesy Ruth Arent.

Pale green print with green trim dress that is cotton and organdy with green flowers, one pocket on front. Fits Patsy Ann. Courtesy Ruth Arent.

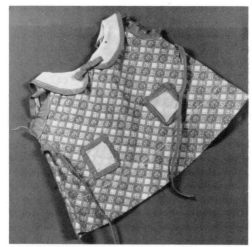

Green and white cotton dress with two pockets on front, ties. Fits Patsy Ann. Courtesy Ruth Arent.

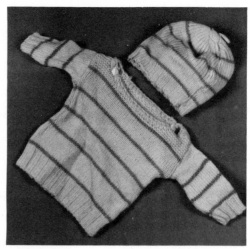

Pink with blue stripe sweater and cap with buttons at shoulder. Fits Patsy Ann. Courtesy Ruth Arent.

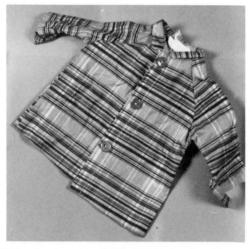

Patsy Ann's green plaid raincoat that is rubberized and tagged: B. Altman & Co./Paris-New York. Courtesy Ruth Arent.

Red Dot print dress, ruffled organdy sleeves, neck and pocket trim for Patsy Ann. Courtesy Ruth Arent.

Green knit ski jacket and cap with white "fur" trim and side buttons. Fits Patsy Ann. Pants missing. Courtesy Ruth Arent.

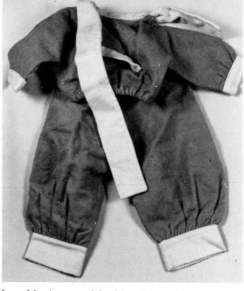

Navy blue/orange felt ski suit, two piece and ties at neck. Fits Patsy Ann. Courtesy Ruth Arent.

This large "Patsy Ruth" has a cloth body with composition arms, legs and head and shoulder plate. She has sleep eyes. The wig may be replaced. Courtesy JoLeen Flack.

21″, 15″ and 15″ all composition and all have glued on wigs and sleep eyes. All are marked Effanbee/Anne Shirley, on backs. All have the open fingers that were designed by Dewees Cockran and are made of hard rubber (latex). 1935-1949. Courtesy Mauldin Collection.

20″ "American Child" designed by Dewees Cochran. All composition with stringing. Long human hair wig. Marks: Effanbee-American Children, on head. Effanbee/Anne Shirley, on back. Sleep brown eyes and closed mouth. Hands will take gloves. She is re-dressed in the correct style. 1936-1940. Courtesy June Schultz.

21″ "Sugar Baby", both have cloth bodies with composition head and limbs. Sleep eyes and open mouths with two upper teeth. Left has molded hair and right, a wig over molded hair. Both have sleep eyes and are marked Effanbee. Both have been re-dressed. 1936. Courtesy Mauldin Collection.

When Amos and Ruby became the "parents" of a baby girl on the Amos 'n Andy radio program, listeners from coast to coast showered gifts on the imaginary baby. Elinor Harriot, who takes the part of Ruby, is showing a few of the dolls that arrived through the mail. Amos (Freeman Gosden) and Andy (Charles Correll) were heard over the NBC network daily except Saturday and Sunday. The Effanbee "Patsy Baby" can be seen included in this arm full of dolls, and peeking from the shelf is a Black Kewpie. The photo is by NBC and dated 12/8/36.

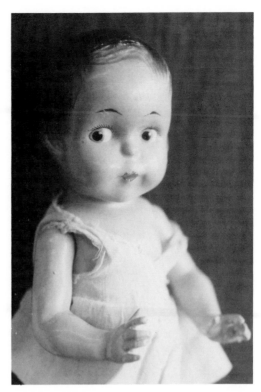

8″ "Button Nose" all composition with brown molded hair, doll on left has brown eyes and deeper molded hair and eyebrows. Doll on right has separated fingers and is slightly longer. Both are marked: Effanbee, on backs and were purchased about 1935 (left) and 1936 (right). Courtesy Dottie Mulholland.

20″ marked: Effanbee/American Children, on head. Mohair wig, painted eyes and feathered eyebrows. Has original heart bracelet. 1936-1940. Courtesy Glorya Woods.

20″ "Sugar Baby". Cloth body with composition shoulder head, legs and arms. Disc jointed and legs are partly cloth. Deeply molded hair, sleep eyes and open mouth with felt tongue and two upper teeth. Marks: Effanbee, on shoulder. 1936. Courtesy Mauldin Collection.

All original "Dutch" from the International Series and a marked "Patsyette". Ca. 1937. Courtesy June Schultz.

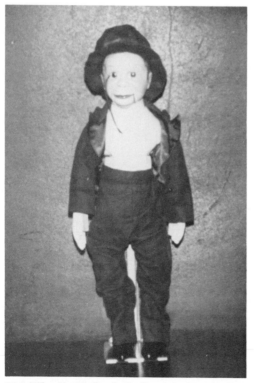

20″ "Charlie McCarthy" all original with cloth body, arms and legs. Composition head, hands and feet. Molded hair and painted eyes. Pull string in back operates mouth. Marks: Edgar Bergen's Charlie McCarthy, an Effanbee Product. 1937. Courtesy Mauldin Collection.

8″ "Button Nose", marked: Effanbee, on body. 1938. Boy has black molded hair and girl has brown molded hair. Boy has painted blue eyes, and girl has brown painted eyes. Spanish boy: black cotton pants and bolero vest stitched in red and white. Multi color sash, white pique shirt with red bow tie, black cotton hat with red braid and black imitation leather shoes. The girl has original shoes and pink cotton slip. The pony is a Steiff. Courtesy Glorya Woods.

Cover of the Effanbee publication "The Patsytown News", Vol. 11, No. 6 and shows the "new" Dy-Dee with rubber ears. Courtesy Margaret Mandel.

This Effanbee doll was listed in the 1938 Wards catalog and is a "Little Lady/Anne Shirley", but has different arms and has magnets in the palms of her hands to hold things. She was called "Magic Hands", and came with parasol, American flag, plush dog, diary, hanky and bouquet. She is 15″, has sleep eyes, and is dressed in pink organdy gown.

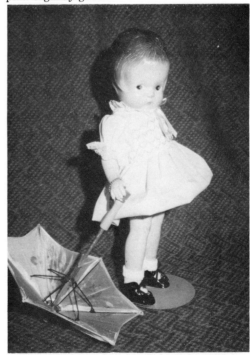

This 18″ "Anne Shirley" with page boy hairdo and dressed in dark brown real fur jacket, wine colored velveteen dress, pill box hat with flowers and a gold necklace was shown in the 1938 Ward's catalog.

This "Patsy" has magnets in her hands and was made in 1938 or 1939. F.A.O. Schwarz, as well as the Effanbee Company made many dolls in their line with the magnets. This doll has been redressed. Courtesy Joleen Flack

Genuine Effanbee Dy-Dee Doll S

The N. Shure Co. of Fall 1938 (wholesale catalog) carried this elaborate DyDee Kin. This same catalog shows four other sets: 13″ or 15″ Dy-Dee Kin packed in a box with pajama suit, and a few accessories. 9″, 11″, 13″ and 15″ called Dy-Dee Wee came in carry case that included a pink organdy dress and cap. One called Dy-Dee-ette in 11″, 13″ and 15″ came in case with layette and dress, plus the doll was on organdy trimmed pillow and mattress combination. The 11″ and 15″ also came in a case with several dresses, coat and hat, as well as regular layette items.

These three dolls were also in the 1938 N. Shure wholesale catalog. The first is 21″ "America's Children" with peasant style dress, guimpe with lace bodice, combination white dimity blouse with broadcloth panties to match dress, white apron. The second doll is "America's Children" and came in 15″, 17″ and 21″ sizes. Paisley print dress, felt roller hat with streamers. The third doll came in 21″ and is an "America's Children" with flowered print dress, silk lined flannel coat with Scotch Plaid cuffs and collar and cap and she has an open mouth.

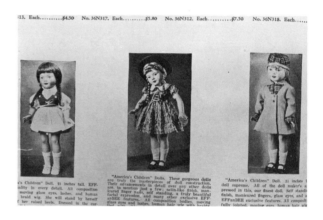

Genuine EFFanBEE Durable Dolls

WE PROUDLY PRESENT THE "AMERICA'S CHILDREN" DOLL LINE
AMERICA'S FINEST DOLL CREATIONS

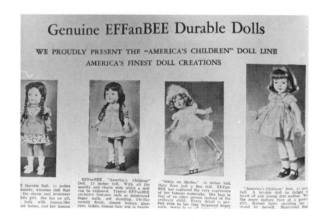

The 1938 N. Shure wholesale catalog carried these four Effanbee all composition dolls with the first being 15″ and the "Patricia" mold (?), the second is 15″ "America's Children" in gingham with organdy pinafore. The third is "Sonja Henie" doll. The fourth doll is 17″ "America's Children" and caption says she has an open mouth and dressed in check pique.

20″ W.C. Fields, 14″, 18″ and 22″ "Charlie McCarthy", 15″ "Clippo" and "Lucifer" (no size given) were all in the 1938 N. Shure wholesale catalog. They have composition heads, hands and feet.

Genuine Effanbee Ventriloquist and Marionette Dolls

14″ "1908 Women's Suffrage Movement" in dark blue with white blouse and trim. Middle. 21″ "1896 Unity of Nation Established" in peachy-pink with white trim, and 14″ "1625 New York Settlement" in two tones of blue and deep rust with yellow ribbon. She has her original price tag of $7.95 and was purchased at Boggs & Buhl. Courtesy Bee Johnson.

14″ Indian that is marked: Effanbee/Anne Shirley, on the back. Original in white buckskins, and decorated with black beads. The fringed leggins come up only to the top of her thighs. She wears brown felt moccasins, has brown painted eyes and is a reddish brown in color. The original box has red and blue stars on a white background and red/white and blue stripped bottom. Historical Doll: 1607 Indian. Courtesy Eloise Godfry.

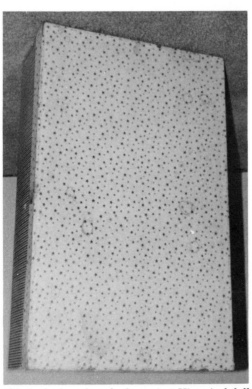

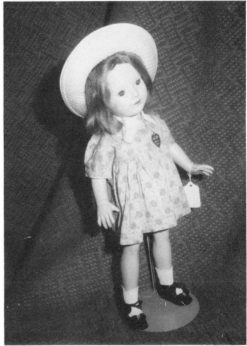

This is the box that the large 21″ Historical doll came in. The lid is white with red and blue stars and the bottom is red/white and blue strips. (Reminds one of a Nancy Ann box). Courtesy Bee Johnson.

15″ that is marked: Effanbee/Anne Shirley, on the back and Effanbee, on the head. She has almond shaped sleep brown eyes, open mouth with four teeth, human hair wig and the typical Anne Shirley/Little Lady hands with pale pink nail polish. This doll came dressed in skating costume and was called "Ice Queen" or "Sonja on Skates", and also dressed in young girl outfits. Courtesy Joleen Flack.

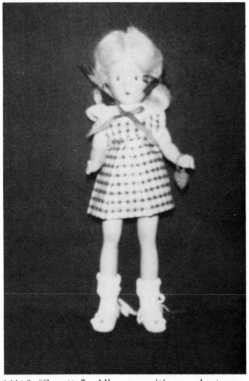

11½″ "Suzette". All composition and strung. Wig and painted eyes, slightly bent arms and wears original metal bracelet. Marks: Suzette/Effanbee USA, on head. Suzette/Effanbee/Made in USA, on back. 1939. Courtesy Mauldin Collection.

11″ "Suzette" girl is all original (may be missing hat), all composition, painted side glance eyes and mohair wig. Marks: Suzette Effanbee USA, on head. Suzette Effanbee/Made in USA, on back. Boy is marked the same, molded painted hair, these dolls are from same original owner, but his clothes may be from an old pattern. The dog is a Steiff "Beggie". 1939. Courtesy June Schultz.

15″ Historial doll "1872 - Economic Development". Deep red broadcloth trimmed in green detachable bustle, tiered skirt. Human hair wig and painted eyes. Marks: "Effanbee/Anne Shirley", on back. 1939. Courtesy June Schultz.

The 1939 set of Effanbee "Amish Man and Woman" that are all composition with mohair wigs and painted features. Her dress is blue and bonnet is white. Shown with the Amish 8″ Alexander-kins by Madame Alexander. Courtesy Glorya Woods.

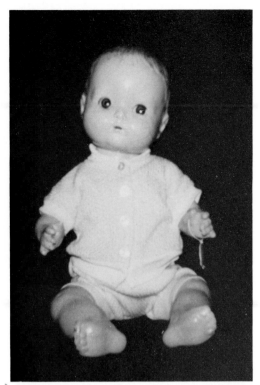

Left. 24" "Sweetie Pie" marked: Effanbee. Caracul wig, brown flirty eyes, cloth body with composition arms and legs in natural curved baby position. Right is a 20" "Sweetie Pie" with blue flirty eyes and is all composition with curved baby legs. Clothes are not original. Courtesy Glorya Woods.

20" "Sweetie Pie". All composition and fully jointed. Molded hair, large brown sleep, flirty eyes and closed mouth. Open hands with two middle fingers molded together. Doll is strung. Marks: Effanbee, on head and back. 1939-1948. Courtesy Mauldin Collection.

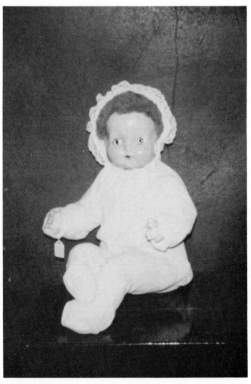

24" "Sweetie Pie-Tousle Tot". Cloth body with composition head, arms and legs. Caracul wig and flirty eyes. Arms are bent and all limbs are disc jointed. Both hands open and two middle fingers molded together. Marks: Effanbee, on head. 1939. Courtesy Mauldin Collection.

16" (Left) composition shoulder head (swivel) and hands, cloth body and limbs. Painted blue eyes, yarn hair and original hat and overalls. (Replaced shirt and shoes). This is "Brother" of 1942 and marked on head: Effanbee Made in USA. Right is 14" "Mickey" all original except missing hat. 1940. Swivel head, cloth body and legs, composition hands with cloth arms. Sleep eyes. No Marks. Both overalls are of woven cotton. Courtesy June Schultz.

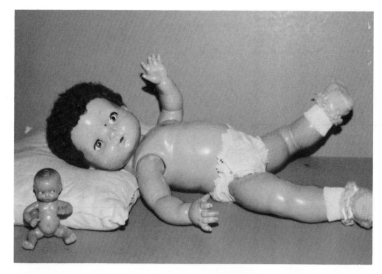

20″ "Sweetie Pie" with all composition body, flirty eyes and caracul wig. Marked: Effanbee. She is holding a 5″ hard plastic baby marked Irwin, U.S.A. Courtesy Glorya Woods.

EFFANBEE Girl Doll and 19-Piece Outfit in Suitcase
• 14-in. doll, sleeping eyes   • Luxurious 19-pc. outfit $4.95
• All composition body   • Packed in sturdy suitcase

Best quality, exquisite EFFANBEE Doll, 14 inches tall . . . and complete outfit of clothes packed in a sturdy suitcase. Doll has finest all-composition body molded by an artist. Sleeping "glass" eyes, real eyelashes. (Read about dolls on Page 44.) She has a new Page Boy hair-do . . . and you can comb it and wave it because it's good quality human hair. Her head tilts and her arms and legs are jointed.

Dolly's extra clothes are fine EFFANBEE quality, too. Her 19-piece outfit includes: Cotton Pique coat, ribbon trimmed white string Hat, nicely starched and blocked, striped Cape to match the party dress she's wearing, Cotton Voile Dress, Percale House Coat, Cotton Broadcloth Pajamas, lawn Slip and Panties, Play Suit, and extra Socks and Shoes. Tiny artificial leather Purse and dainty play Wrist Watch.

In 1939 the Montgomery Ward catalog carried this "Little Lady" style doll that is 14″ and came with a suitcase and wardrobe. The hairdo is page-boy and she is all composition. Note that her hands have wide spread fingers, but are not of the Dewees Cochran design.

11¼″ "Susie" (Suzette) all composition with molded hair and large eyes painted to the side is in the 1942 Montgomery Ward catalog and dressed in checkered gingham jumper with matching poke bonnet. The 11¼″ doll dressed the same was called "Sunbonnet Sue" in the 1938 Ward's catalog.

22″ "Princess Beatrix". 1939, and marked: Ideal. Has molded hair, flirty brown eyes and is cloth and composition, holding 7″ "Baby Tinyette", which is an early one and looks like a Dionne Quint. Marks: Effanbee/Baby Tinyette. Brown molded hair, large painted eyes looking left, delicate coloring and all composition. 16″ "Baby Bright Eyes". Ca. 1940. Marked: Effanbee. Molded hair, flirty blue eyes, cloth body with composition head, curved baby legs and arms with celluloid fingernails. Original outfit and holding 7″ marked "Baby Tinyette" that is a later issue, all composition (pinkish), reddish-brown molded hair and painted eyes straight ahead. Courtesy Glorya Woods.

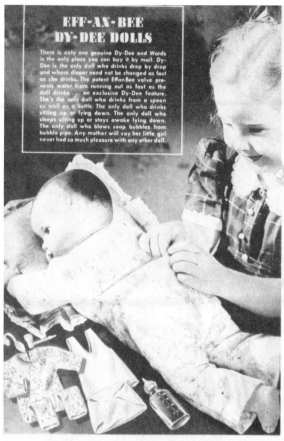

EFF-AN-BEE DY-DEE DOLLS

There is only one genuine Dy-Dee and Wards is the only place you can buy it by mail. Dy-Dee is the only doll who drinks drop by drop and whose diaper need not be changed as fast as she drinks. The patent EffanBee valve prevents water from running out as fast as the doll drinks . . . an exclusive Dy-Dee feature. She's the only doll who drinks from a spoon as well as a bottle. The only doll who drinks sitting up or lying down. The only doll who sleeps sitting up or stays awake lying down. The only doll who blows soap bubbles from bubble pipe. Any mother will say her little girl never had so much pleasure with any other doll.

"HAPPY BIRTHDAY TO *YOU"*

EFFANBEE DOLLS

Look for the golden heart bracelet trademark . . . mark of the world's finest dolls. Composition parts baked longer than cheap dolls; they're not fragile. Sanding and smoothing make mold joints invisible, hand rubbed with several coats of enamel to look like skin. Clothes of fine material, as nicely made as for your own little girl.

$2.59 BEST... Genuine Dy-Dee $7.29
11-in. **Drinking-Wetting Doll** 20-in.

Of all the Drinking-Wetting Dolls, none looks so much like a real baby. Dy-Dee has chubby curves, winsome features, exquisitely sculptured tiny fingers and toes, "peaches and cream" complexion. She feels like a real baby, too. Her body, molded from finest virgin rubber, is soft, smooth and yielding. You can scrub her with soap and water—powder her with talcum—to keep her dainty. Her head, of hard rubber, is practically indestructible; turns and tilts in any direction. Sleeping "glass" eyes framed with long lashes, dark molded hair. Her head, arms and legs are held by strong rubber joints—no rusty springs.

She's dressed in a dainty knitted shirt and a birdseye diaper. Has her own bottle and nipple, bubble pipe, baby spoon and cotton flannelette pajamas.

48 T 2624—11 in. Tall. Shipping weight 2 lbs. $3 Value........$2.59

48 T 2625—15 in. Tall. Ship. weight 3 lbs. 4 oz. $5 Value.........$4.39

48 T 2626—20 in. Tall. Shipping weight 7 lbs. $8.50 Value......$7.29

Regular $7.50 Value $4.95
Magazine Cover Doll

Last year this lovely EFFANBEE Doll made the cover of a leading magazine because her face is so life-like . . . just like a real little girl's.

20 in. tall, "glass" sleeping eyes, real lashes. You can comb the Page Boy bob of first quality Blonde human hair. Fine composition, except arms which are durable hard rubber. Each finger is separate and distinct as on a real hand. Arms, legs turn, head turns, tilts.

Pink Velvet dress. White underslip and panty, White imitation leather slippers, real heels, rayon socks, hair bow.

48 T 2578—Ship. wt. 4 lbs. 8 oz. ..$4.95

NEW! Birthday Doll $6.95
Swiss Music Box

Doll plays "Happy Birthday to You" when Swiss Music Box in body is wound. 17 in. tall, fine composition. Hard rubber hands, arms, distinct fingers. Sleeping "glass" eyes, real lashes, first quality human hair. Arms, legs turn freely. Head tilts, turns. Stands alone.

Clothes of fine material, beautifully made. Med. Blue Velvet dress and hat, dainty lace trim. 4 pearl buttons. Clothes made with real buttons and buttonholes—not pinned together. Ruffled slip, panty. Socks, imitation leather slippers with heels.

48 T 2577—Ship. wt. 4 lbs..... $6.95

19-Piece Dy-Dee Doll Outfit Made by EFFANBEE

Made especially for Dy-Dee Dolls—can be worn by most any rubber or composition baby doll. Nice material, daintily made—up to EFFANBEE standards in every way. White Batiste dress with embroidered collar and lace trimming, batiste bonnet, lawn slip, pajamas and wrapper of printed cotton flannel. Pink eiderdown bathrobe and booties, blanket, crib pad, mercerized shirt, 2 birdseye diapers, feeding bottle and nipple, safety pins, wash cloth, rubber panties . . . just in case—and a booklet, "What Every Young Doll Mother Should Know." All packed in an attractive hinged case, covered with pretty grained paper. The ideal Gift for the little girl who is already "Mother" to a Dy-Dee baby.

$1.89 Small

48 T 2580—For 11-in. Dolls. Shipping weight 2 lbs. 6 oz.........$1.89

48 T 2581—For 15-in. Dolls. Shipping weight 3 lbs. 6 oz........$2.69

48 T 2582—For 20-in. Dolls. Shipping weight 4 lbs...........$3.59

"NOW I LAY ME DOWN TO SLEEP"

Little Tots Love Bedtime When Touslehead Says Her Prayers

$12.95

A tiny Phonograph in her body plays "Now I Lay Me Down to Sleep." Automatic mechanism sets itself, simple enough to be played by a tot. Records are long lasting, replaceable.

Made by EFFANBEE. Touslehead is 18 in. tall, composition head, arms, legs; soft body. Her large "glass" eyes go to sleep, real lashes. Inside jointed arms, legs bent so she kneels. Tousled hair is soft fur skin, clipped short and rumpled—that's where she gets her name—may be washed and brushed. Most lasting type wig made.

She wears pajamas, flowered cotton Flannel bathrobe, soft sole felt slippers. List of additional records included.

48 T 2579 — Shipping weight 5 lbs. 8 oz............$12.95

Time Payments on Any Order of $10 or More

SEE PAGE 12A

WARDS 49

Effanbee Doll Company sent flyers throughout the 1939 year to their store buyers promoting this 17″ "Birthday" doll that has a Swiss music box in her back. The doll is composition with sleep eyes/lashes and has the hard rubber arms. The velvet dress is blue with pearl buttons. This same doll was offered through Montgomery Wards for Christmas of 1939. This page is from the Wards catalog and also show Dy-Dee and the doll Touslehead that is 18″ and has a phonograph player with records in her body.

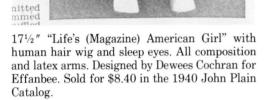

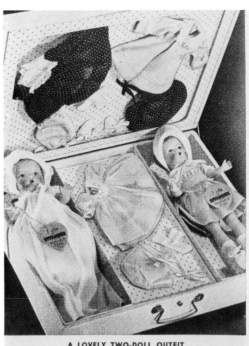

A LOVELY TWO-DOLL OUTFIT

A lovely two-doll outfit, consisting of baby and her grown-up sister. Baby doll measures 8 in. high; dressed in a white organdy dress with matching bonnet. She has on a pink slip, white stockings. When going to a party, dress her in her new pink organdy dress with matching bonnet, trimmed with blue. When it gets cold, you can

17½″ "Life's (Magazine) American Girl" with human hair wig and sleep eyes. All composition and latex arms. Designed by Dewees Cochran for Effanbee. Sold for $8.40 in the 1940 John Plain Catalog.

8″ "Patsy Babykin" and 11″ "Suzette" listed as "Baby and Big Sister" in the 1940 John Plain catalog. The trunk is 15″ x 12½″. The entire outfit cost $8.50 in 1940.

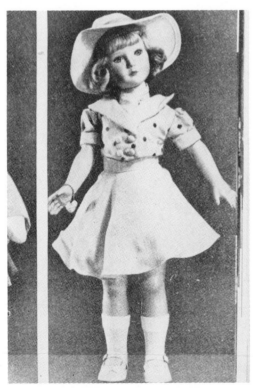

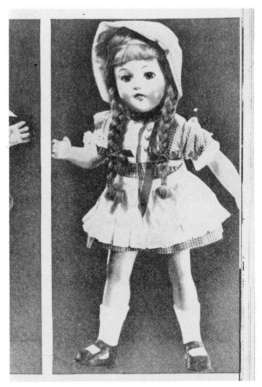

21″ Portrait Doll that is all composition with latex arms and fingers, human hair wig, sleep eyes and in Paris inspired dress with jacket and ascot tie around neck. Sold for original price of $12.50 from the 1940 John Plain Catalog. This is one of the American Children designed by Dewees Cochran for Effanbee.

15″ "Anne Shirley", "a real American girl" that is all composition with sleep eyes/lashes and does not have the Dewees Cochran designed arms and hands. Sold in 1940 from the John Plain catalog for $4.90.

14″ Replica Historical Effanbee that is "1658 Carolina Settlement" using the Anne Shirley doll with latex arms and hands designed by Dewees Cochran. Sale of the Historical dolls ran into 1940. Courtesy Bee Johnson.

13½″ "Suzanne" all composition and strung. Right arm bent, wig, sleep eyes and marked: Suzanne/Effanbee, on head. Suzanne/Effanbee/Made in USA, on back. 1940. Courtesy Mauldin Collection.

16″ Called "Baby Bright Eyes", "Tousle-Tot" and "Sweetie Pie". Composition head and limbs with cloth body. Marked: Effanbee, on head. Sleep blue eyes. Flange neck into cloth body. Old Effanbee dress, but not hers. 1940-1946. Courtesy June Schultz.

23½″ "Baby Bright eyes" with a Steiff "Whatcha-ma-callit". Flirty eyes, caracul wig and not original clothes. Full composition arms and bent legs on cloth body. 1930's. This doll is also called "Sweetie Pie". 1940-1946. Courtesy June Schultz.

22½″ "Patsy Lou". All composition with original early synthetic wig and wears copy of an original outfit, but has original shoes. Sleep brown eyes. Ca. 1940's. Marks: "Effanbee Patsy Lou", on back. Courtesy June Schultz.

A. Talks and sings "London Bridge" with phonograph inside. Dressed in pink and white, is 19″ tall and has sleep eyes/lashes. It is not known if Effanbee made this doll. Sold for $19.75 in 1940. B. "Squeeze Me" and hear music from 18 note music box in cloth body. 17″ with sleep eyes/lashes. Sold for $8.40 in 1940. Maker is not known. C. 17½″ "Patsy" with wind up 18 note music box. Sleep eyes/lashes. Sold for $8.40 in the 1940 John Plain catalog.

"MY NAME IS BEA"

11″ Listed in the 1940 John Plain catalog with caption, "My Name is Bea". All composition with deeply molded hair and painted eyes. The trunk case measures 12¾″ x 7¼″ and this outfit and doll sold for $3.00 in 1940.

20″ "Anne Shirley" or "Little Lady" that is marked on the body with the Anne Shirley/Effanbee, and with Effanbee, on the head. All original with very good quality Scot outfit, mohair wig and blue sleep eyes. Her tam is missing. (Author).

Sales Department - 200 Fifth Avenue ·· Factory - 42-44 Wooster Street ·· Cable Address - Effanbee

EFFANBEE
DURABLE
DOLLS

FLEISCHAKER & BAUM

45 Greene Street ··· New York

PLEASE ADDRESS ALL COMMUNICATIONS
TO 45 GREENE STREET

January 4, 1940

Mrs. Molly Goldman
c/o Hotel New Yorker - Room 1821
New York City

Dear Mrs. Goldman:-

I herewith confirm the conversation we have had yesterday:-

That you will design for Fleischaker & Baum a complete line of doll dresses with hats and bonnets of new, up to date and becoming designs, said samples to consist of a complete sample line of various sizes of the different parts we are going to furnish you with, that is - girl dolls, baby dolls, Dy-Dee dolls and other novelty dolls. Of course, it is understood that these samples must be ready in plenty of time to be able to pass on them and have them ready for display on our dolls at the 1940 Toy Fair.

We agree to pay you $2,000. for such a complete sample line as follows:-

$500. as soon as you start with the designing.
500. upon delivery of a complete Baby sample line in both short and long dresses.
500. upon delivery of the complete samples for Girl dolls.
500. when your sample line is completely finished and delivered to us.

Now, with reference to our discussion of the amount we may purchase, we will enter into a contract with you, agreeing to buy from you $75,000. worth of these dresses after we see your samples and find them satisfactory.

NEW 1941 DY-DEE ★
★
She's Almost Human!
★

SOFT, DAINTY RUBBER EARS AND
REAL NOSTRILS MAKE HER MOST
LIKE A REAL, LIVE BABY

$7⁶⁹   Best of all Drinking- $2⁵⁹
          Wetting Dolls .. Made
20-INCH   by EFFANBEE .. sold   11-INCH
          by mail only at Wards

We've yet to see the Baby who likes to have her ears washed. And this new Dy-Dee is no exception! She'll probably kick and squirm. But secretly she's proud, because Dy-Dee is the ONE AND ONLY drinking-wetting Doll with dainty, soft rubber ears that you can wash behind or clean out with a swab. They're not molded to her head as others. Then, too, this new 1941 EFFaNBEE Dy-Dee has well-defined nostrils . . . two tiny pink-lined holes . . . that little mother can clean out with swabs, same as you would a real baby.
Dy-Dee is the only doll who drinks drop by drop and whose diaper need not be changed as fast as she drinks. A patented valve . . . exclusive with Dy-Dee . . . prevents water from running out as fast as she swallows it.
Dy-Dee is the only doll who drinks from a spoon as well as a bottle; who drinks sitting up or lying down.
Dy-Dee is the only doll who goes to sleep sitting up, and who can keep her eyes open when she's lying down.
Only Dy-Dee can blow soap bubbles from a bubble pipe. You'll love Dy-Dee's chubby curves, dimpled, sculptured fingers and toes. She feels like a real Baby, too. Body molded of finest, virgin Rubber, soft and yielding. Scrub her with soap, powder her with talcum. Her hard rubber head turns, tilts. Finest "glass-like" sleeping eyes, real lashes. Molded hair. Head, arms, legs held by strong rubber joints; no springs to rust. She wears a knitted shirt and birds-eye diaper. Has her own bottle, nipple, spoon, bubble pipe, cotton flannelette pajamas. 3 cotton-tipped swabs.

48 T 2442—20-   48 T 2441—15-   48 T 2440—11-
in. Doll. $5.95   in. Doll. $3 Val-   in. Doll. $3 Val-
Value. Ship. wt.   ue. Ship. wt.   ue. Ship. wt.
7 lbs.....$7.69   3 lbs. 4 oz $4.39   2 lbs....$2.59

The "NEW" Dy-Dee Baby of 1942 came in three sizes (20″, 15″ and 11″) in the Ward's catalog, and in wholesale catalogs of that year. She has a rubber body and ears and a hard rubber head.

THINGS TO DRESS

Dolls are still the most popular single kind of toy and they get more complicated and satisfying every year. A good child-mother today can't be put off with a doll she can only fondle or dress in pantaloons. She wants dolls that do things and ones that have good figures so that they are a pleasure to dress up modishly.

This 3″ long spoon that is "silver" is from the Dy-Dee layettes and is marked: Effanbee-Dy-Dee, on inside of curved part of handle Courtesy Margaret Mandel.

Magnetic Doll has tiny magnets in hands so she can hold things. Doll alone costs $5. There are 28 gadgets—from ice-cream cones to croquet mallets—for her to hold. She can also hold anything with a thumbtack stuck in its handle.

Life Magazine of 1940 carried an article on Christmas toys and included was this "Magnetic Doll". Caption says that 28 gadgets were available for the doll to hold, and that she can hold anything with a thumbtack stuck in it's handle. Shown is "Little Lady-Anne Shirley" marked.

Effanbee dominated the Montgomery Ward's 1942 catalog with five models of "Little Lady-Anne Shirley" that are all composition, sleep eyes and have human hair wigs. A. is 20½" and wears a plum colored coat and hat, along with a blue crepe dress. B. is 21½" tall and dressed in pink rayon crepe, bra and panties. C. is 18" tall gowned in a South American Dancing dress. Her human hair wig is black and the colors in the skirt are (bottom up) red, green, orange, blue and white. D. Came in three sizes: 18", 21½" and 28". The formal is pink marquisette with metallic flowers and bodice is black velveteen . E. is 20½" tall and her gown is Schiffli embroidered net and solid pink net underskirt with white satin bodice.

1942 at Montgomery Wards also included all these Effanbee dolls: E. 19" and 23" flirty eye baby, cloth body and composition head with molded hair and dressed in white organdy with pink ribbon trim. F., G. and H. came in sizes 15", 18" and 21½" with bolero jackets over dotted Swiss dresses in pink, yellow and green. A., B., and C. are 15", 18" and 21½" in pinafore skirts of embroidered cotton broadcloth with batiste blouses and matching bonnets. The colors are pink and blue. D. 19" and 24" flirty eyes and caracul wig, and dressed in white snowsuit with pink trim.

DOLLS SHE'LL TREASURE FOR YEARS

Dy-Dee doll and 20-pc. layette

N., P. and R. 15", 18" and 21½" dressed in wale pique dresses with organdy collars and floral braid trim. Came in red, yellow and green. S. In military outfit of blue cotton and rayon twill. The boots and lining to cape are red. This doll came in sizes 15", 18" and 20½". J. 15", 17½" and 20½" dressed in black velveteen. K., L. and M. in sizes 15", 18" and 21½" dressed in embroidered organdy in blue or red.

Dy-Dee came in sizes 11", 15" and 20" in the 1942 Montgomery Ward catalog with a 20 piece layette in suitcase. Hard plastic head and rubber body. An 11 piece layette was also available.

The McCall Needlework magazine for Winter 1943-44 had an Effanbee Little Lady doll's photo with the wardrobe that could be made for her with pattern #1015 and for the 13¼", 15", 18" and 22" dolls. The grouping included a nurse uniform and air-raid warden's outfit.

18" "Little Lady" that is composition with human hair wig, and all original clothes. Brown sleep eyes. Courtesy Lilah Beck.

In the 1942 Montgomery Ward catalog the 12" Suzette doll was shown in this outfit. This outfit was called "Colonial" and is blue flowered rayon over a pink skirt trimmed with lace. Also shown is 9" "Tousle-Tot" with caracul hair and case with wardrobe.

A. was offered in the 18″ size and is gowned in blue taffeta that is embroidered with pink and blue flowers and human hair wig. B. is 1943 19″ Bride, C. is 18″ in plaid formal of taffeta with white bodice and red trim. The sash and hair bow are both green. D. came in 18″, 21½″ and 27″ with gown of pink rayon with metallic dots and flared peplum of black velveteen, human hair wig. E. in 20½″ size is repeat of 1942.

A and B is now "Sweetie Pie" (Tousle-Tot) and in the 17″ size was dressed dotted Swiss with pink trim and is cloth and composition with caracul wig and flirty eyes. B. is in 19″ and 24″, in snowsuit. C. is in black bra, panties and negligee and has a human hair wig. D. and E. came in sizes 18″ and 21″. In red or yellow flower trimmed pique.

1943 F. and G. "Skippy" all composition with painted on stockings and modeled on shoes. 14″ in Army or Navy suit. H. and J. in 18″ and 21″ size "Little Lady" wears bolero jacket dress of checked cotton broadcloth and matching bow. K. "Sweetie Pie-Tousle-Tot" in the 19″ size with molded hair and flirty eyes. L. 18″ "Majorette" wears red twill skirt lined with white, attached blouse and panties are white cotton twill, white boots with red trim. All three girl dolls are listed as having human hair wigs.

1943 introduced "Brother and Sister" with yarn hair in the 12″ size. Composition head, cloth body, legs and all of arms except hands. He is dressed in blue and she in pink. Shown also in 1944 catalog. They were $6.95 in 1943, and $7.25 in 1944.

1944 saw the #6 in 21½″ and a repeat of the black negligee, panties and bra, but this one has yarn hair, sleep eyes. 7. is 18″ tall in hat and coat of red rayon and cotton twill and under coat is Scotch plaid suspender dress and panties. 9 and 10. in 18″ and 21½″ dressed in pink or blue marquisette with ruffled hems. 8. 18″ in pink pajamas that are two piece of printed rayon and pink plush mules. All these dolls have yarn hair and sleep eyes. These same dolls, along with #1 in yellow gown were offered in 1945 also. So was the Majorette, but 1945 one had yarn wig in rolled under full bangs and rest of hair in pageboy style.

The 1944 Montgomery Ward's catalog is calling "Sweetie Pie", Tousle-Tot again and the doll came in the 20″ size with layette in case, or 19″ and 24″ size in blue snowsuit. Both have flirty eyes and caracul wig and made of all composition. This same outfit with different trim was repeated in 1945.

1944 Montgomery Ward catalog showed all the "Little Lady-Anne Shirley" dolls with yarn hair and still with sleep eyes. 2. Majorette is repeat of 1943 outfit (1943 has human hair wig). 4. and 5. in 18″ and 21½″ in dresses of marquisette in pink and blue. 1. in 18″ dressed in yellow marquisette with red/multi trim. 3. in 18″ wears plaid formal of taffeta, white bodice with red trim, sash and bow. All have yarn hair and sleep eyes.

1944 Montgomery Ward catalog offered the "Little Lady-Anne Shirley" doll as Bride in the 18″ size with yarn hair. Also in the 18″, 21½″ and 27″ with yarn hair and dressed in metallic dotted marquisette trimmed with ruffles and silver ribbon. The cape is black velvet with red lining and is hooded. Both have sleep eyes.

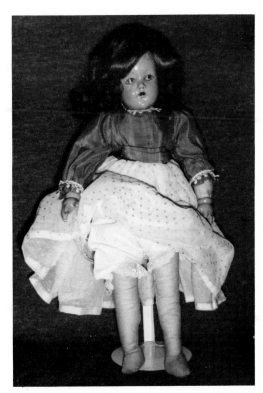

21″ "Today's Girl" (Little Lady). Head and hands are composition with painted eyes and yarn hair. Body, legs and arms to the wrists are cloth stuffed. Note the wide spread, but shorter and stubby fingers. Blonde is original and black hair doll has copy of outfit and was the childhood doll of Nancy Lucas.

17″ "Little Lady" with painted eyes, pink stuffed material body, legs and arms. Gauntlet composition hands and head. Courtesy Lilah Beck.

16″ "Brother" and 12″ "Sister". Both have all cloth bodies, and arms with composition hands, legs on the girls are composition and the boy has cloth legs. Both have original clothes except for shoes and socks. Both have yarn hair and painted eyes and marked: FanB. Heads are a wooden block. Courtesy Jeanne Mauldin.

Right: 18″ Little Lady. All composition and original with woven tag on back of dress: Effanbee Durable Dolls, in a heart-Made in USA. Early synthetic wig of mixture. (1940's). Left: same only with yarn hair and re-dressed. Both dolls are marked head and back: Effanbee U.S.A. Courtesy June Schultz.

1945

ALL WARDS 63

1945 Bride is 18″ and has yarn hair and sleep eyes. The Montgomery Ward catalog also shows 18″, 21″ and 27″ in pink formal of rayon marquisette and white maribou cape and skull cap. The hair is yarn and she has sleep eyes.

Effanbee introduced the sleeping "Babyette" in the 1945 Montgomery Ward catalog. Says the doll is modeled from a four day old sleeping baby. Body, arms and legs are stuffed cotton, and head and hands are composition. Dressed in white marquisette and basket (21″ by 11½″) is pink lined and has blue marquisette around the sides. "Tousle-Tot" is repeat of 1944.

In 1946 Montgomery Ward carried the 21″ Bride with style change and mohair wig, and she still has sleep eyes. Shown next to her is a 20″ "Monica". The A. doll is Bridesmaid that is 18″, has mohair wig and sleep eyes. The gown is blue. Next to her is 14″ Flowergirl by Ideal Doll Co.

Appealing, Life-like Dolls...Dressed

Ⓐ "CANDY KID" IN TRAVELING CASE BY EFFANBEE. This precious Doll is 13 inches tall . . . modeled like an adorable chubby toddling child. Made entirely of smooth, satiny hard-to-break composition . . . round little stomach, short chubby legs and dimpled knees . . . formed with the utmost artistry. Hair molded and painted. Clear, sparkling Glassene eyes "go to sleep"; real lashes.

Wears dainty Pink Rayon Marquisette dress with tucked yoke, ruffled sleeves, ruffled hem, dainty ribbon rosebuds. Ruffles outline her matching bonnet and frame her charming face. Pink rayon underskirt attached to dress. Lace trimmed Pink rayon panties. White rayon socks. Cute Pink imitation lea-

ther slippers. This sweet little doll comes tied with a big Pink ribbon bow in a lovely traveling case. Her extra clothes are nicely arranged inside . . . 2-pc. Pink rayon Satin pajamas trimmed with blue braid. Lace-edged Pink rayon satin panties and bra. Coat-Bonnet-Muff Set of Pink cotton Twill trimmed with Blue wool. Vivid cotton plaid dress with short puffed sleeves and big sash. Extra White rayon socks. Garments carefully made; fasten with tiny buttons. Case of heavy cardboard on wood frame; 17 x 14 x 6 in.; has leather handle, and snap lock. Read more about Effanbee dolls on Page 92.

48 T 3825—13-In. Candy Kid with Extra Clothes in Traveling Case. Ship. wt. 5 lbs. 16.50

FINE QUALITY DOLLS MADE ENTIRELY OF HARD-TO-BREAK COMPOSITION

Ⓑ CHUBBY TODDLER DOLL. Made entirely of smooth, hard-to-break composition with roly-poly body, chubby arms and legs, cute dimpled knees. Hair is molded and painted on. Her "go to sleep" eyes are fine quality Glassene, with thick lashes. Head turns and tilts; arms and legs are jointed. She wears an adorable Blue and White checked Percale dress made like a little girl's with short puffed sleeves, peter-pan collar edged with rick-rack. Matching panties. Matching bonnet has inner ruffle of white. White cotton socks; white imitation leather slippers. About 17 inches tall.

48 T 3948—Ship. wt. 2 lbs. 2 oz. 5.89

Ⓒ "PATSY" BY EFFANBEE. A dainty, lovable little Girl Doll made entirely of hard-to-break composition . . . beautifully modeled like all Effanbee dolls, at a price that is exceptionally low for this fine quality. Pert little face with expressive eyes, rosebud mouth. Her eyes and molded hair are painted on with life-like realism. Head turns and tilts; arms and legs are jointed. She stands alone. Sweetly dressed in Pink checked cotton with embroidered organdy ruffle at shoulders. Panty attached to dress. Cute matching bonnet. White rayon socks and white imitation leather slippers. About 14 inches tall.

48 T 3824—Ship. wt. 1 lb. 14 oz. 3.15

10% DOWN DELIVERS OUR FINEST DOLL. PAY BALANCE ON MONTHLY PAYMENT TERMS. SEE PAGE 189.

The 1946 Montgomery Ward catalog carried the 14″ "Patsy" in pink checked cotton with matching bonnet. Also shown is the 13″ "Candy Kid" with molded hair and sleep eyes and dressed in pink. She came with case and wardrobe. An earlier promotion of Easter saw this same doll/outfit in yellow. (1946) Easter of 1946 saw this special promoted "Candy Kid" dressed in yellow, where it was dressed in pink for the regular 1946 Christmas season. All composition with molded hair, sleep eyes/lashes and is 13″ tall. The Christmas issue of this doll included a cardboard/wood frame trunk with wardrobe.

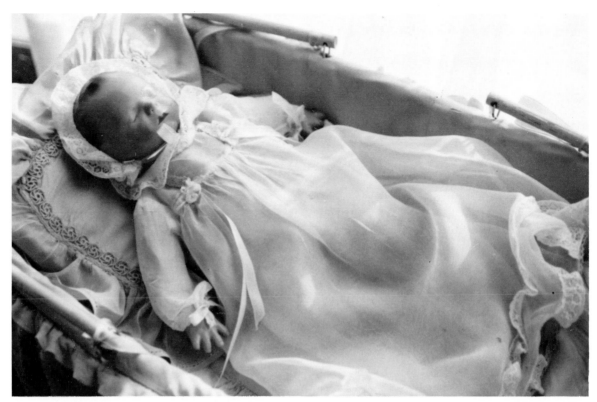

12″ "Babyette" with molded, painted closed a-sleep eyes. Composition head and hands to wrists. Cloth body and limbs. 1945. Original. Courtesy Sheryl Schmidt.

J. is a repeat of the 18″ in black bra, panties and negligee with mohair wig. The remainder of the dolls on this page are made by Ideal Doll and Toy Company. 1946.

Beautifully Made, Beautifully Dressed...

[A] BABY IN LOVELY NET DRESS. Cries "Ma-Ma"; goes to sleep. Composition head, arms, legs. Hair molded and painted. Head turns. Cotton stuffed body. Sleeping Glassene eyes; real lashes. Dress and bonnet are frothy net, beautifully embroidered. Pink slip, panties; socks, shoes. An Ideal doll.
48 T 3949—Abt. 17 in. tall. Wt. 2 lbs....6.89

[B] "FAIRY TALE PRINCESS," BY MONICA OF HOLLYWOOD. REAL HUMAN HAIR "ROOTED" IN SCALP. Snowy white wool felt coat and hat. Dotted swiss dress. Cotton slip and panties. Garments beautifully made with snap fasteners. Rayon socks. Imitation leather pumps; tiny heels. All composition; movable head, arms, legs. Eyes artistically painted by hand.
48 T 3867—Abt. 20 in. tall. Ship. wt. 3 lbs......22.95

[C] SQUEEZE EITHER LEG—CRIES "MA-MA." Voice in body too. Latex (soft rubber) arms, legs; cotton filled. Feels like soft baby skin. Turning plastic head; molded, painted hair. Cotton filled body. Sleeping eyes; real lashes. Organdy dress, bonnet; slip, panties, socks, shoes. An Ideal doll.
48 T 4253—Abt. 17 in. tall. Ship. wt. 2 lbs......5.98
48 T 4254—Abt. 19 in. tall. Ship. wt. 2 lbs. 8 oz..7.98

[D] "THE DOLL SHE DREAMS ABOUT," BY MONICA OF HOLLYWOOD. REAL HUMAN HAIR "ROOTED" IN SCALP. Beautiful Blue Wool Felt coat and poke bonnet. Dotted swiss dress. White cotton slip and panties. Garments carefully made with snap fasteners. Rayon socks; imitation leather sandals with tiny heels. All composition; movable head, arms, legs. Eyes hand painted.
48 T 3864—About 17 inches tall. Ship. wt. 2 lbs. 8 oz.,..............19.95

[E] "MAJORETTE," BY EFFANBEE. Red and White rayon uniform, resplendent with gold color braid, epaulets, buttons. Flared skirt lined with white; blouse, panties attached. High hat with real feather; tiny baton in hand. Military boots (imitation leather) with tiny heels. All composition; movable head, arms, legs. Sleeping Glassene eyes; real lashes. Soft mohair wig.
48 T 3842—About 18 inches tall. Shipping weight 3 lbs..............8.95

[F] EFFANBEE DOLL IN SHEER PINK RAYON MARQUISETTE DRESS with frilly ruffles and dainty ribbon rosebuds. Lace trimmed pink rayon slip and panties. White rayon socks; Pink imitation leather sandals with tiny heels. All composition doll, beautifully modeled, with movable head, arms and legs. Sleeping Glassene eyes with real lashes. Soft, lustrous mohair wig.
48 T 3843—About 21 inches tall. Ship. wt. 4 lbs.....................10.95

[G] CURLY BANGS AND BRAIDED PIGTAILS TIED WITH RIBBON BOWS...just like a sweet little girl. Red and White checked dress of crisp rayon. Sash ties in big bow in back. White cotton slip; panties attached. Rayon socks; Black imitation leather slippers; tiny heels. All composition with movable head, arms and legs. Sleeping Glassene eyes; real lashes. Mohair wig.
48 T 3871—About 18 inches tall. Ship. wt. 2 lbs. 8 oz................6.95

96 WARDS ALL   READ "FACTS ABOUT DOLLS" ON PAGE 92 FOR MORE INFORMATION ABOUT THESE FINE QUALITY DOLLS

1946 Montgomery Ward catalog showed the Majorette in 18" size that is a repeat of the year before and has a mohair wig. (E). Also the 21" size in pink rayon marquisette dress with slightly different trim than year before. (f). B and D are Monica Dolls.

Like Real Little Children

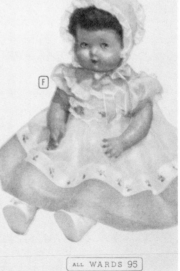

D EFFANBEE'S ADORABLE BABY DOLL, BEAUTIFULLY GIFT PACKAGED WITH EXTRA CLOTHES. A charming, exquisite gift that will delight the most fastidious little girl. So lovable, so life-like, she's almost like a real baby. Her flirting Glassene eyes (with thick lashes) move from side to side and she goes to sleep. Her adorable ringlet wig is finest, softest mohair. About sixteen inches tall. Made entirely of smooth, satiny hard-to-break composition . . . beautifully modeled with cute dimpled face, chubby arms and legs. Head turns and tilts; arms and legs are jointed.

This adorable doll comes to you in a sweet little blue checked romper suit. She's tied in a gift box with a big ribbon bow and her extra clothes are neatly arranged around her . . . a cunning little-girl dress of blue checked Cotton with peter-pan collar, short puffed sleeves; Coat and Bonnet of Pink cotton twill trimmed with blue wool braid; one-piece cotton flannelette pajamas; white rayon socks; white imitation leather baby shoes. Garments carefully made, fasten with tiny buttons and buttonholes. Sturdy Pink box measures 19 by 17 by 5 inches. A once-in-a-lifetime gift for a very special little girl. Be sure to read more about fine quality Effanbee Dolls on Page 92. Use your credit to buy. See Page 189 for details of Wards convenient Monthly Payment Plan.

48 T 3938—Effanbee's 16 inch Baby Doll and Extra Clothes in Gift Box. Ship. wt. 5 lbs......12.95

"TERRI-LEE" PERSONALITY DOLL AND EFFANBEE'S "SWEETIE-PIE"

E "TERRI-LEE" . . . she'll win your heart completely. Actually modeled from a real live 2-year old child. All composition . . . 17 inches tall. Fascinating dimples in her chubby face. Tiny nose, cute little chin, childishly life-like arms and legs, tinted fingernails, beautifully painted eyes and sensitive mouth . . . all combined to give you the most realistic Girl Doll ever made. Head turns and tilts; arms and legs are jointed. Blonde hair made by professional maker of real manikin wigs . . . can be wet and curled like real hair. Blue Rayon Marquisette dress, trimmed with dainty val lace; white cotton slip and panties. White socks; imitation leather shoes. "Terri-Lee" label sewed in clothes. Carries daisy in hand. Gift boxed. Buy on Wards Monthly Payment Plan.

48 T 3873—Shipping weight 3 lbs...........11.50

F EFFANBEE'S "SWEETIE-PIE" BABY DOLL. Curly "tousle-tot" hair is real lambskin . . . won't mat or tangle, can be "shampooed" with damp cloth. Hair is firmly attached to head. Flirting Glassene eyes with real lashes move from side to side. She sleeps and says "Ma-Ma." Head, arms and legs are beautifully molded composition. Soft body is cotton stuffed. Head turns. Exquisitely made dress and bonnet of sheer pink and white Rayon Marquisette with dainty lace frills and embroidered rosebuds. Dress buttons in back; sash ties in big bow. Lace trimmed slip and panties. White socks and imitation leather baby shoes. In attractive gift box.

48 T 3931—24 in. tall. Ship. wt. 5 lbs. 8 oz....16.50
48 T 3932—19 in. tall. Ship. wt. 3 lbs. 12 oz...12.95

ALL WARDS 95

16″ "Sweetie Pie-Tousle-Tot" in all composition was offered in the 1946 Montgomery Ward catalog with flirty eyes and with MOHAIR wig rather than caracul. Sold in box with extra clothes. Romper and dress are blue check, flowered pajamas and pink coat and bonnet with blue trim. The 19″ and 24″ of this same doll was also offered in same pink/white dress and bonnet as year before and has the caracul hair and cloth body.

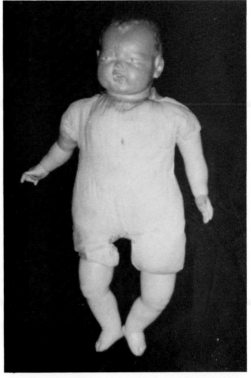

21″ "Lil' Darlin' " with cloth body and early vinyl, molded hair, painted eyes and open/closed mouth with molded tongue. Very frowning face. Left hand is molded open, and right hand has the two middle fingers molded to palm. Marks: Effanbee, on head. Courtesy Jennie Mauldin.

Dy-dee and Magic

(D) EFFANBEE'S "DY-DEE" DOLL. Cries now, with a pacifier that makes a crying noise when you put it in her mouth and squeeze her gently. She drinks, wets, sleeps and blows soap bubbles. All rubber (natural and synthetic). Hard rubber head turns, tilts; molded hair. Clean her soft rubber ears, dainty nostrils with Q-tips. Jointed arms, legs. Glassene sleeping eyes, real lashes. Wears diaper and knit shirt. Has her own bottle, spoon, bubble pipe and Q-tips. Order layette (E) separately.
48 T 4322—20-in. Dy-dee Doll. Wt. 6 lbs. 8 oz.....16.95
48 T 4321—15-in. Dy-dee Doll. Wt. 3 lbs. 8 oz.....12.95
48 T 4320—11-in. Dy-dee Doll. Wt. 2 lbs. 12 oz.....7.65

(E) DY-DEE DOLL LAYETTE. Complete outfit for Dy-dee Dolls above. Pretty white flannelette kimono; lace-trimmed white organdy dress; matching bonnet with ribbon ties; lawn slip with lace at hem; white rayon socks and white imitation leather baby shoes.
48 W 4114—For 20-in. Doll. Ship. wt. 1 lb. 3 oz.....4.89
48 W 4113—For 15-in. Doll. Ship. wt. 1 lb. 1 oz.....3.89
48 W 4115—For 11-in. Doll. Ship. wt. 1 lb.........2.95

(F) IDEAL'S ORIGI
Body of Latex
like baby's skin
hold her. Flexib
plastic head, m
lashes. (Wash w
shirt, panties, or
washcloth, pow
48 W 4018—20-in
48 W 4017—18-in
48 W 4016—16-in
48 W 4015—14-in

(G) LOW-PRICED
stuffed with
her. Jointed ar
molded hair; glo
in. sizes wear k
48 W 4028—18-in
48 W 4027—16-in
48 W 4026—14-in

BE SURE TO READ FACTS ABOUT DOLLS ON PAGE 106. FOR MONTHLY

The 11″, 15″ and 20″ Dy-Dee was offered with molded, painted hair and sold separately. The layette could be ordered separately also. 1948 Montgomery Ward catalog.

Plush "Dydee Bear" and appears to be of late 1950's material of cotton/rayon mixture. Has a felt tongue. Courtesy Joan Meivose and sent by June Schultz.

Effanbee Fine Dolls...Beautifully Made

Effanbee Dolls are among the finest made. They are exquisitely mod-elled—all parts are made carefully, sanded to satin smoothness. Heads turn; arms and legs are jointed; hands have separate fingers, tinted nails, tiny palm markings. Life-like Glassene sleeping eyes have real lashes. They're charmingly dressed. Clothing is made of finest mate-rials, with snap or button closings. Wigs are excellent quality, care-fully made. Read "Facts about Dolls" on Page 106. Use your Credit and buy the Best—See Page 176 for Terms.

A "Honey" With Flirting Eyes, by Effanbee. "Flirting Eyes" move from side to side and close, too. Soft ringlet wig is human hair. All composition body; jointed arms and legs. Head turns. Flower trimmed straw bonnet. White cotton blouse and billowy skirt have "new look." Snap fasteners. Full ruffled petticoat; matching panties attached. Socks, slippers.
48 T 4234—About 21 inches tall. Ship. wt. 3 lbs. 8 oz..............17.95

B "Majorette" by Effanbee. Leads the parade with her tiny baton. Glis-tening braid trims her gay cotton Twill uniform. High flannel hat with plume; black visor and chin strap. Imitation leather boots with heels All composition body; jointed arms and legs. Head turns. Mohair wig.
48 T 4228—About 18 in. tall. Ship. wt. 3 lbs...................9.79
48 T 4227—About 15 in. tall. Ship. wt. 2 lbs. 12 oz.................7.79

C "Party Girl" by Effanbee. All dressed up in her very best clothes—sure to be admired. Sheer Aqua Rayon Marquisette dress over white rayon slip and matching panties—snap closings. Hair band matches ribbon sash. Pink rayon satin party slippers; white socks.
All composition body; jointed arms and legs. Tinted nails; separated fingers. Mohair wig on movable head. Glassene sleeping eyes with real lashes. Ship. wts. 3 lbs.; 2 lbs. 12 oz.
48T3844—Abt. 18 in. 9.79
48T3899—Abt. 15 in. 7.79

110 WARDS xs

D "Pedal Pusher" by Effanbee. Fashionably dressed for town or country cycling and walk-ing. Her gingham dress has attached matching knee-length shorts. Snap fasteners. Wide-brimmed felt sailor hat; woven basket with arti-ficial flowers. Suede-cloth slippers; rayon socks.
Mohair pigtail wig on movable head. Glassene sleeping eyes; real lashes. All composition body; jointed arms and legs. Tinted nails; separated fingers. Ship. wts. 3 lbs.; 2 lbs. 12 oz.
48 T 4226—About 18 inches tall.........11.65
48 T 4225—About 15 inches tall..........9.65

E "Sunbonnet Girl" by Effanbee. Any girl will be proud to introduce this doll best friends. Cotton blouse and panty comb tion under cotton Pique suspender style skirt. Snap fasteners. Bows at back of waist and sun-bonnet. Imitation leather slippers; rayon socks.
All composition body; jointed arms and legs. Tinted nails; separated fingers. Mohair wig on movable head. Glassene sleeping eyes; real lashes. Shipping weights 3 lbs.; 2 lbs. 12 oz.
48 T 3898—About 18 inches tall.........9.85
48 T 3897—About 15 inches tall.........79

A is "Honey" in composition and with flirty eyes. She has a human hair wig, straw bonnet, white/pink trimmed blouse and pink check skirt. B. Majorette was offered in 15″ and 18″ in aqua blue marquisette and pink sash and rib-bon and mohair wig. D. 15″ and 18″ called "Pedal Pusher" outfit in blue/white check with red hat and ribbon running through hem. E. 15″ and 18″ called "Sunbonnet Girl", white blouse and pantie combination under cotton pique suspender style skirt. B, C, D and E are all "Little Lady", all composition, all have sleep eyes and mohair wigs. 1948 Montgomery Ward catalog.

Effanbee's "Dy-dee" and "Sweetie-pie"

(F) ORIGINAL DY-DEE RUBBER DOLL WITH LAYETTE IN CASE by Effanbee. Cryer-pacifier has been added this season to make Dy-Dee more realistic ... now she cries as well as drinks and wets. Dy Dee has patented valve to delay water running out as soon as "swallowed." Slight turn of head permits doll to close or keep eyes open in sleeping or sitting position. Handle Dy-Dee like a real Baby—wash, powder, feed from bottle or spoon, change diapers, use cryer-pacifier or let her blow bubbles. When bathing, wash behind soft rubber ears and use Q-tips to cleanse tiny nostrils. Shampoo her "Tousle-Tot" head with damp cloth ... real lambskin hair.

Jointed arms and legs. Glassene sleeping eyes; real lashes. Wears diaper and knit shirt; cotton coat and bonnet, dotted Swiss dress, slip, extra diaper, 2 safety pins, cryer-pacifier, socks and shoes. Cotton blanket (23x18 in.), washcloth, soap and bubble-bath, Q-tip swabs, spoon, bottle and bubble-pipe. In hinged wood-frame case with handle.

48 T 4319 M—Doll abt. 20 in., with Layette in Case (21¾x15¼x10 in.). Ship. wt. 11 lbs.....35.95
48 T 4318—Doll abt. 15 in., with Layette in Case (18x13x7¼ in.). Ship. wt. 7 lbs.......24.95
48 T 4317—Doll abt. 11 in., with Layette in Case (14¾x10¾x5⅝ in.). Ship. wt. 4 lbs. 8 oz.14.95

EFFANBEE'S "SWEETIE PIE" IN DAINTY LACE-TRIMMED OUTFIT

(G) "SWEETIE PIE" BABY DOLL by Effanbee. She softly calls "Ma-Ma" and rolls her "flirting eyes" to secure a place in the arms and heart of her new "little Mother." A pretty baby from the top of her "Tousle-Tot" head of real Lambskin that may be "shampooed" by wiping with a damp cloth to her dainty feet in white imitation leather

slippers; rayon socks. Dressed in sheer pink and white Rayon Marquisette with flowered embroidery and lace; Organdy slip and panties. Movable composition head, arms and legs on soft cotton-stuffed body. Glassene sleeping eyes; real lashes.
48 T 3931—Abt. 24 in. Wt. 5 lbs. 8 oz.......18.95
48 T 3932—Abt. 19 in. Wt. 3 lbs. 12 oz......14.95

ALL WARDS 111

In 1948 Montgomery Ward offered the Dy-Dee in 11″, 15″ and 20″ with all rubber body and ears with hard rubber head. All three sizes came in suitcases with layette. Also offered was the 19″ and 24″ "Sweetie Pie" with flirty eyes, caracul wig and in same outfit as years before. The Dy-Dee also had a caracul wig.

Christmas for the Children

In 1949 the Marshall-Field catalog carried this Effanbee "Little Lady" that is 18″ and all composition. The Trunk is 20″ and holds an entire wardrobe. Cost in 1949 was $50.

FOR KI... FROM SEVEN TO SE...

DOLL CONTEST WINNERS

We are happy to announce the winners of our Doll Contest:
First Prize: Effanbee Doll. Martha Frances Howell of Tampa, Florida. For longest list of names found in letters of *Everywoman's,* including the prize winning name: *Mayrose.*
Second Prize: Three Dollars. Mrs. G. K. Small of New York, N.Y. For next longest name list.
Third Prize: Doll's sweater and beanie set. Kristin Holmstrom of Aurora, Illinois. For the third longest list of names. Congratulations girls! And thanks to all of you, who sent in splendid long lists along with many compliments for *Everywoman's.* be! Shoes for dolls they aren't rationed,

Mayrose

In the May 1943 issue of Everywoman's Magazine an Effanbee "Little Lady" doll was given away as the result of a contest the magazine held. The winner was Martha Frances Howell of Tampa, Florida for the longest list of names found in letters found in Everywoman's Magazine, which included the winning name of: Mayrose. Instructions were in the magazine monthly for sweaters, skirts, ballgowns, bathing suit and cape.

30″ "Noma Talker" marked Effanbee on hard plastic head (swivel) and shoulder plate. Sleep blue eyes and brown molded hair. Vinyl arms fit in metal socket at shoulders. Vinyl legs and cloth body. Large plastic battery operated talking mechanism in body that is marked: Noma Electric Corp., New York, N.Y. Open mouth, two teeth, felt tongue. Courtesy Nancy Lucas.

27″ "Mommy's Baby" cloth body with cryer in back. Early vinyl arms and legs that are stuffed and disc jointed at shoulders. Hard plastic shoulder plate and head with saran wig over molded, unpainted hair, sleep blue eyes/lashes. Open mouth with two upper teeth, cheek dimples. 1950. Courtesy Pearl Clasby.

Marshall-Field's of 1950 had this 19″ composition Effanbee "Honey". The cost in 1950 was $59.50.

21″ "Dy-Dee'. This size was called "Dy-Dee Louise" and her name is on the paper tag. All original and in original box. Dress and cap are red print on white organdy. Hard plastic head with vinyl body and limbs. The hair is molded and painted. Applied rubber ears. Ca. 1950. Courtesy June Schultz.

Montgomery Ward of 1950 carried the Majorette Honey in all composition and in the 18″ and 16″ sizes. (G). Number K is 21″ tall and also all composition. A smaller "Honey" exactly like K, was offered in hard plastic and she is 18″ tall.

The original Dy-Dee with all rubber body and limbs, and rubber ears on hard plastic head was offered with either molded hair or caracul wigs and all came in 11″, 15″ or 20″ sizes.

1950 Montgomery Ward carried the A. "Mommy's Baby" with curly tousle wig, hard plastic head and latex stuffed body and limbs with cryer in stomach. She came in 16″,19″ , 22″ and 25″. B is 28″ Electronic Talking doll and her price in 1950 was $23.89

14″ "Honey" that is all hard plastic and has original wig, shoes and socks, but has a re-placed dress. Courtesy Lilah Beck.

16″ "Honey" that is all hard plastic with Effanbee, on head and Effanbee/Made in USA, on body. This doll has been beautifully re-dressed as "Prince Charming" by Sally Freeman.

16″ "Honey" all hard plastic with synthetic hair and the same type used for the "Tintair" dolls. All original in beige coat with dark brown velvet cuffs, collar and matching hat. 1951. Courtesy June Schultz.

16″ "Honey" and shows dress that is under the coat in the other picture. Dress is brown and pink check taffeta. Original price tag reads $9.30 Joseph Horne Co. Courtesy June Schultz.

16″ "Honey". All hard plastic with mohair wig in braids. Has the Dewees Cochran style hands and arms, is a non-walker and the modeling of the breasts are very pronounced. Peach color fingernail polish. Organdy dress with white or light pink pinafore. Marks: Effanbee, on head and Effanbee/Made in USA, on back. Courtesy Virginia Jones.

14″ "Honey". All hard plastic with original dress. The wig is mohair and glued on. Marked head and back: Effanbee. Ca. 1951-52. Courtesy June Schultz.

Dolls dressed in French clothes
by couturier Elsa Schiaparelli.

Besides the information listed below the picture, the dolls are Effanbee's Honey Walkers and are all hard plastic. The page is from the November 1951 House and Gardens Magazine and photo credit goes to Grigsey, Miehlmann and Mazzurco. The clothes were designed by French couturier, Elsa Schiaparelli.

In 1951 the "Honey" was used as the "Tintair" doll with dynel wig that could be colored. She came in 14″, 16″ and 18″. This dress is pink with white top/pink and blue dots. From the Montgomery Ward's 1951 catalog.

The 1951 Montgomery Ward's catalog carried the "Mommy's Baby" in sizes: 16″, 19″, 22″ and 25″. She is dressed in yellow and white and came with a caracul wig. Hard plastic head, and the body/limbs were latex. Cryer in stomach that worked when squeezed.

19″ "Honey". All hard plastic walker and all original. The dress is green and white, belt is black, as are the shoes and bow. Courtesy June Schultz.

Dy-Dee Bathinettes

Dy-Dee can be bathed in regular soap and water—naturally, that forms a big part of the "little mother's" play routine. Bathinettes—just like baby brother's—add to the fun. That's why they're so popular.

82

83

Dy-Dee Plastic Diaper Can

500

Dy-Dee needs "changing"—that means diapers, and a diaper set—diaper can, clothes-line, clothes pins and soap—all kiddie-size. Little girls love realism—this is it!

In 1952 these Dy-Dee items were available through the company catalog. The bathinettes came with wood or metal legs and the diaper pails were of plastic.

Mommy's Baby

She's a darling! Effanbee's wonderful talking "mamma doll" with a new, life-like voice. Just hold her, hug her and she'll talk—nothing to wind-up, nothing to go wrong. "Mommy's Baby" really says "Mommy"—so you can actually understand her. She has a beautifully molded plastic head and a Latex Skin body filled with Foam Rubber. She is sure to enchant any little girl.

2771   2774T   2776T   2777T

Nurse and Doctor Kits

Little Doctor and little Nurse can play their games more effectively with Effanbee Nurse and Doctor Kits. Everything they need to treat a doll —clothes, equipment —even a diploma!

1086

1087

The 1952 Effanbee Company catalog illustrated the Nurse and Doctor kits, as well as four models of the "Mommy's Baby" with one being a boy. Hard plastic heads with latex bodies and limbs.

EFFANBEE *Honey Girl*

There is a Honey Girl for every occasion, every mood, every little girl's fancy. Beautiful Honey, beautifully dressed, comes in selection of costumes—in four sizes—with an appropriate hair-do, in nylon, human hair or mohair.

| 7623 | 7621 | 7642 | 7641 | 7622 |

| 7625 | 7626 | 7644 | 7624 |

This page of the 1952 Effanbee Company catalog shows nine outfits that the Honey was available in that year. The doll on the lower left is a Honey, but used for "Lucinda" from the book Roller Skates by Ruth Sawyer.

8621

8661

EFFANBEE

Honey Girl

Formal

Cinderella
8523

Prince Charming
8524

The Effanbee Company catalog shows the Cinderella and Prince Charming, along with two Honey dolls in formals.

8963

8965

8642

8964

Honey is shown in formals on this page of the 1952 Effanbee catalog. Sizes are not given, but three of these dolls are large.

66

65

EFFANBEE
Portrait
Dolls

275

67

70

"Pretty as a picture"
—that's the portrait dolls,
sweet little miniatures,
prettily packaged, each
in its own frame-box
—an Effanbee exclusive.

This page shows the little Portrait dolls made in 1952 and shown in the Effanbee Company catalog. Each was packed in a frame style box.

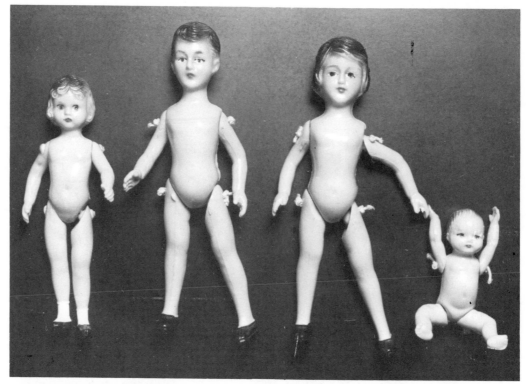

4¾", 3¾" and 2½" Doll House dolls that are all heavy plastic with molded, painted brown hair, painted features and string jointed. Molded on shoes. (Socks on girl). Baby has bent legs. All are marked: F AN B/ MADE IN CANADA. A set exactly like this is also marked: F an B/ MADE IN U.S.A. Girl has original stringing, rest have been re-strung. Courtesy Marge Meisinger.

18" "Honey". All hard plastic in original pink ruffled flaired gown with black ribbon and bows. Blonde mohair, sleep blue eyes/lashes. All fingers wide spread. Ca. 1952. Bonnet missing. (Author).

10" Old store stock. All hard plastic and the doll is strung. This doll is totally unmarked, but is surely an Effanbee. Courtesy June Schultz.

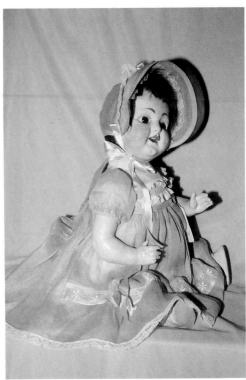

12″ head circumference bisque head incised Effanbee, on composition baby body. Open mouth with four top teeth, dimples and glass eyes. 16″ long. 1919. Courtesy Jimmy and Fay Rodolfos.

18″ "Bubbles" marks: Effanbee/Bubbles/Copyr.-1924/Made in U.S.A. Composition shoulder head with very deep shoulder plate, kapok stuffed body, tin sleep eyes and molded, painted hair. Open mouth, cheek dimples. Doll modeled by Bernard Lipfert. The smaller doll is a 14″ "Bubbles" with same markings as the larger doll. Original clothes, but replaced hat. This one was called "Dolly Bubbles". There were also Betty Bubbles, Charlotte Bubbles and the only difference between the dolls was the size and structure of the legs. Courtesy Rose Albanese.

29″ "Mae Starr" composition talking doll. Kapok stuffed body with talking phonograph devise in center of body. Takes wax cylinder records. Doll was available as a premium for selling subscriptions to "The Philadelphia Ledger". Doll was on the market only a short time. 1928. Composition shoulder head and limbs, open mouth, four teeth, sleep eyes and human hair wig. Courtesy Rose Albanese.

19″ "Patsy Ann", all composition with sleep eyes and molded red hair. Marks: Effanbee/"Patsy Ann"/Pat. # 1283558, on back. 1929. Courtesy Mary Sweeney.

31″ "Mary Lee" with cloth body and composition head, shoulder plate and limbs. Original clothes and wig. Courtesy Naomi Hennig.

17″ 1925 Rosemary's. White girl with original red check dress and Black version in organdy dress. Courtesy Naomi Hennig.

14″ "Patsy" that is all original including her pin and wig. Courtesy Marge Meisinger.

9½″ "Wee Patsy" was used as the Colleen Moore Castle doll house doll in 1932. Her box and pin present the famous doll house. Courtesy Marge Meisinger.

A "Patsy" group with 20″ Patsy Joan in back right. All composition and marked: Effanbee. 1930-1946. Not original clothes. She has a bent right arm, swivel head and jointed hips and shoulders. Brown sleep eyes and painted and molded hair. Back left is 22½″ Patsy Lou and so marked. All composition, came with mohair wigs or painted hair, sleep eyes and fully jointed. Not original clothes. In front are Patsy Babyette Twins. All composition, 8″ tall, with molded brown painted hair, blue sleep eyes with lashes. All original outfits and marked: Effanbee/Patsy Babyette. The standing doll is 9″ tall, all composition, molded and painted hair, bent right arm. Also came with wigs. Marks: Effanbee/Patsyette Doll. Not original clothes. Courtesy Rose Albanese.

18½″ Patsy look-a-like. All composition. Marks. AN-EE-GEE doll. Box is also marked AN-EE-GEE doll. EEGEE is the trademark used by E. Goldberger Doll Corp. Came with Scot's outfit and pink party dress. Painted upper and lower lashes, blue tin sleep eyes/lashes. White canvas shoes tie with buckle. Courtesy Diane Hoffman.

9″ "Patsyette". All composition with painted eyes, painted upper lashes and bent right arm. Molded hair under light brown mohair wig. 1931. Original clothes. Courtesy Diane Hoffman.

5½″ "Wee Patsy". all composition with molded on shoes and socks. Painted eyes and molded hair. 1930. Courtesy Diane Hoffman.

16″ "Patsy Joan", composition with molded hair under original brown human hair wig, brown glass sleep eyes/lashes and lashes painted top and bottom. Head is unmarked, body marked, "Effanbee Patsy Joan". Dressed in clothes from 1930's Patsy patterns. Heart bracelet. The "Uncle Wiggley" is 18″, all cotton stuffed, molded and hand painted face, black glass eyes. Game by Howard R. Garis, author of the bedtime stories by Milton Bradley Co. 1930-1946. Courtesy Margaret Mandel.

9″ "Patsy Baby", all original shown with "Patsy Babyette" that is all composition with blue glass sleep eyes/lashes, wig over molded hair and is marked: Effanbee, on head and "Patsy Babyette", and 1932, on body. Teddy Bear is 11″, early wool plush, rigid body with haunches and tin nose. Childhood bear of owner. Courtesy Margaret Mandel.

9″ "Patsy Baby", cloth body, legs and arms with gauntlet celluloid hands. Composition head swivels, brown tin sleep eyes, molded painted hair. Original white organdy christening dress, original pink silk coat from 1932 on. Steiff tiger is 30″ and early mohair. "Little Orphan Annie" marked 'Harold' and is a 1930's wood toy. Courtesy Margaret Mandel.

All composition, straight legs "Baby Tinyette". All original. Made by Effanbee. 1932. Courtesy Marge Meisinger.

13″ "Patsy Baby", all composition with molded hair under original blonde mohair wig, brown tin sleep eyes/lashes and painted lashes top and bottom. Marks: "Patsy Baby", on head and "Patsy Doll", on body. Favorite childhood doll of owner and dressed in clothes from 1930's Patsy pattern. Unusual to find a Patsy Baby on toddler legs. Heart bracelet. The book "Goldilocks and Three Bears" with 1923 copyright was published by Sam'l Gabriel Sons & Co. New York from 1932 on. Courtesy Marge Meisinger.

10″ "Patsy Baby" with head marked: Effanbee Patsy Baby and jointed composition body is marked: Effanbee Patsy Baby. Brown sleep eyes, brown molded, painted hair, closed mouth. 1932. Courtesy Jimmy and Fay Rodolfos.

10″ Black "Patsy Baby/Amosandra" marked: Effanbee Patsy Baby. Closed mouth, painted to the side eyes, black molded, painted hair with three string pigtails. Original dress. 1936 used as Amosandra doll. Courtesy Jimmy and Fay Rodolfos.

14½″ "Patricia", all composition with both arms slightly curved, brown sleep eyes, original heart bracelet, original shoes, blonde mohair wig with no molding underneath. 1932. Dressed as cowgirl. Original Effanbee outfit purchased in 1935, sold separately in stores. (Would fit either Skippy or Patricia). Courtesy Margaret Mandel.

14½″ "Patricia" in dark brown composition. Human hair wig in long pigtails. Original dress and shoes. 1932-1933. Courtesy Marianne's Doll House. (Billie McCabe).

9″ "Martha Washington" (Patsyette). All composition and original with painted eyes and bent arm. Marks: Effanbee, on head and back. 1931-1932. Courtesy Barbara Male.

17″ "American Children". All composition with human hair wig, closed mouth, dimples, multi-stroke eyebrows, brown sleep eyes. Designed by Dewees Cochran for Effanbee. Marks: Effanbee/American Children, on head. Effanbee-Anne Shirley, on body. 1936. Courtesy Barbara Jean Male.

"Charlie McCarthy", composition head and hands and feet with cloth body and limbs. Open and close ventriloquist mouth. Shown is original book that came with doll. Marks: An Effanbee Product. 1937. Courtesy Rose Albanese.

14½″ "Ice Queen" & "Sonja on Skates". All composition hair wig. Marks: Effanbee, on head and Effanbee/Anne Shirley, on body. Tag on arm: The Ice Queen/Effanbee Durable doll. Feather trimmed white satin outfit. Designed by Dewees Cochran. 1938. Courtesy Barbara Jean Male.

14″ Historical dolls of 1939 (see Chronology). Left to right: 1492 - "Primitive Indians". 1565 - St. Augustine Settlement. 1607 - "Indian Squaw with braids". Courtesy Naomi Hennig.

The 1939 14″ Historical dolls are, left to right: 1608 - Virginia Colony. 1620 - Plymouth Colony. 1625 - New York Settlement. Courtesy Naomi Hennig.

Left to right: 1632 - Maryland Colony. 1658 - Carolina Settlement. 1666 - Massachusetts Bay Colony. All courtesy Naomi Hennig.

1939 14″ Historical dolls are, left to right: 1682 - Quaker Colony. 1685 - Later Carolina Settlement. Missing is 1711 - Colonial Prosperity. 1720 - The Pioneer American Spirit. Courtesy Naomi Hennig.

Left to right: 1740 - Benjamin Franklin influence. 1760 - Pre-Revolutionary Period. 1750 - The Development of Culture. Missing is 1777 - Revolutionary Period. Courtesy Naomi Hennig.

Left to right: 1804 - Louisiana Purchase. 1816 - Monroe Doctrine. 1840 - Covered Wagon Days. Courtesy Naomi Hennig.

Left to right: 1841 - Pre-Civil War Period. 1864 - Civil War Period. 1868 - Post-War Period. Courtesy Naomi Hennig.

Left to right: 1872 - Economic Development. 1873 - Industrial South. Courtesy Naomi Hennig.

Left to right: 1888 - Settling the West. 1896 - Unity of Nation Established. Courtesy Naomi Hennig.

Left to right: 1908 - Women's Suffrage Movement. 1938 - Modern Miss America. 1939 - Today. Courtesy Naomi Hennig.

Box end of the "Little Lady" doll belonging to Margaret Mandel.

17″ "Little Lady", all composition with glued on blonde human hair wig in original set, blue glass sleep eyes/lashes. Marks: Effanbee U.S.A., on body and head mark is indistinct. Original clothes and box. Box is marked: #7520 and price tag: $4.95. Clothes are blue and white cotton dress/bonnet, blue socks, black leather Mary Jane shoes with center tie. Childhood doll of owner and Christmas present in 1939. Shown in picture is owner in 1940 wearing Dutch dance costume. Owner's mother copies child's costume for doll. Courtesy Margaret Mandel.

18″ Boy and girl from the American Children Series. Designed by famous doll artist Dewees Cochran. Courtesy Naomi Hennig.

21″ "Little Lady-Anne Shirley". All composition with sleep eyes and closed mouth. Original dress, glued on wig. Has lashes painted under the eyes. 1939. Courtesy Diane Hoffman.

27″ "Snow White" (Little Lady). All composition with sleep eyes, painted lower lashes and very black human hair wig. 1939. Courtesy Diana Hoffman.

14″ "Mickey" of 1940. Composition head and gauntlet hands with rest cloth. Marks: F an B, Made in USA, on head. Original clothes. Brown sleep eyes and mohair wig. Courtesy Pam Ortman.

16½″ "Little Brother" which is the largest size. Composition, swivel head on cloth body and limbs with gauntlet composition hands. blue decal eyes, molded hair under red string wig. Completely original in blue cotton overalls, check shirt, blue knit cap and white tie shoes. Marks: F & B Made in USA. The Ferdinand is 13″ long, 12″ high and the first that is all straw stuffed, early black cotton plush, gold mohair, velvet nose with stitch for flower. Celluloid disc eyes. Courtesy Margaret Mandel.

27″ "Little Lady" made during World War II, and has yarn hair. All composition. Courtesy Sheryl Schmidt.

"Suzanne" shown in another original outfit. All composition with sleep eyes and glued on wig. 1940. Courtesy Marjorie Uhl.

"Suzanne". All composition with sleep eyes and glued on wig. All original. 1940. Courtesy Marjorie Uhl.

Standing is 14″ "Suzanne". 1940. All composition with human hair wig. Sleep eyes and also came with painted eyes. One hand points down and the other out. Marks: Suzanne/Effanbee/Made in U.S.A. Largest doll is 18″ "Rosemary". Cloth body with composition shoulder head, arms and quite chubby legs. Gren tin sleep eyes, open mouth with four teeth. Human hair wig. Not original. Marks: Effanbee/Rosemary/Walk-Talk-Sleep, in oval. 1925. The other doll is 13″ "Baby Dainty" with cloth body and composition shoulder plate, arms and legs. Painted blue eyes, molded hair. Not original. 1912-1925. First issue with the Effanbee in script had cloth legs.

The second production has the mark: Effanbee/Baby Dainty. This doll was also used and marked: Patsy. (First Patsy). Courtesy Rose Albanese.

14″ "Patricia" and so marked. All composition and this close up shows the detail of the face. Replaced clothes and restyled wig. Courtesy Eileen Harris.

16″ "Tommy Tucker". All composition and using the same doll as the Baby Bright Eyes, which has molded hair. The sleep eyes are large, and flirt. Original outfit, but wig may be a replacement. Ca. 1940. Courtesy Eileen Harris.

18″ "Honey Bride". Ca. 1948-1949. All composition and wears original bride's gown. Courtesy Pam Ortman.

17″ "Honey". All hard plastic with sleep eyes/lashes and glued on wig. In original trunk with wardrobe. Ca. 1950-1953. (Author).

16″ Prince Charming and Cinderella of 1953. First made in 1950 and made through 1954. All hard plastic "Honey" with glued on wigs. Both are original and Cinderella has a golden crown that can stand up on top of her head. Courtesy Shirley Bertrand of Shirley's Doll House.

18″ "Honey" all hard plastic with Effanbee on back of head. All original with platinum mohair wig, blue sleep eyes/lashes. Has blue leather Mary Jane shoes with white ribbon bow. Wears blue underpants with attached white organdy blouse and taffeta skirt. Individual fingers have very pale pink nailpolish. Ca. 1951. Courtesy Elizabeth Montesano.

All hard plastic Honey Walkers and all are marked: Effanbee. Honey came in many sizes and outfits, and was a very popular doll. Front left is "Cinderella" 16″ with wrist tag (paper). There is a matching Prince Charming, also. On the right is a 14″ Honey Walker in party gown of blue with fancy hair set. The gown is ruffled organdy. In back is 18″ Honey, and her gown originally belongs to American Character's "Sweet Sue". Courtesy Rose Albanese.

19″ "Honey Walker". All hard plastic with glued on blonde saran wig, blue sleep eyes, and all original in blue and white cotton dress trimmed with red ribbon, red plastic belt and red straw hat. Black patent, center snap shoes. Ca. 1951-1954. Courtesy Margaret Mandel.

17″ "Honey Walker". All hard plastic with glued on saran wig. Sleep blue eyes, closed mouth. All original. 1954. (Author).

24″ "Honey Ann" all hard plastic walker, blue sleep eyes, blonde saran wig and original pink/-purple/white rayon dress. 1952-1954. Courtesy Margaret Mandel.

10″ "Fluffy Bluebird". Insignia is silk screened on cap. Vinyl with dark brown rooted hair, blue sleep eyes/molded lashes. Toddler legs with dimpled knees. Marks: F & B and circle 1964. Steiff is "Crabby" and 11″ short mohair stuffed lobster elaborately decorated. Courtesy Margaret Mandel.

10½″ "Mickey - The All American Boy". 1956 on. All vinyl, fully jointed, painted features and molded on hair/hats. Came in 20 different outfits over the years. Pictured are Fireman, Football and Baseball. 8″ Fluffy is all vinyl with rooted hair, sleep eyes and fully jointed. 1957 on. Came with various costumes. Shown is regulation Brownie and Campfire. These, as well as Mickey, came in white or black. These uniforms were discontinued thereby making the dolls out of date. Courtesy Rose Albanese.

10″ "Fluffy". All vinyl with rooted hair and sleep eyes. Original ballerina outfit. Ca. 1957. Courtesy Eileen Harris.

17″ "Dy-Dee Baby". All vinyl with full head of blonde rooted hair with center part and bangs. Blue sleep eyes. Original pink brushed rayon play suit. Marks: Effanbee 56 71 on head, Effanbee 1967, on body, but still being made. Doll drinks and wets. Excellent modeling detail of body and toes. The bear is 7″, unjointed and a synthetic plush. Courtesy Margaret Mandel.

18″ "Suzie Sunshine". Plastic and vinyl and original including the 8″ "Babykin" doll she holds. Ca. 1967. Courtesy Eileen Harris.

11″ "Pum'kin". Plastic and vinyl with sleep eyes and rooted hair. Both are original. Courtesy Eileen Harris.

16″ "Baby Face". Plastic and vinyl with sleep eyes and rooted hair. All original. Courtesy Eileen Harris.

18″-19″ "Suzie Sunshine" of the Innocence Collection. The black one was made in 1978 only, and white was made during 1978 and 1979. Both are original. Courtesy Eileen Harris.

This group has . . . in back: Gumdrop 16″ "Pioneer Series" costume. 18″ "Suzie Sunshine" Freckles, sleep eyes, rooted hair and original. She was available in many costumes, and is still available (also comes as a boy). In front center is Half Pint 11″ that has been available in many different outfits (also as a boy) and is still on the market. Next (left) is the girl "Pun'kin". This doll came as boy and also in black. First released in 1966 and marked with that date. Pictured is the "Colonial Pun'kin" and the boy is from the same series. Courtesy Rose Albanese.

30" "Mary Jane". Plastic and vinyl with rooted hair, sleep eyes and original clothes. 1955-1956. Courtesy Marjorie Uhl.

One of the early Grand Dames and most likely from 1975. Courtesy Eileen Harris.

15" "Peaches and Cream" of the Grand Dames Collection of 1976. (Chipper). Came either black or white. Courtesy Eileen Harris.

15" 1974 "Country Cousins" (red/white/blue) using the Chipper doll is shown with 15" Chipper that is black and part of the Touch of Velvet Collection of 1978. The white version was only made in 1977. The Country Cousin set also included 16" Baby Face, 11" Pun'kin and 13" Butterball. Courtesy Eileen Harris.

18″ "Miss Chips" from the Granny's Corner Collection. Beige pants, burgandy slippers, pale pastel print gown with beige cotton ruffles, lace trim. Hair pulled back and tied with wide burgandy ribbon. 14″ "Chipper" dressed just like the larger doll. Courtesy Beverly Harrington.

19″ "Suzie Sunshine" of the Granny's Corner. 1975 and 1976. Long lace trimmed gown with velveteen vest and bonnet. This page shows the series except for an 11″ Pum'kin in long gown and cap, 20″ Sugar Plum in dress and bonnet and 15″ Little Luv in dress and bonnet. Also to this set is one of the "Floppsies" 21″ with cloth body and limbs. There are a total of nine dolls in the collection. Courtesy Beverly Harrington.

11″ "Pum'kin" boy and girl from the Granny's Corner Collection. Boy: one piece burgandy velveteen pants with beige shirt attached, beige socks, burgandy slippers, cap and bow at neck. Red rooted hair, freckles. She: beige pantaloons, short socks with burgandy slippers. Matching gown to larger dolls with beige cotton bonnet with burgandy ribbon, no freckles, blue sleep eyes and ash blonde rooted hair. Courtesy Beverly Harrington.

14″ "Pint Size" of the Granny's Corner Collection of 1975 and 1976. Burgandy/blue and beige print cloth body and limbs with vinyl head. Lace trimmed short dress and cap with velveteen trim. Courtesy Eileen Harris.

18″ "Bride" (Miss Chips) from the Heirloom Collection. All beige cotton and lace trimmed, full lace overskirt tied at waist with wide beige ribbon. Beige pantaloons, hose and beige-tan slippers. Net cotton half slip with wide ruffle that matches gown. Wide lace shawl collar is separate, veil is double, tied to top with beige satin ribbon with bow to side. Beige lace with rose tied to wrist. 11″ "Bride" matches the large bride and is from the same set. She has a one piece slip and bodice with lace sleeves and lace covered front bodice, wrap full lace skirt tied in back with beige ribbon, beige pantaloons, hose and tan slippers. Double veil with same treatment as large doll. Courtesy Beverly Harrington.

17″ "Countess" from the Regal Heirloom Collection and marked: Effanbee/1969/9469, on head. Body tagged: All new material, etc. Cloth body with cryer, vinyl head, arms and legs. Rooted hair, sleep blue eyes. Beige panties, long white stockings, royal blue side snap shoes. Plain beige dress with sleeves and royal velveteen coat and bonnet with lace trim, beige bow and ties on bonnet. 14″ Chipper of the Regal Heirloom Collection. Beige pantaloons and short socks, slippers and side snap spats. Royal velveteen dress with beige lace trim and beige satin ribbon around waist with beige rose. Matching bonnet with double tied satin ribbon tied at top. Courtesy Beverly Harrington.

"Regal Heirloom Series". 1976. All original and all are vinyl dolls. Beautiful deep blue velveteens with ecru lace trim. The "Queen Mother" is Suzie Sunshine 17″, and the baby she carries is a "'Pun'kin" 8″. The small "Crown Prince and Princess" are 10″ Pun'kins. The Baroness is 15″ Chipper, and the "Duchess' is 18″ Miss Chips. All courtesy Rose Albanese.

11″ "Miss Spain and Spanish Boy" from the International Collection. She is 1976 on and he is 1979 and 1980 only. Courtesy Eileen Harris.

Shown are two of the 11″ Internationals, Miss Scotland of 1976 and Miss USA of 1976. Courtesy Eileen Harris.

1976 Bi-Centennial boy and girl. She has panties, but no slip. Red skirt with white bodice and sleeves. Attached white apron with red and blue trim. Red bow at neck, blue vest, white bonnet with blue trim. Marks: Effanbee 1966, on head. F-B, on back. He: has freckles only. Shirt attached to red pants, blue vest and felt hat, white socks and shoes. Courtesy Beverly Harrington.

14″ "Ma Cherie" of the Grand Dames. 1976. Net cotton half slip and another with stiff grosgrain backing to ruffled inset. Peach satin over gown, pulled up and tacked with three roses. Ribbon tied around sleeves. Matching circle bonnet, white hair pulled back in sausage curls. Fan tied to wrist. (Chipper). Courtesy Beverly Harrington.

These two dolls are part of the "Passing Parade" series and are: Gay Nineties, 1978, and Gibson Girl, 1977. Courtesy Rose Albanese.

14″ "Downing Square". Cotton pantaloons, open net half slip, plus cotton half slip with applied rose. Pink check gown with rows of lace trim. Matching circle bonnet. (Chipper). Part of Grand Dames Collection of 1978. Courtesy Beverly Harrington.

11″ "Miss Holland" of the International Collection and this one was issued in 1977. Courtesy Eileen Harris.

"Passing Parade" series included these two dolls: Civil War, 1977, and Hour Glass Figure, 1978. Courtesy Rose Albanese.

Shows the black "Four Seasons" (Summer and Autumn) for the year 1977. Courtesy Eileen Harris.

"Four Seasons" (Winter and Spring) are shown in the 1977 issue that was available in black. Courtesy Eileen Harris.

11″ "Florence Nightengale" from the 1977 collection of Historical dolls that also included: Betsy Ross, Martha Washington, Davy Crockett, Pavlova Ballerina and Pocahontas. Courtesy Eileen Harris.

11″ "Little Bo Peep" is from the 1977-1978 series of Storybook Dolls, as is the other one, "Mary, Mary", only she is from the year 1978. The first Mary, Mary dolls carried a basket of flowers. Courtesy Eileen Harris.

11″ "Robin Hood and Maid Marion" from 1978. These dolls were part of the Historical Collection. Courtesy Eileen Harris.

11″ "Miss Black America" (to 1979) is shown with "Pocahontas" of 1978. Courtesy Eileen Harris.

11″ "Cinderella" of 1978. Part of the Storybook Collection. Courtesy Eileen Harris.

11″ "Cleopatra". All vinyl with sleep eyes and made by Effanbee. 1978. Courtesy Renie Culp.

"Grand Dames of 1975". They come in three sizes: 11″, 15″ and 18″. Most of the older Grand Dames are discontinued now. Pictured are the "Four Seasons". 11″, and only 11″, in this series. They are Spring, Summer, Fall and Winter. The marks are Effanbee and the date of series on backs of necks. They are very finely dressed and represent famous women. There are 27 in series, up to and including 1979. Courtesy Rose Albanese.

11″ "Miss Italy" of 1978, and "Miss China", also from 1978. Both are from the International Collection. Courtesy Eileen Harris.

15″ "Madame DuBerry" from the Grand Dames Collection of 1978. Courtesy Eileen Harris.

14″ "Cinderella" made for Disneyland-World. Marks on head: Walt Disney Prod./Cinderella. Plastic and vinyl with rooted hair and sleep eyes. Original. 1977-1978. Courtesy Renie Culp.

14″ "Alice in Wonderland" made for Disneyland-World. Marks on head: Walt Disney Prod./Alice in Wonderland. Plastic and Vinyl with rooted hair and sleep eyes. Original. Courtesy Renie Culp.

14″ "Snow White" made for Disneyland-World. Plastic and vinyl with rooted hair and sleep eyes. Marked on head: Walt Disney Prod./Snow White. Original. Courtesy Renie Culp.

14″ "Sleeping Beauty" made for Disneyland-World. Plastic and vinyl with sleep eyes and rooted hair. Marked on head: Walt Disney Prod./Sleeping Beauty. Courtesy Renie Culp.

Ringbearer from the 1979 "Bridal Suite Series".
Courtesy Eileen Harris.

11″ "Jack and Jill" from the 1979 Storybook
Collection. Courtesy Eileen Harris.

11″ "Miss Ancient Egypt" from the Historical
Collection of 1979. Same doll as used for
Cleopatra, but different design of clothes.
Courtesy Eileen Harris.

15″ "Magnolia" in the Grand Dames Collection
of 1979. Also available in White. Courtesy Eileen
Harris.

1979 series called "Gigi Growing Up". All are vinyl and marked Effanbee and have human or saran rooted hair. This series shows the different stages of a young girl growing up. Left to right: Papa's Pet, School Girl, Ingenue, Femme Fatale, Mama and Grand Mere. All beautifully costumed. This was a very novel idea by Effanbee. Courtesy Rose Albanese.

15″ "W. C. Fields". A special doll made only during 1980, the Centennial year. This is an excellent likeness, and is sure to be a great collector item in years to come. Courtesy Eileen Harris.

This is the "Crowning Glory" made for the Limited Edition Doll Club. 1978. Courtesy Renie Culp.

15″ "Susan B. Anthony" Commemorative Doll that was the Limited Edition Club doll of 1980. No more than 3,485 were made. Head is marked: S.B.Anthony/Limited Edition/Effanbee. Body is marked: Susan B. Anthony/Effanbee Doll/Ltd. Edition/1980. A Commemorative dollar is included with the doll. Courtesy Eileen Harris.

Left is 18″ "Little Lady", all composition and mint in red/white taffeta dress and metal heart bracelet. Right is 18″ "Honey Walker" all hard plastic and original that is green and white. Has paper tag and woven tag in dress. 1953. Courtesy June Schultz.

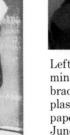

Effanbee put out these four puppets in 1952, and each had a record that had the voices for each one of them. Top: Jambo and Kilroy. Bottom: Toonga and Pimbo.

21″ "Cuddle Up". 1953. Vinyl head and limbs and vinyl coated, kapok filled body. Rooted hair, open mouth with two teeth. Marks: Effanbee, on head. Original, but missing hat. Courtesy June Schultz.

Molded Hair		
9552 — 20″ —	9.95
9752 — 23″ —	12.95
9952 — 27″ —	15.95

Rooted Hair		
9582 — 20″ —	13.95
9782 — 23″ —	16.95
9982 — 27″ —	19.95

In corded cotton checked overalls with matching hat with pom-pom; under her overalls, Cuddle-Up wears a Basque-type jersey shirt with matching pants; shoes and socks. And her precious plush pet is dressed in matching overalls!

Effanbee means finest ♥ and best

Rooted Hair Only		
2582 — 20″ —	
2782 — 24″ —	18.95
2982 — 29″ —	23.95

In fine quality organdy pinafore dress, with embroidered braid and rick-rack trim; lace trimmed slip and panties; lace and rick-trimmed bonnet; ankle strap shoes and white socks.

Effanbee means finest ♥ and best

The 1954 Effanbee catalog had the Cuddle-Up baby with either molded or rooted hair in the 20″, 23″ and 27″ sizes. She came in a snow suit, taffeta dress with embroidery trim, a printed nylon party dress with ruffle just above the hem line, and a nylon fleece coat and bonnet with a taffeta dress. This Cuddle-Up version in corded cotton check overalls, matching hat and with a stuffed animal dressed the same.

In 1954 "Candy Ann" in 20″, 24″ and 29″ sizes was shown in the Effanbee Catalog in a fine organdy pinafore dress with trim and ankle strap shoes.

Rooted Hair Only		
2583 — 20″ —	
2783 — 24″ —	19.95
2983 — 29″ —	24.95

Dressed in washable taffetta Nylon coat and flower and ribbon trimmed straw bonnet; crisp printed washable Nylon dress with matching panties; ankle-strap shoes and white socks. Her precious pet toy wears a cute little straw bonnet too.

Effanbee means finest ♥ and best

7442 — 15″ —	7.95
7642 — 19″ —	9.95
7742 — 21″ —	12.95
7942 — 25″ —	15.95

In striped taffeta dress and matching panties; straw hat; ankle-strap shoes and socks.

Effanbee means finest ♥ and best

1954 also had this "Candy Ann" dressed in taffeta nylon coat, straw bonnet and print nylon dress. She came in sizes 20″, 24″ and 29″.

The 15″, 19″, 21″ and 25″ "Honey Walker" came dressed in stripped taffeta with straw hat in the Effanbee catalog of 1954.

HONEY WALKER — *one of the pig-tail crowd*
in gingham & lace

7443 — 15″ — 9.95	Checked gingham guimpe dress with lace trimmed
7643 — 19″ — 11.95	white organdy blouse; lace trimmed slip and panties.
7743 — 21″ — 14.95	Straw beanie hat with ribbon and flower trim. Her
7943 — 25″ — 17.95	beautiful Saran hair is combed in pigtails which are
	tied with flower-trimmed ribbon bows; she wears suede-
	cloth shoes and white socks.

Effanbee means finest 🖤 and best

The "Honey Walker" in the Effanbee 1954 catalog came in a check gingham guimpe dress with lace trimmed white organdy blouse, straw beanie and pigtails.

HONEY WALKER — *in charming chintz afternoon frock*

7444 — 15″ — 9.95	Printed chintz with braid and button trim, with white
7644 — 19″ — 11.95	yoke and sleeves and printed chintz collar and bow tie;
7744 — 21″ — 14.95	black patent leather belt; flower and ribbon trimmed
7944 — 25″ — 17.95	straw hat; lace trimmed petticoat and panties; suede-
	cloth shoes and white socks.

Effanbee means finest 🖤 and best

The 15″, 19″, 21″ and 25″ "Honey Walker" of 1954 was dressed in printed chintz with braid and button trim, patent belt and straw hat. Effanbee catalog reprint.

HONEY WALKER — *girl and pup ready for rain*

7446 — 15″ — 11.95	In smart plastic rain slicker and rain hat and matching
7646 — 19″ — 15.95	plastic rain boots. Under her slicker Honey Walker
	wears a very pretty print dress with matching panties,
	and her boots cover her pretty shoes and socks. Her
	little pet plush doggie on a leash, wears raincoat and
	boots to match her own. And she comes packed in a
	clearvue gift box.

Effanbee means finest 🖤 and best

The 15″ and 19″ "Honey Walker" in the 1954 Effanbee catalog wears a rain coat and hat and boots that are plastic. Print dress and had a little dog on a leash with rain cape and boots to match the dolls.

HONEY WALKER — *radiant, refreshing — but*
still the blushing bride

8413 — 15″ — 10.95	Here Comes The Bride! In beautifully fashioned satin
8613 — 19″ — 15.95	gown with a very full skirt ending in a graceful train;
8713 — 21″ — 18.95	looped fringe trim around flattering shawl-bib collar;
8913 — 25″ — 24.95	her satin bridal bonnet is floral trimmed and crowns
	her traditional bridal veil, and like all brides, she car-
	ries a bouquet of flowers. She wears a taffeta petticoat
	over crinoline, taffeta panties and white satin bridal
	slippers. And—she wears a borrowed Blue Garter!

Effanbee means finest 🖤 and best

The Effanbee catalog of 1954 shows this Bride (Honey Walker) that came in 15″, 19″, 21″ and 25″ sizes. The gown is satin. This same catalog shows the Bridesmaid in the same sizes and dressed in a sheer nylon gown with eyelet embroidery trim and flowers across the front of her hair.

PATRICIA WALKER — *pretty as a picture*

Rooted Hair	
7681 — 19″ — 14.95	Organdy party dress, with striped organdy ruffle trim-
7781 — 21″ — 17.95	ming and yoke; straw hat, flower trimmed; ankle strap
7981 — 25″ — 21.95	shoes and white socks; lace trimmed slip and panties.

Effanbee means finest 🐾 and best

The "Patricia Walker" came in sizes 19″, 21″ and 25″ in the 1954 Effanbee catalog dressed in organdy party dress and straw hat. Vinyl, with rooted hair.

PATRICIA WALKER — *ready for a stroll*

Rooted Hair	
7683 — 19″ — 15.95	This young lady will walk right into your heart! Dressed in her stunning velvet coat with matching leg-
7783 — 21″ — 18.95	gings and bonnet. And when you remove her outer garments, you will find she wears smart slacks and a
7983 — 25″ — 24.95	blouse. And to keep her hands warm, she carries a dear little white plush muff.

Effanbee means finest 🐾 and best

"Patricia Walker" of 1954, in the Effanbee catalog, dressed in velvet coat with matching leggings and bonnet and under it she wears slacks and a blouse. She came in the 19″, 21″ and 25″ sizes. Vinyl with rooted hair.

PATRICIA WALKER — *a vision to behold*

Rooted Hair	
8481 — 15″ — 12.95	Glamorous Formal metallic striped nylon gown with silver metallic-cloth bodice; taffeta and crinoline petti-
8681 — 19″ — 17.95	coat and taffeta panties; simulated pearl necklace and bracelet; silver dancing slippers; straw formal bonnet,
8781 — 21″ — 19.95	flower trimmed. #8481, 8681 and 8781 carry colorful little fans. #8981 carries a ruffle trimmed striped nylon
8981 — 25″ — 37.95	parasol to match her gown.

Effanbee means finest 🐾 and best

"Patricia Walker" with rooted hair (vinyl) came in this metallic striped nylon gown with silver metallic cloth bodice, straw bonnet with the 15″, 19″ and 21″ carrying colorful little fans, and the 25″ with a matching parasol (as shown). Effanbee catalog.

LITTLE LADY — *pert & pretty in pinafore and pantaloons*

7487 — 15″ — 15.95

All vinyl doll, fully jointed, with go-to-sleep eyes. Rooted hair that can be combed and washed and set and reset. Her hair is set in old-fashioned hairdo with curls at the back, and bangs. In long-sleeved dress, braid trimmed, with dotted organdy pinafore, lace and ruffled petticoat, lace and rick-rack trimmed pantaloons; long white stockings and 2-tone suede-cloth button shoes.

Packed in attractive gift box, with "Little Lady Toiletries—cologne, per- fume, shampoo, soap, talcum powder, bubble bath, powder puff, comb, mirror, curlers.

*Toiletries designed by Helene Pessl, Inc.—originators of children's toiletries.

Effanbee means finest 🐾 and best

The "Little Lady" came in only the 15″ size and was all vinyl with rooted hair and dressed in a long sleeve dress, braid trimmed, with dotted organdy pinafore, pantaloons, long white stock- ings and two tone suede cloth button shoes. In gift box with "Little Lady" Toiletries which were designed by Helene Pessl, Inc., the originators of children's toiletries. Shown in the 1954 Effanbee catalog.

HONEY WALKER — *come rain — come shine*   HONEY WALKER — *ready for travel — "Bon Voyage"*

7401 — 15″ — 17.95

Here's Honey Walker in attractive gift carrying case with metal catch and handle — and she comes to you prepared for Rain or Shine! Dressed in cotton gabardine shorts, white broadcloth blouse and red leather belt, red suede-cloth play shoes, with red ribbons in her beautiful Saran Hair. Layette consists of raincoat and hat, golashes, real miniature umbrella, shoebag with satin bedroom slippers and patent leather shoes, shoehorn; 2 piece pajamas; printed dress and panties; plastic hangers, comb, brush and mirror set; bobby pins, barrettes, necklace; bouquet of flowers; braided straw bonnet; sun-glasses; pocket book, curlers.

Effanbee means finest 🎔 and best

The 15″ "Honey Walker" of 1954 was shown in the Effanbee catalog in a carry case that included many clothes, rain coat, umbrella and accessories.

7403 — 15″ — 19.95

HONEY WALKER IN STEAMER TRUNK. In sturdy steamer trunk, all wood and metal construction, with simulated leather trimmings. Honey Walker wears a flock-dot organdy party dress trimmed with lace, ribbon and flowers; lace trimmed lawn slip and panties, suede-cloth slippers and white socks, with ribbon bows in her magic-fibre Saran hair.

Her wardrobe consists of plaid raincoat, felt coat, 2-piece printed cotton pajamas, all on plastic hangers. Also, felt hat to match her coat, suede-cloth carryall handbag and matching belt, bedroom scuffs, dress shoes, play shoes, comb, brush and mirror set, curlers.

Effanbee means finest 🎔 and best

The 15″ "Honey Walker" in the 1954 Effanbee catalog also came in a steamer trunk that contained clothes and accessories.

Here is Dy-Dee in a novel wood-frame convertible suitcase with a metal catch-lock and plastic handle. As you open the suitcase, Dy-Dee is automatically raised up on a plastic quilted pad, surrounded by the accessories that make her so much fun to play with — her bubble pipe, cry-pacifier, plastic rattle, Q-Tips, sipping straw, feeding spoon, bottle and nipple, rubber sponge duck, bubble bath powder and powder puffs. She is dressed in shirt and diaper and tied with ribbon bow onto the quilted, lace-trimmed pad. Dy-Dee's layette was selected to make her the very best-dressed baby! There's a dainty short dress, slip, shoes and socks; a darling satin coat and bonnet, flannel pajamas, feeding bib, wash-cloth, soap. And a booklet entitled "What Every Young Doll Mother Should Know" which tells you how to get the most fun and take care of your Dy-Dee Doll.

Effanbee means finest 🎔 and best

The DyDee of 1954 in the 11″ size only, with or without caracul wig came in a display box that looked like a play crib and the 11″, 15″ and 20″ with molded hair or caracul wig came in a carry case with layette. This baby was also available in a wood frame suitcase that looked like a portable sewing machine case, only opens at the center and when the sides are open, they contain her layette. (This case available only with the 15″ and 20″ shown). There was another deluxe wood frame carry case with lift out tray that held her clothes also shown in the Effanbee catalog.

CANDY-KID — *a sweet two-some*

341 — Candy Kid Twin — 12″ Tall — 9.95

All vinyl dolls, fully jointed with tiltable head — completely washable from head to toe.

Brother is dressed in red & white checked gingham pants with white shirt with check collar and cuffs, with matching hat. Sister in matching checked lace-trimmed dress, panties and bonnet. Both wear white shoes and socks. Packed in clearvue gift box.

Effanbee means finest 🎔 and best

12″ "Candy Kid" twins, boy and girl. All vinyl and fully jointed. Deeply molded hair and inset glasseen eyes. Dressed in red check gingham. He has wooden yo-yo and she carries tiny stuffed monkey.

17″ "Lawrence Welk's Champagne Lady". Vinyl high heeled doll that is all original and complete with gold heart wrist tag, purse and original green satin dancing dress. Marks: Effanbee Doll. 1957. Courtesy E. Samec. Nationwide newspapers reported on April 26, 1981, that, in Dallas, Mrs. Alice Lon Bowling, who was Lawrence Welk's first network TV "Champagne Lady" was dead at age 54.

Company flyers to toy store buyers touted this "Patsy Ann" doll of 1959 as the "July 4th" winner for Summer sales. She is 15″, all vinyl with rooted saran hair and has sleep eyes. The head is marked Patsy Ann/1959, and the name Effanbee is not on the doll. The tam and bodice are bright red and the skirt is white. She also has red shoes. Courtesy June Schultz.

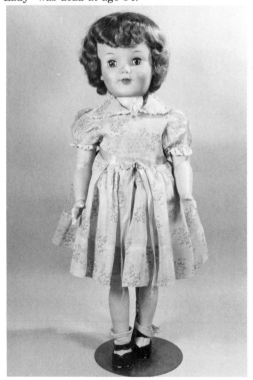

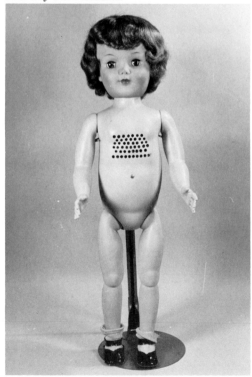

27″ "Melodie" marked with her name and Effanbee on the head. Hard plastic with vinyl head, rooted hair and sleep blue eyes/lashes. Thin legs are jointed at the knees and she is a walker. Plastic door in back opens to reveal a record player and is battery operated. Original dress has bloomers attached and snaps closed all the way down the back. Dress is organdy with roses and pink ribbon trim. Imitation leather pumps. arms only go shoulder high. 1953. Courtesy Beverly Harrington.

10″ "Mickey" shown in various outfits. Some have molded on hats, and the boxer eye color is in the vinyl. All are courtesy Miriam Knox.

All these "Mickey's" and the two lower, "Happy Boy" were on the market a number of years. All are courtesy Miriam Knox.

11″ "Happy Boy". All vinyl and jointed. Marks: 1960/Effanbee, on head and 10 Effanbee B, on back. Re-dressed. Courtesy June Schultz.

The first set of "The Most Happy Family" were made with the teen doll, Tiny Fluffy and Babykin. Later ones also included Mickey. This is one of the first sets in it's original box that is made like a living room. Courtesy Doris Richardson.

The Most Happy Family of 1957 included 20″ Mother, 11″ Sister (Fluffy), 11″ Brother (Mickey) and 8″ Baby (Babykin). The cost of the four dolls was $22.95. The clothes shown in this 1957 Ward's catalog are blue and this set was also available in red clothes. (No coats).

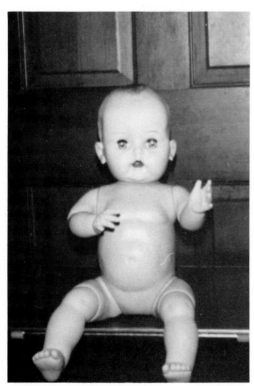

20″ "My Precious Baby" of 1958 came with molded or rooted hair. All vinyl, flirty eyes and has extra joints at elbows and knees. Courtesy Jeanne Mauldin.

GIRL DOLLS

ALICE
No. 7364 15″ tall...$10
No. 7564 19″ tall...$13
All vinyl girl doll with luxuriant rooted Saran hair that can be washed, combed and set in pigtail or ponytail style. Dressed in organdy pinafore and organdy dress, polished cotton slip and panties, shoes and socks. Carries mirror in her hand. Ribbon bow in her hair.
Moving arms, legs and eyes.

JR. MISS BALLERINA WALKING DOLL
No. 7431 15″ tall...$10 (jointed ankles)
No. 7631 21″ tall...$14 (jointed ankles and knees)
Plastic body and legs, vinyl arms and head. Moving arms, legs and eyes. Has rooted Saran hair that can be washed, combed and set. Wears net ballerina costume with nylon stockings and ballerina slippers. Has decoration in her hair. Carries acetate hatbox containing leotard and walking shoes.

LITTLE LADY
No. 7563
All vinyl girl doll with moving arms legs and eyes. Has rooted Saran hair, braided in pigtails, that can be washed, combed and set. She is dressed in checked gingham dress, which has organdy puffed sleeves trimmed with lace. Over the dress, she wears organdy apron trimmed with embroidery. Also wears flower-trimmed straw sailor hat, cotton slip and panties, shoes and socks. 19″ tall. $14

No. 7563

No. 7564

No. 7631

JR. MISS DOLL
No. 8651
21″ tall—Made of rigisol vinyl plastic. Has moving legs, arms, head and eyes. Her rooted Saran hair can be washed, combed and set. Dressed in flowered nylon formal with flower-trimmed picture hat, long taffeta slip, matching panties, nylon stockings, high heel shoes, nylon gloves, simulated pearl earrings and necklace, and carries corsage in her hand. $15

BRIDE DOLL
No. 8653
21″ tall—Rigisol vinyl plastic body, legs, arms and head. Moving eyes, arms, legs. Has rooted Saran hair that can be washed, combed and set. Dressed in long, white satin dress with three-tier overskirt, trimmed with Venice lace, ruffled slip, panties, nylon stockings, high heel shoes, nylon gloves, ring, necklace and earrings. Wears head piece trimmed with flowers and long net veil. Carries corsage in her hand. $15

The "Jr. Miss" doll is shown in the 1958 Effanbee catalog as Bride and Bridesmaid. Both are 21″ tall. The Bridesmaid is dressed in flowered nylon and the Bride's gown is satin.

"Little Lady" in the Effanbee 1958 catalog came in the 19″ size and was all vinyl with joints just above the elbows. Wears dress, organdy apron and straw sailor hat. Also shown is "Alice" who came in 15″ and 19″. She wears organdy dress and pinafore and carried a mirror in her hand. The arms are one piece. This same doll was offered as a ballerina called "Jr. Miss" that came with jointed knees and could be ordered also with jointed ankles. She came in 15″ and 21″.

Alyssa

ANOTHER EFFANBEE ORIGINAL WITH THE CONTINENTAL FLAIR!

LITTLE LADY
No. 8673

No. 638

No. 7788

No. 7781

No. 637

No. 0636

OFFICIAL GIRL SCOUT (PATSY ANN)
Style No. 638

15" all vinyl girl doll fully jointed with moving eyes and rooted saran hair that can be washed, combed and set. Has freckles around nose.

Dressed as Official Girl Scout. Her uniform and panties are made of the authentic material used by the Girl Scouts of America. She wears a green beret, yellow tie, green socks, brown shoes and

Patsy Ann

PATSY ANN BOX SET
Style No. 0636

Patsy Ann is dressed in organdy dress, taffeta slip and panties, shoes and socks. Extra outfits consist of:
a) ballerina outfit and slippers
b) 2 pc. slack suit and matching slippers
c) lace trimmed school dress with nylon petticoat and beret

1959 was the first year that "Patsy Ann" was used as the official Girl Scout and Brownie. She was also offered in a gift pack set. The Bride is 20" "Little Lady" and the other two are 23" and called "Alyssa" and she is jointed at the elbow.s

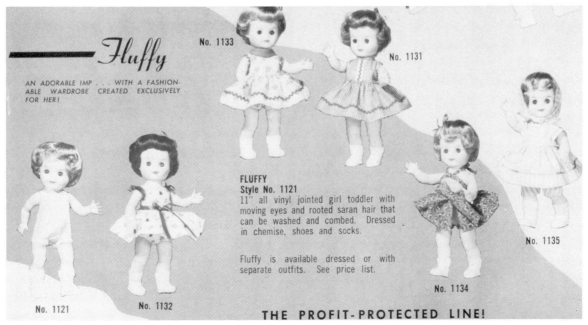

Fluffy

AN ADORABLE IMP . . . WITH A FASHION-ABLE WARDROBE CREATED EXCLUSIVELY FOR HER!

No. 1133

No. 1131

FLUFFY
Style No. 1121

11" all vinyl jointed girl toddler with moving eyes and rooted saran hair that can be washed and combed. Dressed in chemise, shoes and socks.

Fluffy is available dressed or with separate outfits. See price list.

No. 1135

No. 1134

No. 1121

No. 1132

THE PROFIT-PROTECTED LINE!

The "Fluffy" is 11", all vinyl and came in six different outfits. 1959.

Two very unusual dolls made an appearance in the 1959 Effanbee catalog. 28″ Boudoir-Playmate dolls that have a nylon cloth body and vinyl head and limbs.

32″ "Mary Jane". Plastic and vinyl with rooted hair, flirty sleep eyes and walks. All original. Marks: Effanbee/Mary Jane 1960, on head. 1960. The dog is "Snobby", a Steiff. Courtesy June Schultz.

The 1959 Effanbee catalog carried the 15″ girl doll "Suzette" that is all vinyl, has posable head and came dressed as a Bride, Bo Peep and five other outfits. Also shown is the 32″ "Mary Jane" with flirty eyes and a walker.

Suzie Sunshine

THE MOST IMPISH .. THE MOST DELIGHTFUL!
TO SEE HER IS TO LOVE HER.

18″ all vinyl and plastic toddler, fully jointed with tiltable head, flirting eyes and rooted hair that can be washed, combed and set.

SUZIE SUNSHINE Style No. 1812
Dressed in two (2) piece snow suit consisting of cotton pants and fleecy jacket with fleece scarf and matched hood. White boots.

SUZIE SUNSHINE Style No. 1813
Dressed in printed cotton tunic dress with lace trim and matching panties; flower and ribbon in hair; shoes and socks.

SUZIE SUNSHINE Style No. 1814
Dressed in lace trimmed printed cotton top with solid color slacks, patent shoes and socks; ribbon in hair.

SUZIE SUNSHINE Style No. 1815
Dressed in lace trimmed gingham checked sun dress with matching panties and play sandals; ribbon bow in hair.

SUZIE SUNSHINE Style No. 1817
In printed plaid pinafore with matching bonnet and solid color broadcloth dress with slip and panties, shoes and socks.

SUZIE SUNSHINE Style No. 1818
In printed cotton dress with matching lace trimmed pantaloons and lace trimmed, dotted Swiss pinafore. Knee length socks and shoes. Ribbon bow in hair.

SUZIE SUNSHINE Style No. 1819
Dressed in polished cotton striped dress with lace trimmed organdy pinafore and matching panties. Ribbon in hair, patent leather shoes and socks.

SUZIE SUNSHINE Style No. 1821
Dressed in printed cotton dress and Cordana Coat, hat and leggings set with fur-like plush trim and muff. White Boots.

SUZIE SUNSHINE Style No. 1822
In white pique dress and coat set with rick rack trim. Slip and panties. Straw hat, patent leather shoes and socks and carries a straw handbag.

The 18″ "Suzie Sunshine" introduced in the Effanbee catalog of 1959 is unique in that she has flirty eyes. Plastic and vinyl, she came with long or short hair and as a blonde or a brunette and was available in nine different outfits.

16″ Unmarked Patsy-type. Blue sleep eyes. Vinyl arms and head with body and legs plastic. No marks and not original. Courtesy Nancy Lucas.

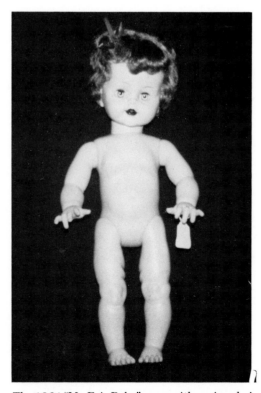

The 1964 "My Fair Baby" came with various hair colors and was sold through Montgomery Ward. The doll was made from 1960 and will be marked 1960. Courtesy Jeanne Mauldin.

11″ "Pum'kin" that wears her original dress of pink pleated chiffon. Marks: Effanbee/1966. Courtesy June Schultz.

16″ "Twinkie", both black and white of 1966. These dolls came with either rooted or molded hair. The two on the right are original. Courtesy Jeanne Mauldin.

Left: 17″ "New Dy-Dee". All vinyl with fairly straight legs and marked only Effanbee, on head. Right: 15″ "Peaches" with cloth body and vinyl head and limbs. Marks: Effanbee 1965, on head. Courtesy June Schultz.

This 23″ doll dressed for Sears and Roebuck in 1963 was called "My Baby Doll". Cloth body with vinyl head and limbs. Also dressed in white and red. Part of the "Sugar Plum" collection.

The Effanbee dolls for Sears and Roebuck in 1963 were dressed in red and white. The red was velveteen and the white was either cotton or organdy. Dolls shown are: 18" "Suzie Sunshine", 15" "Gumdrop", 15" "Twinkie". "Suzie Sunshine" in the 13" size was called "Mary Jane" and #5 is another 15" "Twinkie". They were called the "Sugar Plum" collection.

The 1963 Sears and Roebuck catalog shows the 18" Suzie Sunshine used as "Schoolgirl Writing Doll" with especially molded hand to hold a crayon. She is all vinyl with a ball jointed arm that can move in any direction.

Sears of 1964 featured this "Sweetie Pie" on dark pink pillow and dressed in white eyelet, rosebud trimmed, and bow of dark pink. All vinyl, open mouth/nurser. Came with ID bracelet with her name. 16" tall.

1964 Sears carried 6 other dolls that were dressed in velveteen: top to bottom: 12″ "Cupcake", all vinyl, open mouth/nurser dressed in bloomers and white eyelet short dress. 18″ "Sugar Plum" in pink and white. 16″ "Gumdrop" in green and white, 11″ "Candy Kid" in pink and white, 24″ "Sugar Pie" in pink and white "fur" trim and muff, white eyelet dress and cloth body, and 18″ "Honey" (Suzie Sunshine) in green and white.

16″ "Baby Peaches" with all vinyl body and limbs was featured in the 1965 Sears catalog dressed in white organdy with peach flower trim, on white pillow, and with bracelet. Not in Effanbee catalog.

Effanbee dolls called "Peaches 'n Cream" were sold through Sears in 1965. Shown are: "Dy-Dee" in white and tied to blanket with peach satin ribbon and is 16″. 18″ "Sweetie Pie" with cloth body, white dress and peach coat. 16″ "Gumdrop" with white hair and peach coat dress. 16″ "Gumdrop" with reddish hair and white dress with peach ribbon trim. Not in Effanbee catalog.

Sears has

Our pink and pretty doll family . . $14⁹⁹
includes two Big Sisters and Baby

1965 Sears carried the 16″ Gumdrop in pink check nightgown, 11″ Candy and 8″ Babykin as a "family". The cradle is white wire frame, 10x7x9″. Not in Effanbee catalog.

Charlee

13″ All vinyl toddler, fully jointed with moving eyes and rooted hair that can be washed and combed.

#6431 – Striped cotton batiste dress with matching panties.   Retail $7.00
#6434 – Plaid percale dress with leotards and cotton panties.   Retail $7.00
#6436 – Printed flannel pajamas & cap.   Retail $6.00

#6431

#6434

#6436

Half Pint

13″ All vinyl toddler, fully jointed with moving eyes and rooted hair that can be washed and combed. Tiltable head.

#6211

#6212

#6211 – Printed cotton batiste dress, lace trimmed with matching panties. Retail $5.00
#6212 – Lace trimmed velveteen dress with taffeta panties.   Retail $5.00
#6213 – Lace trimmed, printed batiste dress with ruffle trim; matching panties.   Retail $5.00

#6213

13″ "Charlie". All vinyl toddler, with sleep eyes to the side, and freckles across the nose came in three outfits in 1966. Striped cotton batiste short dress and panties, plain dress with leotards, spats, and printed flannel pajamas and cap.

The 1966 Effanbee catalog shows "Half Pint" available in three outfits. Lightly printed batiste dress with lace on the bodice and matching panties, lace trimmed velveteen very short dress and taffeta panties and lace trimmed batiste dress with printed flowers and matching panties.

Little Gum Drop

#1428 — 14″ All vinyl toddler with moving eyes and rooted hair; fully jointed. Shoes and socks. 8″ vinyl Babykin; drinks and wets; bottle. Both in checked gingham. Retail $7.00

Gum Drop

16″ All vinyl toddler, fully jointed with moving eyes and long rooted hair that can be washed and combed. All with shoes and socks, ribbon bow in hair. Available colored.

#1631 — Striped cotton dress with velvet bodice; matching panties. Retail $6.00

#1641 — Velveteen jumper with white cotton blouse and white cotton panties. Retail $7.00

#1642 — Navy and white polka dot cotton dress; White pique pinafore with red trim; polka dot panties. Retail $7.00

#1646 — Flannel nitey with matching panties and bedroom scuffs. She holds an 8″ Babykin dressed in flannel sleeping bag. Retail $8.00

14″ "Litle Gum Drop" came carrying a Babykin, both dressed in check gingham, pants with check bands and sandals.

The regular 16″ "Gumdrop" of 1966 came in a flower print flannel nightgown and carrying an 8″ Babykin in matching sleeping bag. Striped cotton dress with velveteen bodice, strip sleeves. Velveteen jumper with white cotton blouse with trim down front. Navy and white polka dot cotton dress, white pique pinafore.

nightgown nties and e holds an lly jointed nd molded ching flan-tail $10.00

mmed or-ith cotton ured hose. ail $10.00

"Suzie Sunshine" of 1966 was available in flannel nightgown and carrying an 8″ Babykin in matching sleeping bag. Also in a velvet trimmed organdy party dress and textured hose.

17″ "Miss Chips" of 1966 was available in six outfits: striped blazer jacket over white cotton dress with pleated skirt, textured hose and hat; oatmeal sack slack suit with pink cotton blouse; linen dress with front panel, four buttons, white collar and matching hat, also textured hose; white vinyl raincoat with polka dot trim, polka dot dress, boots and babushka; nylon Bridesmaid gown with rosebud trim, textured hose, taffeta slip and ribbon in hair; and Bride with three rows of scalloped lace at hem and lace on bodice.

Chipper

15″ All vinyl girl doll, fully jointed with side glance moving eyes and rooted hair that can be washed and combed.

#1531—Two-tone printed percale dress & hat; matching panties and textured hose. Retail $6.00

#1532 — Cotton dress with cotton braided panel in front; matching panties and textured hose. Retail $6.00

#1535 — Lace trimmed tulle bridal gown with taffeta slip and panties; crinoline and long textured stockings. Bridal veil. Retail $9.00

#1532

#1531

#1535

15″ "Chipper" of 1966 came in cotton dress with cotton braid panel down front, matching panties and textured hose, two-tone print cotton dress of percale, matching hat, textured hose. She was also available as a Bride with double, scalloped hem, textured stockings, and lace trimmed veil.

EFFANBEE DURABLE DOLLS

Pun'kin

11″ All vinyl toddler, fully jointed with moving eyes and rooted hair that can be washed and combed.

#1315 — Velveteen dress with matching panties. Retail $4.00

#1317 — Long flannel nitie with matching panties. Retail $4.00

#1318 — Lace trimmed organdy party dress with cotton slip and panties. Retail $5.00

#1319 — Checked coat and hat over cotton dress and panties. Retail $5.00

#1319

#1315

#1317

#1318

11″ "Pun'kin" came in a velveteen dress, pleat in front, matching panties and daisy. Long flannel nightgown with wide ruffle at hem and matching panties. Lace trimmed party dress, cotton slip and panties. Check coat and hat, over a cotton dress and panties.

EFFANBEE DOLLS

Twinkie

TWINKIE. An adorable drink and wet baby. 16" all vinyl doll — fully jointed with moving eyes and rooted hair and voice. Dressed in long, organdy dress with embroidered hemline and velvet bodice, lace trimmed taffeta slip; diaper and booties. Velvet bow in her blonde hair. She lies on a velvet pillow with embroidered organdy ruffle. Wt. 2 lbs.
2523TEF697 .... $10.00

HALF PINT. An 11" all vinyl toddler, fully jointed with tiltable head, moving eyes and rooted hair. She's dressed in a two piece printed flannel pajamas and shoes. In her blond hair she has two bright bows and carries a hair brush in her hand. She'll be the favorite of some lucky girl. Wt. 1 lb.
6217TEF370 ......$5.00

MISS CHIPS. Dressed in all lace bridal gown with taffeta slip, crinoline, nylon hose and slippers. Has blue garter and bridal bouquet. 17" vinyl doll with moving eyes and rooted hair.
1768TEF896—Wt. 1 lb. $13.00

HONEY BUN. 18" Kapok stuffed doll with vinyl arms, legs and head—moving eyes and rooted hair and voice. Dressed in gingham checked cotton "A" line dress with panties, shoes and socks.
9553TEF697—Wt. 2 lbs. $10.00

BABY FACE. An appealing 16" all vinyl toddler, fully jointed with moving eyes and rooted hair that can be washed and combed. Dressed in an organdy dress with pleated Bertha collar; lace trimmed cotton slip and panties; shoes and socks. A ribbon bow in her blonde hair. Weight: 2 lbs.
2623TEF497 ......$7.00

During 1967 these Effanbee dolls were listed in catalogs: "Half Pint" in flower printed two piece flannel pajamas, 17" "Miss Chips Bride", 18" "Honey Bun" with cloth body in check gingham dress with white sleeves and collar, 16" "Baby Face" in pink organdy dress and 16" "Twinkie", all vinyl, open mouth/nurser in pink and white.

17" "Miss Chips" with trunk and wardrobe, along with black 11" "Half Pint" as Flowergirl dressed in pink with white lace, and boy in black and white shirt were shown in the 1967 Marshall-Fields catalog. The other two dolls shown are one in coat from Italy and black doll in pink gown is an Alexander Leslie.

Lil Sweetie

steals your heart away.
Feels so REAL..
looks so REAL..
even drinks and
wets like a
REAL BABY

DRINK 'N
WET DOLLS

$9⁹⁹

This lovable, realistic-looking infant
drinks from her own little bottle.
Then she'll wet her didy. Lil Sweetie
is all soft vinyl and fully jointed.
Her soft, blonde baby hair is rooted,
can be brushed or combed. She comes
in a long christening gown with lace
and embroidered rosettes. Sweater,
cap and booties are hand-crocheted.
Pillow trimmed with embroidery, organdy ruffle. 18 in. tall.
49 N 3160—Wt. 2 lbs. 10 oz..$9.99

Three different outfits

1 **Bunting Outfit.** Take Lil Sweetie
for an outing in this warm blanket, jacket and cap. All are trimmed
with lovely satin binding.
49 N 3287—Shpg. wt. 12 oz..$3.99

2 **Robe.** Made of soft printed flannelette to keep Lil Sweetie warm
after her daily nap.
49 N 3286—Shpg. wt. 10 oz..$1.99

3 **Bath Towel.** White terry cloth.
Has its own hood to keep Lil
Sweetie warm after a bath. Shell
stitch trim.
49 N 3285—Shpg. wt. 10 oz..$1.19

NOTE: Doll not included with outfits

590 Sears PCBKM AEDSLG

18″ "Lil Sweetie" is one of the most collectable of the Effanbee babies and was shown in the 1967 Sears catalog dressed in white christening gown with pink sweater and cap, pink bunting with white trim, printed flannel robe and
diaper, and in pink diaper with white bath towel.

Sears in 1968 carried this 18″ "Baby Button Nose" dressed in white with lace trim, and a ribbed pink coat with wide collar and rosette trim, plus a matching bonnet. Three separate outfits were: pink dress with white trim, and pink knitted sweater with bonnet, all pink flannel gown, bonnet and bunting, and a pink flower printed pajamas with white robe.

16″ "Baby Winkie" came in this beautiful party dress that is pale pink with three rows of embroidered pink flowers and scalloped hem, plus had three extra outfits available, a white flannel bunting, printed one piece pajamas and pink flannel robe, plus a pink coat and bonnet. 1968 J. C. Penney's catalog.

The 1968 Sear's catalog had the 18″ "Dy-Dee Darlin' " dressed in white eyelet, two tiered dress with matching bonnet.

DY DEE DARLIN'
dressed like the little angel she is . .
drinks her own bottle, wets her diaper . .
when you pick her up she coos with delight
$9⁹⁹

Eyes bright with wonder, cheeks kissed by sun . . and all decked out for special occasions in a tiered cotton batiste dress that's lavished with dainty eyelet embroidery. Matching cap topped with delicate rose bud. Flannel diaper. Satin shoes, socks. 18-inch vinyl body fits right into your arms. Soft vinyl head, arms, legs. Comb her glossy rooted hair. Eyes open and close.
49 N 30194—Shipping weight 2 pounds 8 ounces.....................$9.99

BABY DOLLS

Sears

 *Half Pint*

11" All vinyl toddler, fully jointed with moving eyes and rooted hair that can be washed and combed.

11" "Half Pint" of 1968 came as two sets of boys and girls. One set in velveteen, which was available in both black and white, also in striped and dotted cotton. She also came in a flowered dress and matching panties with white sleeves, and in two piece printed flannel pajamas (black or white).

8" "Babykin" of 1968 came as twins in flannel jacket with hood and diapers, in flannel bunting. This doll was also available as singles in same outfit, plus three other outfits. Courtesy Beverly Harrington.

18" "Suzie Sunshine". Vinyl head and arms, plastic body and legs. She has been re-dressed in a very nice outfit, but what makes her unique is her left hand is cupped to hold something. She may have been one of the dolls that hold an 8" "Babykin" and a bottle in cupped hand. Marks: Effanbee/1961. Courtesy June Schultz.

Miss Chips

17" All vinyl girl doll, fully jointed with side glance moving eyes and rooted hair that can be washed and combed.

#1742 — Plaid jumper and white blouse; straw hat, cotton slip and panties; textured stockings and shoes.

#1742N — Same as above — NEGRO.

#1743 — Printed voile dress with tucked bodice; cotton slip and panties; textured stockings and shoes.

#1743N — Same as above — NEGRO.

#1745 — Cotton dress; maribou trimmed velveteen coat and hat; textured stockings and shoes.

#1746 — Vinyl raincoat with polka dot trim; polka dot dress with matching panties; polka dot boots and babushka.

#1748 — Lace and tulle bridal gown over taffeta slip; panties; crinoline, stockings and satin shoes. Lace trimmed bridal veil with flowers on crown.

#1748N — Same as above — NEGRO.

#1746 Retail $10.00

#1748 Retail $13.00

#1748N Available negro Retail $13.00

#1745 Retail $13.00

17" "Miss Chips" of 1968 came dressed as a Bride with ornate crown veil (also in black), in vinyl raincoat with polka dot trim, boots and head scarf, in a cotton dress with coat of velveteen and maribou trim. She also came dressed in plaid jumper, white blouse and straw hat (black, also), and in printed voile dress with tucked bodice (also in black).

Chipper

15" All vinyl girl doll, fully jointed with side glance eyes and rooted hair that can be washed and combed. All with knee socks and shoes except #1554 Bride.

#1551 — Ruffled voile party dress with matching panties.

#1552 — Printed cotton dress with lace trimmed pinafore and matching panties; straw hat.

#1554 — Lace and tulle bridal gown over taffeta slip and panties; crinoline, stockings and satin shoes. Lace trimmed bridal veil with flowers on crown.

#1555 — Printed voile dress with tucked bodice; cotton slip and panties.

#1551 Retail $7.00

15" "Chipper" of 1968 was available with three different hairdos and came dressed as Bride with five rows of lace, matching lace on veil with flowers at crown, printed voile dress with tucked bodice and wide ruffle at hem, printed cotton dress with lace trimmed pinafore and straw hat. Two ruffles at hem of party dress of voile with flowers on sash, and "poodle" hair style.

#1552 Retail $8.00

#1554 Retail $9.00

#1555 Retail $7.00

16″ "Baby Face" is shown in the outfit that was sold through the J. C. Penney stores (not in the catalog) during the 1969 Christmas season. She has red flannel skirt, white organdy bodice with red trim, and red ribbon in hair. The 8″ "Babykin" is in white flannel with red trim. (Author).

18″ "My Fair Baby" was sold through the J. C. Penney's catalog in pink dress with white band trim, and pink and white knitted sweater and bonnet. 18″ "Sweetie Pie" came in pink ribbed nylon coat, matching hat and muff, and under her coat is a pink nylon crepe party dress. Three separate outfits were available for these two dolls: printed pajamas and pink flannel robe, pink trim on white party dress with lace at neck, and sleeve edges and in a pink and white two piece playsuit. 16″ "Twinkie" came in pink diapers at top tied to a pink print on white quilted blanket. 16″ "Lil' Darlin' " was dressed in nylon with two scalloped trims at hem and row of embroidered flowers, and lace trim.

11″ "Half Pint" boy that is marked: Effanbee/1966, on back of head. Original black body suit and white shirt. 1968, 1969 and 1970. Also came in black. Courtesy Renie Culp.

"Sunny" (on tag) toddler that is 18″ tall, jointed with vinyl head and arms and plastic body and legs. Open/closed "rosebud" style mouth. All original. Marks: 15 Effanbee 1968/9305, on head. (Button Nose). Courtesy June Schultz.

In 1969 the J. C. Penney catalog sold 16″ "Twinkie" in white organdy gown with pink ribbon trim, sash and bow in hair, on a bright pink velveteen pillow with lace trim.

A. is an Effanbee called "Lynn" in the 1969 Marshall-Field's catalog, dressed in pink snowsuit with muff. B. is "Suzie Sunshine" in printed dark pink long gown and white pinafore, and D. and E. are Effanbee "Brother and Sister" dressed in blue. C. is an Italian doll "Orietta", and F. is Alexander's "Michael and Bear".

In 1969 the Marshall-Field's catalog had the 18″ "Miss Chips", but called her "Chris", along with wardrobe and trunk, called "Chris Going To Prom", L. is also an Effanbee, but called "Lucinda", with small wardrobe and trunk.

#1724
Retail $16.00

#1724N
Retail $16.00

#1725
Retail $15.00

Miss Chips

17" All vinyl girl doll, fully jointed with side glance moving eyes and rooted hair that can be washed and combed.

#1724 — Eyelet embroidered organdy bridal gown over cotton slip, panties and crinoline; nylon stockings and shoes. All tulle bridal veil w/ flowers on crown; bridal bouquet.

#1724N — as above — NEGRO.

#1725 — Eyelet embroidered organdy bridesmaid gown over contrasting colored cotton slip and panties; crinoline, stockings and shoes. Flowers in hair and bouquet in hand.

#1514
Retail $12.00

#1513
Retail $9.00

Chipper

15" All vinyl girl doll, fully jointed with side glance eyes and rooted hair that can be washed and combed.

#1513 — Long dotted cotton granny gown w/eyelet lace trimmed pinafore; matching panties, shoes and socks.

#1514 — Eyelet embroidered organdy bridal gown over cotton slip and panties; nylon stockings, shoes. All tulle bridal veil w/flowers on crown; bridal bouquet.

17" "Miss Chips" of 1969 is shown in Bride's gown with eyelette embroidery on bodice and two rows on skirt, along with the Bridesmaid. Both have flowers in hair. 15" "Chipper" as a "Bride" has one row of embroidered eyelette trim, and was also sold in gown of dotted cotton with pinafore.

Toddletot

13" All soft vinyl drink and wet toddler; fully jointed with moving eyes and molded hair. Has plastic drinking bottle.

#6313 — Two piece lineen suit w/matching cap/shoes and socks.

#6314 — Lace trimmed cotton voile dress w/matching bikini panties; hat and coat; shoes & socks.

Baby Face

16" all vinyl toddler, fully jointed with moving side glance eyes and rooted hair.

#2642 — Crepe top and nylon tulle tutu, stretch tights and satin slippers.

#2642N — as above — NEGRO.

#2644 — Lace trimmed gingham checked cotton nitie w/matching panties and slippers. Has plastic hair brush. Double pony tail hairdo.

#2647 — Cotton dress with eyelet cotton pinafore; matching panties; shoes and socks.

#2642N
Retail $8.00

#6313
Retail $7.00

#6314
Retail $7.00

#2644
Retail $9.00

#2647
Retail $8.00

16" "Baby Face" shown in the 1969 Effanbee catalog came dressed in three outfits: lace and ruffle trimmed check gingham gown, cotton dress with eyelette/ribbon trim and as a ballerina, which was also available in black.

The 1969 Effanbee Catalog shows 18″ "Suzie Sunshine" in flower print Granny gown and white pinafore, daisy covered flannel nightgown, holding 8″ matching "Babykins", and also an entirely different doll as "Suzie" in fleece snowsuit, cap and muff.

11″ "Half Pint" was sold in six different outfits in 1969: lace trimmed long check gown (also came in black), eyelette top with long cotton overalls and bonnet (also in black), lace trimmed velveteen dress and matching panties, white cotton shirt and velveteen pants boy (also in black), lace trimmed organdy party dress and as ballerina.

#9 is a "Baby Twinkie" in case with wardrobe. The suit case is pink and white check. #11 is 11″ "Half Pint" in blue long pants and white top with blue bonnet. (Also sold this outfit in 1969). #12 is an 11″ "Half Pint" dressed in old fashioned outfit all white with pink sash and ribbon in straw hat, black shoes with white side snap spats.

11″ "Pun'kin" of 1969 came in three outfits: short lace trimmed check dress with straw hat, pleated nylon dress with cotton slip, and in long printed flannel nightgown with wide ruffle. (Also in black.)

16″ "Twinkie" in the J. C. Penney's 1970 catalog was sold two ways: in pink eyelette trimmed dress on pink pillow with matching trim, and in pink coat and bonnet with a cotton dress.

1970 carried this 18″ "Suzie Sunshine" in white long gown and multi-colored pinafore, along with 15″ "Miss Chips" (name in catalog, actually a "Chipper"). The Bride's gown has three wide rows of lace, lace sleeves and flowers in veil.

15″ "Gumdrop" marked: 1962 Effanbee, on head. Box is marked: #1643. All original in yellow gown with black and red apron, and matching bonnet. From the Frontier series. Courtesy Renie Culp.

18″ Black "Suzie Sunshine". Dress is red, yellow and navy. All original. Marks: Effanbee 1961, on head. One of the Frontier series. 1971. Courtesy Renie Culp.

16″ "Dy-Dee Baby" was sold from Sear's catalog in pink, lace trimmed outfit, tied to pink flannel, lace trimmed blanket, and with extra clothes. 14″ "Baby Butterball" came in pink flannel outfit, in pink lace trimmed bunting. 17″ and 14″ "My Fair Babies" (two different dolls) came in white dresses with pink trim, or sweater and cap.

14″ "Chipper" wears blue panties and nightgown with lace trim, applied blue roses and beige ribbon trim. White hair and blue bonnet. Marks: Effanbee/1966, on head. 1971. 17″ "Miss Chips" also came in same gown, but hers was pink. Courtesy Beverly Harrington.

A Baby Doll's
Country Look,
Warm as can be...

Cuddly dolls dressed in
patchwork-patterned prints, plus
furniture with colonial styling

They have vinyl heads
and arms, rooted hair,
and eyes that close

1 Baby Face Doll. She has her own tiny baby. Baby Face is 16 in. tall with long blond hair. She wears a cotton lace trimmed party dress with a patchwork-pattern checked skirt, wide hem, white cotton panties and slippers. She carries a tiny 9-in. baby doll and plastic bottle in a white sleeping bag.
X 921-4495 A—Mailing wt. 1.40 lbs. 12.88

2 Chipper. Lifelike Chipper has long blond rooted hair you can brush, comb and braid. She wears a cotton party dress with a white lace trim on top, a ruffled red and white patchwork-patterned skirt. White cotton panties with cotton lace trim, white slippers and a ribbon in her hair. She's 15 in. tall.
X 921-4503 A—Mailing wt. 1.40 lbs. 9.88

3 Butterball Baby Doll. She coos and drinks from her own plastic bottle. She rests on her own cotton pillow that matches the patchwork-patterned trim on her white cotton dress. She wears cotton flannel diapers, too. 13 in. tall.
X 921-4560 A—Mailing wt. 1.50 lbs. 8.88

Hardwood Doll Furniture—
Dark maple finish,
real wood turnings

Butterball Doll
has her own pillow

J. C. Penney's in 1973 carried the Country Look in three Effanbee dolls: "Baby Face" 16″ and carrying a 9″ baby, "Chipper" who is 15″ and "Butterball", 13″. All are dressed in red and white.

The Anniversary of 1973 for the Ward's Co. carried several re-introduced dolls, and listed from 1934 was their "new" Dy-Dee Baby. 17″ tall dressed in white with white blanket and tied with pink ribbons.

11″ "Half Pint". 1973 to 1975. Cotton panties with lace trim, hand crocheted dress in blue with white and roses on front. Marks: Effanbee 1966, on head. Effanbee/2400, on back. Outfit tagged: 100% acrylic fibre. Effanbee hand made Korea. Courtesy Renie Culp.

A. THRU C. CARRIAGES. Superbly built! Chrome accents!

A. "CINDY." Red vinyl padded carriage with 27" mattress, 27" body length. 27" high to handle. 10" wheels. Ship. Wt. 28 lbs.

E. THRU H. DOLLS. Effanbee "Highland Fling" adorables! Moving eyes, rooted (asst. blonde 'n platinum) hair. In scotch plaid and organdy—lace 'n satin trims!

E. SUZIE SUNSHINE. 19" vinyl

These four dolls of the "Highland Fling" collection of 1973 were sold through the F.A.O. Schwarz catalog in 1973, and included "Suzie Sunshine", "Pun'kin", "Little Luv" and "Butterball".

18" "Suzie Sunshine" with head marked: Effanbee 1961. All original red/blue plaid pinafore. Red trim on sleeves and bottom of skirt. 1973. "Highland Fling" collection. Blue sleep eyes and platinum rooted hair. Courtesy Renie Culp.

17" "Miss Chips" Country Cousins. 1974. Vinyl and plastic with sleep eyes and rooted hair. Marks: Effanbee/1965/1700. Courtesy Renie Culp.

Such rollickin' times you'll have a ball, when

COUNTRY COUSINS

come to call!

(10 thru 13) Country Cousins have smooth vinyl skin, large moving eyes and shiny rooted hair. Dolls are fully jointed.

10 16-inch Baby Face. Red and white dot dress with navy print apron. Black shoes, white spats, white leotards. Wt. 1 lb. 5 oz.
49 N 32094 ....$14.99

11 15-inch Chipper. Navy print dress with accent trim. White leotards, shoes.
Shpg. wt. 1 lb. 8 oz.
49 N 32095 ....$12.99

12 11-inch Pun'kin. Red and white dot dress, navy print apron, bonnet. White leotards, shoes.
Shpg. wt. 1 lb. 3 oz.
49 N 31637 ....$9.99

13 13-inch Butter Ball. Red and white dot dress, lace trim. Print diaper. Drinks and wets. Bottle. Wt. 1 lb. 4 oz.
49 N 31636 ....$9.99

NOTE: Items (10 thru 12) for ages 3 to 10. Not recommended for ages under 3, due to small parts. Item (13) for ages 6 months to 6 years.

PBLSCOM
KDGAE 2 [Sears] 433

Part of the "Country Cousins" group was sold through the 1974 Sear's catalog and included 16″ "Baby Face", 15″ "Chipper", 11″ "Pum'kin" and 13″ "Butterball". All are in red/white and blue.

Soft, little baby dolls, Pun'kin and Pint-Size

$9.99 each

6 11-inch Pun'kin. Dressed in a cozy, pink nylon fleece sleeper with delicate lace and ribbon trim. She hugs a tiny vinyl teddy bear. Lovely brunette rooted hair with two top curls. All vinyl body is fully jointed so you can pose her. Movable eyes. Ages 3 to 10.
49 C 32059—Shpg. wt. 14 oz. $9.99

7 14-inch Pint-Size. Cloth-body doll covered in cuddly nylon fleece. Vinyl head. Dress, sleep cap trimmed in lace. Ribbon trim also on cap and at ankles. Rooted hair, movable eyes. She squeaks when you squeeze her. Ages 3 to 10.
49 C 34103—Shpg. wt. 1 lb...$9.99

PBCOM
KDGAE [Sears] 449

11″ "Pun'kin" and 14″ "Pint Size" were both dressed in pink fleece for the Sear's 1975 catalog. "Pun'kin" came with a white vinyl Teddy Bear, and "Pint Size" had an all cloth body covered in fleece.

15″ "Chipper Bride" and 19″ "Suzie Sunshine" of the "Americana" collection wearing a blue check dress, white bonnet and pinafore with multi-color trim were offered through the Marshall-Fields catalog of 1975.

Wards is where the Dolls are!
All kinds...all sizes...all prices

Here's our own Suzie in a doll-age and size for every little girl

A-E **Suzie at 5 doll-ages from Baby to Bride.** Quality dolls from a foremost American manufacturer. Lifelike vinyl heads, delicate coloring, go-to-sleep eyes. All 5 make a wonderful gift for a lucky child—or doll collector. Set sold below at a savings.

A **Newborn Suzie.** Sweet little baby is all soft vinyl, fully jointed. Molded hair. Drinks and wets. Wears printed flannel diaper set, wrapped in fleecy blanket.
48 G 10049—About 11 in. Ship. wt. 12 oz............6.99

B **Suzie's Christening Day.** Long white dress with lace and embroidery trim, dainty gingham pillow. Cuddly, fully-jointed vinyl body. Drinks and wets. Rooted hair.
48 G 10051—About 12 in. Ship. wt. 1 lb. 2 oz.........12.99

C **Little Girl Suzie.** Coos happily when she's hugged! Cushion-soft body is cotton stuffed. Vinyl head, arms, legs. Rooted hair. Frilly print party dress, booties.
48 G 10072—About 15 in. Ship. wt. 1 lb. 6 oz..........14.99

D **School Girl Suzie.** Smart and perky in plaid coat, straw hat. White dress, panties, shoes, socks. Fully jointed, can stand alone. Long silky rooted hair to comb and set.
48 G 10206—About 16 in. Ship. wt. 1 lb. 4 oz.........16.99

E **Suzie's A Bride!** Lovely in traditional gown with embroidered organdy yoke and skirt panel. Filmy veil, satin slippers, nosegay, blue garter! Fully jointed, stands alone.
48 G 10207—About 17 in. Ship. wt. 1 lb. 14 oz.........19.99

SAVE $12. All Suzie Dolls, Baby to Bride. 71.95 separately.
48 G 10212—Five Dolls. Ship. wt. 6 lbs. 6 oz.......set 59.95

1974

358 WARDS ALL

In 1974 Ward's "Suzie" at five doll ages from baby to Bride. A. "Newborn Suzie" 11″, B. "Suzie's Christening Day" 12″, C. "Little Girl Suzie" 15″, D. "School Girl Suzie" 16″ and "Suzie Bride" 17″. Each could be bought separately or as a group for $59.95.

189

This is the all black Effanbee Bridal Party that was made in 1975 as a special for a customer. Very few sets were made. Courtesy Renie Culp.

All from 1975 "Duck, Duck, Goose" collection. 12″ "Butterball" marked: Effanbee/1969/6569, on head and back. White flannette diaper pants, blue dress with lace trim. White geese and orange ducks embroidered on hem. Blue matching pillow tied to neck, blue ribbon in hair. Blue sleep eyes and rooted hair. Tag: All new/polyester/Effanbee/Doll Corp/New York, N.Y. 17″ "Suzie Sunshine" with white panties, blue dress with organdy sleeves, lace trim and blue ribbon. Straw hat tied with blue ribbon. Embroidered ducks and geese at hem line in yellow and orange. Freckles and sleep blue eyes. Marks: Effanbee/1961, on head. 15″ "Baby Face" with white panties, yellow dress with yellow ribbon at waist and on matching bonnet. Lace trim, organdy short sleeves. White geese embroidered at hem line. Bonnet ties wrapped around and tied at top of head. Marks: Effanbee/1967/2600, on head. Courtesy Beverly Harrington.

25″ "Precious Baby" used for the first Limited Edition Club doll. 1975. Cloth body with vinyl head and limbs. Head is marked: Effanbee 1967, metal heart on dress: Effanbee Durable Dolls, and dress tagged: Effanbee Limited Edition Doll. Courtesy Renie Culp.

11″ "Autumn" of the Four Seasons Collection. Marks: Effanbee/1975/1176, on head. EFF & BEE, on back. The skirt section is pleated beige with brown braid trim, golden brown coat and bonnet with braid trim. Lace neck and cuffs, net ties on hat. 1976 only with skirt cut to waist and hat. 1977 to 1980 has V'ed out section of skirt and tied on head bonnet.

11″ "Winter" of the Four Seasons Collection. Doll is marked: Effanbee/1975/1176, on head. EFF & BEE, on back. Gown is white with red trim and coat is red with white trim, as is the bonnet. Bonnet trim and scarf are white "fur". 1976 set, but remained the same to 1980. Courtesy Renie Culp.

11″ "Summer" of the Four Seasons Collection. Marks: Effanbee/1976/1176, on head. EFF & BEE, on back. All white organdy with lace trim and pink ribbon sash, roses on hat and in basket tied to wrist. 1976, but remained the same to 1980. Courtesy Renie Culp.

11″ "Spring" of the Four Seasons Collection. This is from the 1976 set only. From 1977 to 1980 gown is green where this one is yellow with black trim. The blouse is white as is the hat. Marks: Effanbee/1975/1176. Courtesy Renie Culp.

All vinyl "Tiny Tubber" used for the "Baby Classics" of 1975, tied to a small pillow and gown has red strawberries printed on it. Courtesy Beverly Harrington.

11½" "Baby Winkie" in pink flannel sacque with pink ribbon and white lace trim. Wears white diaper pants, white flannel sweater with pink trim and has baby bottle tied to wrist. All vinyl with sleep blue eyes/lashes. Open mouth/nurser and has wide spread toes. Molded hair and separate flannel bonnet. Marks: Effanbee /1971/6171. 1976. Courtesy Beverly Harrington.

18" "Sweetie" of 1976, (came either black or white). Was sold in pink christening gown or blue flowered dress with pink knit sweater with matching bonnet and booties. Courtesy Jeanne Mauldin.

12" "Butterball". Beige cotton diaper pants, beige dress with bonnet, blue ribbon trim and applied blue roses. Molded hair, blue sleep eyes and white ribbon tied to wrist. Marks: Effanbee/1969/6569, on head and back. 1976. Courtesy Beverly Harrington.

11″ "Caroline" (#1185) of the 1976 Bridal party. Lace trimmed organdy with lace "bertha" collar. Head is marked: Effanbee/1976/1476, and on back: EFF & BEE. Courtesy Renie Culp.

14″ Black "Chipper Bride" from the 1976 Bridal Suite Collection. Marks: Effanbee/1966, on head.

11″ "Pum'kin" 1975, 1976, Crochet Classics. She is dressed in pink with white fringe, matching bonnet and white shoes. Courtesy Renie Culp.

11″ "Pum'kin Flowergirl". Head is marked: Effanbee/1966. F-B, on back. 1976 doll. Courtesy Renie Culp.

12″ "Pint Size". All red stuffed body and limbs with tag: All new materials, etc./Effanbee Doll Corp. Doll is marked on head: Effanbee/1968. Wrap around white removable pinafore that snaps in back and ties with red ribbon around neck. Straw hat, reverse tied with red ribbon and red ribbon in hair. Black sleep eyes to the side. 1976. Courtesy Beverly Harrington.

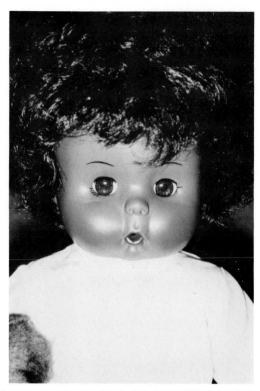

18″ "Black Dy-Dee". All vinyl with nurser mouth, sleep eyes and rooted hair. Marks: 15/Effanbee/56 71, on head. Effanbee/1967, on back. Teddy Bear came with this doll and the outfit has "Effanbee" written all over it (print). 1976. Also white. Courtesy Renie Culp.

11″ "Half Pint" of the Crochet Crowd Collection. 1976. White full, sleeveless body suit. White side snap spats over black slippers. Crocheted pale blue sweater with attached hood and muff. Black sleep eyes to side. Tag: 100% Acrylic Fibre/Effanbee Hand Made/Korea. Head marked: Effanbee/1966. Courtesy Renie Culp.

16″ "Patsy" of 1976 and the Limited Edition Club doll for that year. Head is marked: Patsy/Limited Edition/1976 and back: Effanbee/Patsy/Limited Edition/1976. Dress is tagged: Effanbee Limited Edition/1976 and she wears a metal heart on wrist: Effanbee Durable Dolls. Courtesy Renie Culp.

"Half Pint" is dressed in white leotards with blue velveteen dress and matching bonnet with white lace trim and sleeves. Pink rose on bonnet. Black slippers and separate white spats with side snaps. 1976. Courtesy June Schultz.

16″ "Baby Face" of 1976 was dressed in blue velveteen dress with lace trimmed slip, matching hat with flower, pantaloons, shoes, socks and spats. Courtesy Lilah Beck.

18″ "Suzie Sunshine". Head marked: Effanbee/1961. Box: #1856, and price of $22.98. Purchased in 1976 and made in 1975. Mint and original including Teddy Bear. Courtesy June Schultz.

11″ "Half Pint" in white eyelet with applied rose, bright pink ribbon sash and ribbon on hat, plus two ribbons in dark brown hair. Sleep black eyes to side. White leotards, spats with side snaps and black slippers. Marks: Effanbee/1966. 1976. In 1977 sash is red and wears cap. 15″ "Baby Face" dress is same material with matching bonnet. Marks: Effanbee/1967/2600, on head. 1976 and in 1977 the sash and bonnet trim were red. Courtesy Beverly Harrington.

11″ "Miss U.S.A." 1976 to date. One piece red/white check body suit with long sleeves, brown velveteen skirt, vest, cuffs. White fringe/red trim. White boots and hat with brown string ties. Long blonde hair with full bangs. Red belt with gold buckle and red kerchief. Marks: Effanbee/1976/1276. Courtesy Beverly Harrington.

11″ "Miss Germany". Black leotards and slippers, cotton half slip and patch work flowered dress. Red velveteen vest with navy trim, white apron/multi color trim is attached at the waist. Head band with two ribbons on the sides. Marks: Effanbee/1976/1276. 1976 with head band only. Courtesy Beverly Harrington.

The 11″ "Martha Washington" was made in 1976 and 1977, but the head will be marked: Effanbee 1975/1476. She was part of the "Historical Collection" and is dressed in deep blue with white trim, shawl and bonnet with blue trim. Courtesy Renie Culp.

11″ "Paul Revere". White leotards with black slippers and silver buckles. Tan velveteen knee pants and attached beige cotton shirt with lace trim. Green velveteen vest and brown velveteen cap. Carries tan bag over shoulder. Very long, straight hair pulled back with rubber band. Black belt/gold buckle. Marks: Effanbee/1976/1276. 1976 only.

This is the "Granny's Corner" of 1976, although the dolls are also made in 1975. All are in a pale paisley print with red velveteen ribbons and trim. The boy has red velveteen pants, shoes and hat. Shown on another page is the 16″ "Baby Face" in pale paisley with white pinafore, trim on bonnet and black shoes with white side snap spats.

The 1976 Americana Collection included: top: 15″ "Chipper" in white gown and blue check pinafore, bonnet; 15″ "Little Luv" in white with pink check; 19″ "Suzie Sunshine" in white with blue check in either black or white. Bottom: 15″ "Chipper" in black; 13″ "Butterball" in pink check; 11″ "Pun'kin" in blue check, and available in either black or white and the red/white/blue "Spirit of '76" boy and girl.

In 1975 Effanbee introduced a set of the "Grand Dames" using both the "Chipper" and the "Miss Chips" dolls. These same dolls were used in 1976 except for "Mam'selle" 18″ with white hair, multi color stripe skirt and trim, and red with black trim coat and bonnet. In 1976 she was replaced with sandy color, plain skirt and green coat/bonnet. (1734) Top, left to right: Peaches and Cream, Ma Cherie, Southern Belle. Lower: 1975 Mam'selle and 1976 Mam'selle. See the other two from this collection on the last page of the 1976 section: Mint Julip and Victorian Lady.

The 1976 Regal Heirloom Collection top to bottom: Bride is 18″ "Her Royal Highness" in antique color laces; 15″ "Baroness" in royal blue velveteen, white lace and pink ribbons; 16″ "Countess" baby in antique color dress, royal blue coat and bonnet; 18″ "Duchess" in royal blue gown and hat; 11″ "Crown Princess" in antique color lace bridal gown; 17″ "Princess" in antique color christening gown, blue pillow.

The Ragamuffins Collection of 1976 included top, left to right: 21″ Floppy in plain/paisley print dress, pantaloons and high snap shoes; 14″ Pint-size in pink/white check with white bonnet and red ribbon trim; 21″ in red/white check, red ribbon and white pantaloons and pinafore dress; 14″ in paisley body with white dress and bonnet. All these dolls have an all cloth body. Lower: 14″ Button Nose in pink/white check; 14″ Pint-size in red polka dot and white pinafore dress, straw hat; 14″ Button Nose either black or white; and 21″ Floppy with pale pink body, dress and bonnet.

18″ Grand Dame's "Mint Julip" dressed in pink with white over dress of lace and matching bonnet was used in 1976 only. Courtesy June Schultz.

18″ "Victorian Lady". 1975, 1976 and 1977 Grand Dames. Burgandy and off-white. Open net cotton half slip and satin full slip, pantaloons. Open crown hat with pale blonde hair pulled through in ringlet curl. Drawstring bag tied to arm. (Miss Chips). Courtesy Beverly Harrington.

16½″"Dewees Cochran" the 1977 Limited Edition doll. Head is marked: Effanbee/Ltd. Ed./1977 and back: Effanbee/Limited Edition/1977/Dewees Cockran. Courtesy June Schultz.

11″ "Pum'kin Ring Bearer" of 1977. Head is marked: Effanbee/1966. F-B, on back. White pants, blue shirt, red hair and freckles. Courtesy Renie Culp.

The 1977 set of Grand Dames were 1538: 15″ "Coquette" in red with lace tiered lower skirt, 1535: 15″ "Madame DuBarry" in pale blue with white over skirt and hair, 1537: "Lady Ashley" in white with deep wine bodice and ribbon on straw hat and lower skirt trimmed with tiny pleats. 1536: 15″ "Violetta" in all dark lavender with pale lavender trim and two roses on bonnet. 1735: 18″ "Champagne Lady" in all antique lace and was also available in black.

1734: 18″ "Mam'selle" was in antique satin with dark green overskirt and bonnet with puff hand bag. 1731: 18″ "Victorian Lady" came in deep red with inset panel of rows of lace in front and lace bonnet with red trim. 1736: 18″ "Fluerette" came in rose flowered print on beige with red ribbon trim.

15″ "Passing Parade - Gibson Girl". Navy blue skirt, matching jacket, lace ruffled organdy blouse, straw hat, slip, pantaloons, belt and pumps. 1977 and 1978 only. Courtesy Renie Culp.

15″ "Passing Parade - Colonial Lady". 1977 and 1978 only. Flowers printed on blue background with white trim overskirt, white cap, slip, pantaloons and pumps. Courtesy Renie Culp.

14″ "Flapper" of the Passing Parade Collection. This one from 1977 and 1978 only. The 1979 has dark brown "fur" muff and collar and no fur trim on hat, plus has a black belt and buttons at side of skirt. This one has black leotards, burgandy coat dress and slipper and hat. Short brown hair and blue sleep eyes. Courtesy Renie Culp.

15″ "Passing Parade 70's Woman". 1977 only. Gown of dusty-rose chiffon type material. Gold purse. The doll shown in 1978 catalog is different and has white chiffon blouse and black velveteen skirt. Courtesy Renie Culp.

15″ "Passing Parade - Civil War Lady". White organdy dress with rows of lace and multi-color embroidery, picture hat, black velvet neckband with cameo, black ribbon sash, slip, pantaloons and pumps. 1977, 1978 and 1970. Became part of Grand Dames Collection for 1980. Courtesy Renie Culp.

15″ "Passing Parade - Frontier Woman". Gray cotton dress and shawl with fringe. Matching bonnet, slip, pantaloons, pumps and velveteen carpetbag that is red with black fringe. 1977 and 1978 only. Courtesy Renie Culp.

19″ "Suzie Sunshine" #1824 of Americana Group - 1977. Head is marked: Effanbee 1961. Gown is rusty-orange and yellow with matching bonnet. The apron is yellow with multi-color trim. White lace cuffs. Freckles and blue sleep eyes. Courtesy Renie Culp.

16″ "Gumdrop" Americana - 1977. Gown is yellow with black background, apron with white/orange/yellow flowers. The bonnet matching the apron. Head is marked: Effanbee 1961, although doll was used in 1977. Courtesy Renie Culp.

11″ "Miss Germany". Marks: Effanbee /1975/1176, on head. Effanbee, on back. Braids tied with red and blue ribbon and brought to back with rubber band. Black leotards, black slippers. White half slip, gown is yellow/blue /white print on red, with attached apron and self trim and eyelet lace. Separate navy vest with red tie. 1977 and 1978 with braids down with ribbons intertwined. 1979 has braids coiled and 1980 has loose hair and hat. (Author).

11″ "Miss Switzerland" of the International Collection. Head marked: Effanbee/1975/1376. EFF & BEE, on back. This 1977 version has red skirt and ribbons, white lace attached apron and blouse. Green felt hat with yellow feather, black vest. Multi color trim on blouse. Courtesy Renie Culp.

11″ "Miss Black America" of 1977. Marks: Effanbee/1975/1976, on head and on back: EFF & BEE. There will be a variation of print. Discontinued 1980. Courtesy Renie Culp.

11″ "Pocahontas" that was made in 1977 and 1978 only. She is dressed in brown velveteen with blue trim. Marks: Effanbee 1975/1475, on head and EFF & BEE, on back. Courtesy Renie Culp.

11″ "Miss Holland" 1977. Marks: Effanbee/1975/1476, on head. EFF & BEE, on back. Blue gown with white attached apron. Red ties, ribbons and trim. White sleeves and Dutch bonnet. Wood shoes. Courtesy Renie Culp.

In 1976 three dolls made up the "Historical Collection": "Paul Revere", "Martha Washington", and "Betsy Ross". The 1976 "Betsy Ross" had a very small flowered pattern gown and this 1977 version had a larger "bouque" pattern. Courtesy Renie Culp.

11″ "Bo Peep" that is marked: Effanbee 1975/1475, on head and EFF & BEE, on shoulders. From 1977 to date. The panniers are pink, as is the bodice and ribbons. There is a small pink and blue flower print on white for the rest of the gown. Courtesy Renie Culp.

11″ Black "Tiny Tubber" that is marked: Effanbee, on the head. Dressed in white fleece flannel with blue lining and ribbons. 1977. Courtesy Renie Culp.

The 1977 Regal Heirloom Collection varied in dolls and not in colors used. The large Bride was the same, with the smaller one having an extra tier of lace at the waist, and a new style bonnet veil. The 18″ "Duchess" (available in black, too), and the "Baroness" both were given new head gear and had the skirts cut and lace inserts. The "Princess" not only had a change of gown, but a change of dolls, and the "Countess" baby came in all one color with shirred bonnet. The new one added was the 19″ "Queen Mother" in royal blue and feathers in bonnet, and cameo at neck. She holds a baby in antique color christening gown.

The Country Bumpkin Collection of 1977, eight dolls with two being offered in black. All were dressed in blue and a small blue and pink flower design material. They were: 11″ "Pun'kin" boy and girl, 18″ "Miss Chips", 19″ "Suzie Sunshine", 14″ "Pint Size", 13″ "Butterball", 18″ "Sweetie Pie".

In 1977 Effanbee offered the Vanilla Fudge Collection of six dolls that were all dressed in brown and white check with white bib fronts with brown buttons and trim. They included 11″ "Pun'kin", 19″ "Suzie Sunshine", 21″ "Floppy", 13″ "Butterball", 15″ "Little Luv" and 20″ "Sugar Plum".

Yesterday's Collection in 1977 included eleven dolls with two being offered in black (15″ "Little Luv" and 15″ "Chipper"). All were in white and dark red flowered material with black bands and trim. 11″ "Pun'kin" boy and girl, 15″ "Chipper", 18″ "Miss Chips", 19″ "Suzie Sunshine", 21″ "Floppy", 17″ "Twinkie", 14″ "Pint Size", 15″ "Little Luv", 18″ "Sweetie Pie", 20″ "Sugar Plum".

11″ "A Night on the Hudson" from the Currier and Ives Collection. Pale blue satin pantaloons, half slip and gown with white trim. Blue bonnet with white net tie, flowers and bow on top. Blue sleep eyes and brown hair. 1978 only. Courtesy Renie Culp.

11″ "Plymouth Landing" of the Currier and Ives Collection. Beige pantaloons and half slip, deep burgandy with burgandy trim. Lace on front with burgandy tie and cameo. Matching bonnet with net tie and trim. 1979 and 1980 only. The 1979 issue has wider spaced trim at hem and a shorter lace "bib". Courtesy Renie Culp.

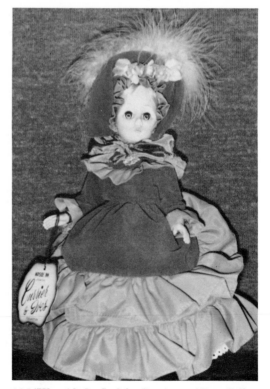

11″ "Life in the Country" of the Currier and Ives Collection. White cotton pantaloons and half slip, beige flowered gown with burgandy and lace trim and waist wrap with same trim. Matching bonnet with same trim, and cameo at neck. 1978 and 1979. Discontinued in 1980. Courtesy Renie Culp.

11″ "Wayside Inn" of the Currier and Ives Collection. Blue half slip and pantaloons with white trim. Blue ruffled gown with wide ruffle collar and sleeves. Royal blue bodice and waist wrap with wide satin ruffle. Royal blue bonnet with wide satin ruffle and four flowers and leaves. 1978 with 1979 dressed same but in green. Discontinued in 1980. Courtesy Renie Culp.

11" "Charleston Harbor" of the Currier and Ives Collection. White cotton slip and pantaloons, black slippers. Pink skirt and wrap overskirt with black trim. Pink and black hat with feather. A few came with black and beige flowers. 1980 only. Courtesy Renie Culp.

11" "Central Park" of the Currier and Ives Collection. Beige pantaloons and half slip with lace trim, tan slippers. Beige satin gown and waist wrap with two ruffles at hem. Fringe trim at sleeves, lace at neck, plus green ribbon trim and sash. Flower and green ribbon trim on waist wrap and bonnet with brown feather. 1978 only. Courtesy Renie Culp.

Boy and Girl "Skaters" from the Currier and Ives Collection. 11" boy has no lip color. Dressed in blue and white with black trim. 1978 to 1980 only. Courtesy Renie Culp.

11" "Miss Ancient Egypt". Black hair to below the waist and full bang. Extra eyebrow and eye detail and the eyes are blue. Black topless style body suit, large gold trim collar, wrap around skirt, gold strap slippers and gold head piece that snaps under chin. 1978 and 1979 only. (Author).

11" "Pavlova". White leotards and satin slippers tied with pink ribbons. Rose trim across white ballerina tutu. Pink ribbon tie at neck. Brown hair and blue sleep eyes. 1977 and discontinued in 1979. (Author).

11″ "Tinkerbelle". 1978. White boots and dress with gold trim and white net wings with gold trim. Courtesy June Schultz.

11″ "Maid Marion". 1978 and discontinued in 1979. From the Storybook Collection. Black with gold trim. Courtesy Renie Culp.

14″ "Chipper Bride". 1978 from the Bridal Suite Collection. White cotton panties and slip, hose and garter with white satin slippers. White eyelet cotton gown and head piece with net veil. Marks: Effanbee/1966, on head. (Author).

11″ "Spain" boy and girl. She has been made since 1978 to date, and he was made in 1979 and 1980 only. Both will have the same marks: Effanbee 1975/1475, on head, and EFF & BEE, on backs. Courtesy Renie Culp.

In 1978 The Passing Parade Collection included eight dolls: 1504: "Gay Nineties" in dark grey. 1503: 15″ "Civil War" in white with black trim. 1502: 15″ "Frontier Women" grey gown and shawl. 1501: 15″ "Colonial Lady" in flower print cotton and white cap. 1505: 15″ "Hourglass Look" light brown walking coat, fur trimmed bonnet and cape. 1506: 15″ "Gibson Girl" in navy blue and white. 1507: 15″ "Flapper" in red with grey collar and muff. 1508: "70's Women" black skirt and white fluffy bodice, black bow in back of hair.

11″ "Prince and Princess" were added to the Regal Heirloom Collection of 1978, which was the last year for this collection of dolls.

1535

1540

Gra
Dames

Our GRANDES DAMES coll
the "CONTINENTAL LOO
craftsmanship to create a br
ficent beauties are beyond con

1535 — 15" MADAME DU BARRY —
blue taffeta dress with embroidered panel.
Lace-trimmed organdy overskirt. Touches
of ribbon and lace in her hair. Slip, pantaloons, pumps, hankie.

1540 — 15" LADY GREY — multi-ruffled
taffeta dress with fringe and lace-trimmed
velveteen overskirt and bodice. Cameo at
neck. Matching hat with marabou. Slip,
pantaloons, pumps, pocketbook.

1735 — 18" CHAMPAGNE LADY —
organdy dress with layers of lace,
matching ruffled bonnet. Slip,
pantaloons, pumps, hankie.

1737 — 18" NICOLE — embroidered
dress with velveteen overskirt caught at side

®ALL TRADE NAMES
REGISTERED EFFANBEE 1978

*1539

1538

des
Collection

tion combines the elegance of
" with superb EFFANBEE
thtaking effect. These magni-
are!

1538 — 15" COQUETTE — dress with rows
of ruffles and lace. Scalloped velveteen
overskirt. Matching velveteen hat. Slip,
pantaloons, pumps, pocketbook.

*1539 — 15" DOWNING SQUARE — pleated
velveteen dress with lace-trimmed hem and
bodice, marabou collarette. Matching ruffled
velveteen hat. Slip, pantaloons, pumps,
pocketbook.

1736 — 18" FLEURETTE — floral print
cotton sheer dress and hat. Cameo at neck.
Slip, pantaloons, pumps, hankie.

1738 — 18" BLUE DANUBE — woven
floral taffeta dress with matching coat,
lace jabot. Straw hat with marabou. Slip,
pantaloons, pumps.

The Grand Dames Collection of 1978 included eight dolls: 1535: 15″ "Madame DuBarry" with white hair, blue gown with white overskirt. 1540: 15″ "Lady Grey" with two rows of antique color satin ruffles at hem and dark grey over skirt and purse, black trim. 1737: 18″ "Nicole" embroidered lace underskirt and deep maroon gown caught at sides with roses, cameo at neck and maribou feather in hat. 1735: 18″ "Champagne Lady" organdy gown with antique and brown color overskirt, matching bonnet and carries hankie. 1539: (Also available in black) 15″ "Downing Square" with vertical pleated skirt and wide lace at hem, bodice and sleeves; carries purse and has matching bonnet. 1538: 15″ "Coquette" with rows of ruffled lace at hem, red over dress, bonnet and purse. 1736: 18″ "Fleurette" in floral print cotton sheer gown and hat with burgundy ribbon trim. 1738: "Blue Danube" woven blue taffeta gown, puff sleeves, lace at neck, straw hat, maribou feathers.

14″ "Chipper-Auto-Train Hostess". Tag: Hi! I am Pammi your hostess doll. Welcome aboard. Marks: Effanbee/1966, on head. Purple pants with red slippers, purple back snap jacket top with red cotton inset sleeves. Yellow and red trim. Purple hat with cloth tag on front: Auto-Train. Blonde hair and blue sleep eyes. The Auto-Train ran between New York City and Miami, Florida, for a short period of time, offering to take your car aboard while you rode in the comfort of the train, and allowed you to have your car while being in Florida. (Author.)

The Limited Edition of "Skippy" and for the year of 1979. (No more than 3,485 to be made.) Head is marked: Effanbee/Ltd. Edition/Skippy/1979/-Skippy Inc/1979. Same marks are on body. Shown also is a Steiff Boxer dog. Courtesy June Schultz.

11″ "Pun'kin" from the Crochet Classics of 1979, which includes 10 dolls, but this year the "Pun'kin" came with a two piece set rather than just a dress. Also in 1980 and 1981. The outfit and bonnet are pink with a tiny blue flower near the top on one side. Courtesy June Schultz.

15″ "Lil' Suzie Sunshine" in pink cotton panties, white slippers and white gown with attached pink slip. White bows tied in hair. Of the Rainbow Parfait Collection of 1979.

11″ "Jack & Jill" with both heads marked: Effanbee/1976/1376, on heads and backs: EFF & BEE. White leotards, bodice/shirt and attached apron. Rest is blue/white check. Both carry red pails. 1979 and 1980. Courtesy Renie Culp.

11″ "Goldilocks" that has been made since 1979. The skirt is yellow, with yellow and green flowered, attached apron, white top and blue vest and ribbon in hair. Doll will be marked Effanbee 1975/1475, on the head, EFF & BEE, on the back. Courtesy Renie Culp.

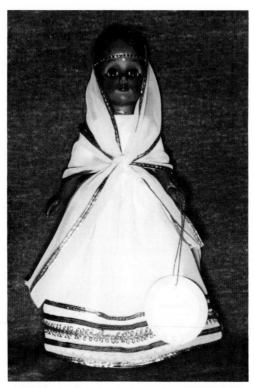

11″ "Miss India" that is dressed in blue with gold and blue trim. She was first made in 1979 and is still available. The doll will be marked Effanbee 1975/1475, on head and EFF & BEE, on back. Courtesy Renie Culp.

This 19″ "Suzie Sunshine" is from the 1979 Innocence Collection that included 11″ "Caroline" (Chipper), 15″ "Chipper", 18″ "Miss Chips", 16″ "Li'l Sizie Sunshine", 19″ "Suzie Sunshine", 11″ "Half Pint", 17″ "Twinkie", 15″ "Buttercup" and 18″ "Sweetie Pie". All are dressed in white with pink ribbon sash and trim. Only the 18″ "Sweetie Pie" was offered in black. (Author.)

14″ "The 70's Women" of the Passing Parade Collection. All these dolls are marked: Effanbee/1979/1578, on the head. Black panties and attached half slip with lace trim. Black net gown with black satin bow in front and in hair. 1979 only. Blonde hair and blue eyes. (Author).

14″ "The Hourglass Look" in 1979 only. The 1978 one has pleated ruffle at hem, "fur" trim down front and around skirt, a bonnet with brown trim and yellow gold ruffles around face. This one has off white pantaloons and half slip, gold gown with off white bodice, gold jacket with black cuffs and trim. Gold hat with large black and gold bow. Black bag tied to arm. (Author).

1979 18″ "Lady Snow" of the Grand Dames Collection. Woven floral taffeta walking coat, trimmed in black fringe and braid, matching hat. Head marked: Effanbee/1978/1776. Courtesy Renie Culp.

11″ "Castle Garden" from the Currier and Ives Collection. White cotton pantaloons and half slip. Pale blue skirt and sleeves with deep purple bodice and wrap around overskirt. White hat with blue tie, purple bow and blue flower, blonde hair and blue eyes. White shoes. 1979 and 1980 only. (Author).

1531

*1532

Gra
Dames

Our GRANDES DAMES c₀
the "CONTINENTAL L₀
craftsmanship to create a b
ficent beauties are beyond c

1531 – 15" BLUE BAYOU – pleated
taffeta dress with lace-trimmed hem
and velveteen jacket. Matching chapeau
with marabou. Slip, pantaloons, pumps,
purse.

*1532 – 15" MAGNOLIA – tiered taffeta
and lace-trimmed dress. Matching bonnet.
Slip, pantaloons, pumps, fan.

1731 – 18" LADY SNOW – woven
floral taffeta walking coat, trimmed
in fringe and braid. Matching taffeta
and velveteen hat with marabou. Slip,
pantaloons, pumps, purse.

1732 – 18" CHERRIES JUBILEE –
ruffled print dress with velveteen overskirt and bodice. Matching velveteen
hat. Cameo at neck. Slip, pantaloons,
pumps, purse.

*Black dolls are available in this style.

1533

1539

ndes®

Collection

lection combines the elegance of
₀K" with superb EFFANBEE
eathtaking effect. These magni-
mpare!

1533 – 15" EMERALD ISLE – taffeta
dress with lace and pleated underskirt.
Matching taffeta hat with flowers. Slip,
pantaloons, pumps, handkerchief.

1539 – 15" DOWNING SQUARE –
pleated velveteen dress with lace-trimmed
hem and bodice. Velveteen jacket.
Matching velveteen hat with marabou.
Cameo at neck. Slip, pantaloons, pumps,
purse.

1733 – 18" CRYSTAL – lace-trimmed
taffeta coat dress with embroidered oval
medallion on bodice. Matching taffeta
hat. Slip, pantaloons, pumps, handkerchief.

1737 – 18" NICOLE – embroidered
dress with velveteen overskirt caught
at sides with flowers. Matching veiled
chapeau. Cameo at neck. Slip, pantaloons, pumps, purse.

The Grand Dames of 1979 were: 1531: 15″ "Blue Bayou" in blue with black trim, lace near hem, jacket and purse. 1532: 15″ "Magnolia" (which also came in black) dressed in pink tiered lace with matching bonnet. 1731: "Lady Snow" in woven floral white walking coat with black fringe trim and buttons down front. 1732: 18″ "Cherries Jubilee" in ruffled, floral print skirt and red over skirt and matching bonnet. 1533: 15″ "Emerald Isle" all green taffeta gown with three rows ruffled lace at pleated hem, matching bonnet. 1539: 15″ "Downing Square" in brown pleated skirt with wide lace edging, brown feather shawl and purse. 1733: 18″ "Nicole" same as 1978. 1737: 18″ "Crystal" all in blue with white trim and oval embroidered medallion on bodice.

Keepsake® Collection

These exquisite keepsakes of yesteryear are sure to grace every collector's mantel. These timeless miniatures recall the old-fashioned days and ways of elegance and beauty.

In 1979 the Royal grouping was changed to the Keepsake Collection using the two Brides with blue flowers in bouquets, and the baby's dress is same color, but changed in design. Added are the 11″ "Pun'kin" boy in blue with black trim, spats, and girl in antique color dress, bonnet with blue ribbon trim, also with spats.

Faith Wick's dolls in vinyl. There are two sets "Anchors Aweigh" (shown) and "Party Time" which is same doll in velvet party outfits (boy and girl). Marks: Effanbee. 1979-1980. Courtesy Rose Albanese.

The 16″ "Party" boy and girl designed by Faith Wick were both available for 1979 and 1980. The girl is dressed in burgandy and the boy in blue.

1561

1562

The Passing Parade®

1561 — 15" COLONIAL LADY — calico print dress and embroidery trimmed overskirt, cap. Cameo at neck. Slip, pantaloons, pumps.

1562 — 15" FRONTIER WOMAN — gingham dress with apron and fringe-trimmed shawl. Matching bonnet, slip, pantaloons, shoes, carpet-bag.

1565 — 15" THE HOUR GLASS LOOK — lace-trimmed velveteen skirt and jacket. Blouse with tucked jabot. Cameo at neck. Matching velveteen lace-trimmed hat. Slip, pantaloons, pumps, purse.

1566 — 15" GIBSON GIRL — braid-trimmed skirt, with tucked and lace-trimmed "gibson" blouse. Cameo at neck. Buckled belt, braid and velveteen-trimmed straw hat. Slip, pantaloons, pumps.

EFFANBEE'S salute to the American Woman. A sparkling array of classic beauties depicting changing styles in an ever-changing world. Every doll lover is sure to long for each and every one of the "PASSING PARADE".

1563

1564

1563 — 15" CIVIL WAR LADY — white organdy dress with rows of lace and multi-color embroidery, picture hat, cameo at neck. Slip, pantaloons, pumps, fan.

1564 — 15" GAY NINETIES — fringe-trimmed velveteen skirt, lace-trimmed velveteen jacket, lace jabot, cameo at neck. Matching velveteen bonnet with marabou, slip, pantaloons, pumps, purse.

1567 — 15" FLAPPER — Velveteen coat dress with pleats and fur collar. Buckled belt. Velveteen cloche. Fur muff, stockings, pumps.

1568 — 15" THE 70'S WOMAN — "point d'esprit" net ruffled gown, overlying a lace-edged taffeta slip. Dress accented with satin bow and jewels. Panties, stockings, pumps.

The Passing Parade dolls of 1979 included: 1562: 15″ "Colonial Lady" in blue flowered cotton. 1561: 15″ "Frontier Women" in blue/white check, gown and poke bonnet, white apron, dark brown shawl and deep beige purse with dark brown fringe. 1565: "The Hour Glass Look" in deep gold with black trim. 1566: 15″ "Gibson Girl" with black skirt with white trim, white blouse and hat with black trim. 1563: 15″ "Civil War Lady" in white organdy and a "Scarlett" look, pink ribbon on hat and black ribbon at waist and wrist. 1564: "Gay Nineties" in blue with black trim and buttons down front, matching bonnet, and black jacket style bodice with lace. 1567: 15″ "Flapper" in red with three side buttons and black vest, deep brown fur collar and purse. 1568: 15″ "The 70's Women" all in black with stand up collar and ribbon in hair.

1979 18″ "Bride" with the Nicole face, 15″ "Bridesmaid", with the Caroline face and the boy and girl "Pun'kin" from the Bridal Suite Collection. The Bridesmaid, Ringbearer and Flowergirl are in white over blue slip and have blue on the bodice, blue flowers and blue pillow. Courtesy Hazel Adams.

1979 "Bride" with the Caroline face. There was a matching 15″ "Chipper Bride" with the "Chipper" being available in black. From the Bridal Suite Collection. Courtesy Hazel Adams.

This 11″ "Miss Black America" is from the 1979 International Collection, and the last year this doll was made. The print is grey, white on rust. Courtesy Hazel Adams.

1979 15″ "Little Lovums" in white wicker bed on wheels and with handle. Dressed in long christening gown and on pink pillow with wide organdy ruffle.

The "Ship Ahoy" Collection was not offered through the Effanbee catalog in 1980, but were offered through a special flyer sent to all customers. They are all dressed in red/white and blue and tagged with each dolls name. (Author)

15″ "Susan B. Anthony Commemorative Doll" that was the 1980 Limited Edition Club doll. (No more than 3,485 made). Head is marked: S.B.Anthony/Limited Edition/Effanbee. Body is marked: Susan B. Anthony/Effanbee Doll/Ltd. Edition/1980. A Commemorative U.S. Dollar is included with the doll. Courtesy Renie Culp.

11″ "Sunday - Is bonny, blithe, good and gay" from the Day by Day Collection. Head marked Effanbee/1980/1480 and back: F-B. Red choir robe with white top and tied with red bow. 1980, 1981. Courtesy Renie Culp.

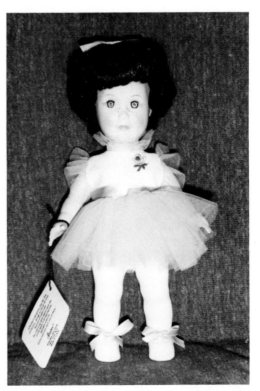

11″ "Monday - Child is fair of face" of the Day by Day Collection. Marks: Effanbee/1980/1480, on head and F-B, on back. White pantaloons and pinafore with pink ribbon trim. The dress is pink, slippers are white and she carries a blue mirror. 1980, 1981. Courtesy Renie Culp.

11″ "Tuesday - Child is full of grace" from the Day by Day Collection. Head is marked: Effanbee/1980/1480 and back: F-B. Blue net skirt on tutu as well as sleeves, neck, ribbon in hair and ties on slippers. Bodice and slippers and leotards are white. 1980, 1981. Courtesy Renie Culp.

11″ "Wednesday - Child is free of woe" Day to Day Collection. Dress is red and white check ruffled hem and sleeves, plus red rickrack and buttons. Red ribbons in hair, straw hat tied with black ribbon. Carries jump rope. 1980, 1981. Courtesy Renie Culp.

11″ "Thursday - Child has far to go" from the Day by Day Collection. Dress/coat is green with matching bonnet, white "fur" trim on bonnet and scarf. White ribbon and rose on hat. Marks: Effanbee/1980/1480. 1980, 1981. Courtesy Renie Culp.

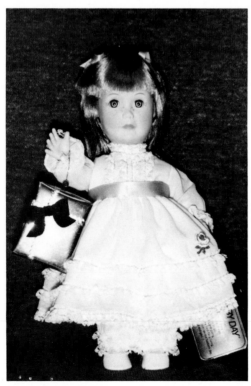

11″ "Friday - Child is loving and giving", Day by Day Collection. Dress is all white with applied blue rose on skirt, blue ribbon at waist and in hair. Carries gift box tied to wrist. 1980, 1981. Courtesy Renie Culp.

11″ "Saturday - Child works hard for a living", Day by Day Collection. Head is marked: Effanbee 1980/1480. Marked on back: F-B. The dress is multi color patch work with white pinafore apron with red trim. The scarf is yellow and she carries a red plastic bucket. 1980, 1981. Courtesy Renie Culp.

"Clown". White vinyl head with painted features. All original and marked: Effanbee/1979/Faith Wick, on head and: Faith Wick Originals/Clown, on back. Courtesy Renie Culp.

"Girl Clown". All vinyl with rooted red hair and blue sleep eyes. Original. Designed by doll artist Faith Wick. Marks: Effanbee/1979/Faith Wick, on head. No marks on body. Introduced in 1980. Courtesy Renie Culp.

11″ "Half Pint" boy and girl from the Cotton Candy Collection. Heads are marked: 10ME/Effanbee/1966. Dress, shirt and bonnets are pink/white check. White shoes and socks. 1980. Courtesy Renie Culp.

11″ "Crystal Palace" of the 1980 only Currier and Ives Collection. Marks: Effanbee/1979/1279. On back: EFF & BEE. Bonnet is ringed with brown feather fur, cameo at neck and wide beige sash around waist. Courtesy Renie Culp.

11″ "Davy Crockett". Brown and tan with green bodice, "fur" hat, brown sleep eyes, with no lip color. Marks: Effanbee/1975/1176, on head. Effanbee, on back. Brown hair is shoulder length with full bangs. 1977 and 1978 only. 11″ "Prince Charming" white leotards, black slippers with silver buckles. Royal blue body suit, white sleeves, gold belt. Royal blue cape with gold trim. Lace collar and royal blue hat with feather. Blonde with full bangs. Blue sleep eyes and no lip color. 1980. (Author).

11″ "Cinderella" of 1980. Head is marked: Effanbee/1975/1476 and back: EFF & BEE. The gown is white with silver dots and silver crown. Courtesy Renie Culp.

11″ "Miss Brazil" with basic black gown with red/yellow/green and white. The doll will be marked Effanbee 1975/1475, on head. EFF&BEE, on back. Introduced in 1980 and still available. 1980 saw the beginning of using a new style wrist tag on the International dolls. Courtesy Renie Culp.

11″ "Greece" (Soldier) that was made in 1980 only. He is dressed in white with red and has gold trim. The mustache is painted into the vinyl. (Author).

16″ "Monique" in all antique color with blue sash and ribbons has brown hair, and 11″ "Mimi" wears blue under white lace with red hair. Both are from the Petite Filles Collection that was made in 1980 only. (Author).

16″ "Giselle" with burgandy dress that has a two tier skirt, blonde hair and lace trim, and 11″ "Madeleine" dressed in red with white lace trim are both from the Petite Filles Collection and only made in 1980. (Author).

16″ "Lili" from the Petite Filles Collection, dressed in white with pink trim and ribbons. Made in 1980 only. (Author).

16″ "Gabrielle" in deep green with white trim and red hair, and 11″ "Babette" in antique color satin with floral print and dark brown hair are from the Petite Filles Collection and made in 1980 only. (Author).

11″ "Brigitte" of the Petite Filles Collection. Marks: Effanbee/1966. Using the Half Pint doll in 1980 only. Courtesy Renie Culp.

11″ "Pun'kin" from the Rhapsody in Blue Collection of 1980, white bodice, deep blue skirt and ribbon and much lace trim. Also in this collection, and dressed in the same manner were: "Miss Chips", 20″ "Sugar Plum", 18″ "Sweetie Pie", 16″ "L'il Suzie Sunshine", 15″ "Buttercup" and 15″ "Chipper". (Author).

"Baby Lisa" who is all vinyl, 11″ tall and modeled beautifully. Designed by Astry Campbell the past president and member of the National Institute of American Doll Artists (N.I.A.D.A.). The first Baby Lisa was made in porcelain, and is part of a permanent collection at the Smithsonian Institute. She was also available in diaper/top and tied to blanket and in a wicker basket with layette. (Author).

Created exclusively for the Smithsonian Institution.

"My Friend" doll, created for the Smithsonian by Effanbee, looks very much like the coy young Miss wearing a flowered bonnet in the 19th-century lithograph, "My Friend and I." The hand-colored print, part of the Peters Collection in the Cultural History Collections at the National Museum of History and Technology, was made by E. B. and E. C. Kellogg in New York. The taffeta gown with lace ruffles captures the sentimentality and charm of this Victorian print.

The above is from the card that comes with the doll. Courtesy June Schultz.

11″ "My Friend" doll was made especially for the Smithsonian Institute during 1980. The doll looks very much as the 19th Century lithograph "My Friend and I". Dressed in red taffeta with lace ruffles on pink satin and matching bonnet. The doll did not come with a certificate, but was limited to the 1980 production year. Photo is from the Smithsonian catalog for 1980.

The Grand Dames of 1980 included 1574: 15″ "Hyde Park" in deep blue with wide lace collar and trim. 1774: 18″ "Night at the Opera" . . . see separate photo. 1773: 18″ "La Vie en Rose" . . . see separate photo. 1573: 15″ "Magnolia" in pink satin, sash, bonnet and white lace. 1771: 18″ "Coco" in antique lace and black coat, wide V collar and beige feather in hat. 1571: "Jezebel" which is same doll that was used in the previous Passing Parade Collection. 1572: 15″ "Ruby" and only one available in black . . . see separate photo. 1772: "Carnegie Hall" in antique satin gown and deep green bonnet, cape, coat, purse.

18″ "La Vie en Rose" came in floral print soft satin with two rows of ruffles at hem, burgandy sash and came with both plain white hat and one with ribbon around crown. 1980 only. (Author).

15″ "Ruby" of Grand Dames of 1980 is dressed in red with black lace, short black jacket and hat with large red bow. (Author).

18″ "Night at the Opera" is dressed in black and has a wide lace portion to skirt. There is a variation to the lace used. Black cape with maribou at neck. (Author). 1980 only.

This is the black version of the Grand Dames "Ruby" of 1980. Courtesy Hazel Adams.

18″ "Coco" from the 1980 Grand Dames Collection. She is shown in the Effanbee catalog as having the Nicole face, but this one has the enlarged Caroline face. Courtesy Hazel Adams.

In 1980 the "Civil War Lady" from the discontinued Passing Parade Collection was added to the Grand Dames Collection as "Jezebel". She is 15″ tall. Courtesy Hazel Adams.

11″ Black "Bride" from the Keepsake Collection of 1980. Limited Edition of only 50 dolls. Uses the smaller Caroline face. Courtesy Hazel Adams.

15″ Black "Chipper" from the Cotton Candy Collection of 1980. In pink and white check with white pinafore and flowered embroidery trim. Courtesy Hazel Adams.

15″ "Bride" from the 1980 Bridal Suite Collection. Uses the Caroline face. Was also available in white. Courtesy Hazel Adams.

18″ "Bride" using the Nicole face from the 1980 Bridal Suite Collection. Courtesy Hazel Adams.

Rhapsody In Blue Collection of 1980. All the dolls are dressed in royal blue and white and their names and sizes appear under each doll.

11″ "Mother Goose" from the Storybook Collection. The skirt is yellow with attached white apron, bodice and blue trim and shawl with deeper blue fringe. The hat is peaked with a yellow tip, blue band and white ruffle, plus blue tie. Along with new (1980) wrist tag is a tag with "Tales of Mother Goose" that contains verses from various favorites. New in 1981. (Author).

11″ "Mother Hubbard" of the Storybook Collection dressed in green with white pinafore apron and multi color trim. The bonnet is yellow with white lace. New in 1981 is the wooden handled broom. She was introduced in 1980. (Author).

11″ "Mary Had A Little Lamb" was introduced in 1981 and is one of the prettiest of the Storybook Collection. Very soft material dress that has a very light embossed "Effanbee" printed on it, along with tiny pink hearts and flowers. Matching poke bonnet and pink braid trim. A paper lamb is tied to her wrist. (Author).

The 11″ "Pinocchio" has an elongated red nose, deeper cheek color and lips, short brown hair and is dressed in dark orange short pants attached to yellow top with wide white collar. Black vest and buttons with orange felt hat with yellow feather. White felt mitts on hands and over-size black shoes. The bow tie is blue. New in 1981. (Author).

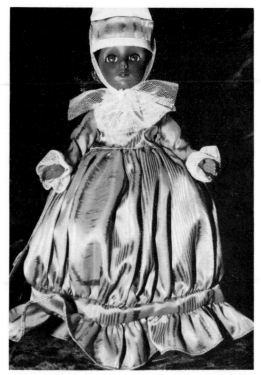

11″ "Francoise" of the Grand Dames Collection. A black doll that was limited to 125, and came with certificate and number. They were made exclusively for Treasure Trove (19 Village Road, Manhasset, NY 11030) and Effanbee is now producing a Limited Edition of 300 black "Miss Black United States", dressed in cowboy outfit. Courtesy Hazel Adams.

11″ "Peaches and Cream" of the Grand Dames Collection and limited to 125. Made in 1981 for Treasure Trove. Courtesy Hazel Adams.

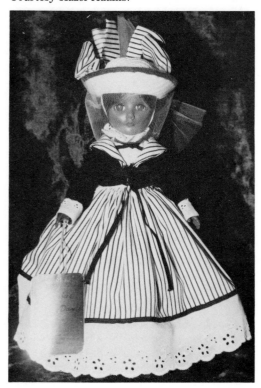

11″ "Saratoga" of the Grand Dames Collection and made in 1981 exclusively for Treasure Trove. Limited to 125. Courtesy Hazel Adams.

11″ "Lady Ascot" of the Grand Dames Collection and limited to a 125 production especially for Treasure Trove. Courtesy Hazel Adams.

11″ "Heidi" of 1981 with dark blue dotted skirt, white bodice with lace. The embroidered floral band is attached to waist and head gear is matching with a black back, and red ties. The 1980 version had a floral and striped skirt. She was first introduced in 1980. There can be a variation of skirt and trim during both years. (Author).

There were three "Huggables" or "Floppies" in 1981. This one is "Alice In Wonderland". There were also "Little Bo Peep" and "Little Red Riding Hood". All pink cloth stuffed bodies and limbs with removable blue dress with white pinafore. blue ribbon and braid trim. Blue ribbon in long blonde hair. Black patent high tie up shoes. (Author).

16″ "Renoir's Girl With the Watering Can" is the 1981 Effanbee's Limited Edition Club doll, and their seventh presentation. She has painted eyes. the marks are: Effanbee/Ltd. Edition/Renoir/-1981, on head. Effanbee/Ltd Edition/Renoir/-1981, on back. Courtesy Renie Culp.

15″ in catalog, but actually only measuring 13″ is this 1981 Bridesmaid from the Bridal Suite Collection. She wears a blue slip under a white organdy gown with pale pink, yellow and blue bands and has blue and pink flowers over her head. Courtesy Hazel Adams.

Grandes Dames™ Collection

1758 — 18" TOPAZ
1759 — 18" TURQUOISE
1556 — 15" CHANTILLY
1559 — 15" SHAUNA

The 1981 Grand Dames Collection included: 1758: "Topaz" in brown with deep lace collar and tall hat. 1759: 18″ "Turquoise" in rich blue with sides pulled up to reveal lace over blue at hem. 1556: "Chantilly" in pink with wide lace hem, cameo at neck and bonnet. 1559: 15″ "Shauna" is dressed in all green with side ruffle drape and beige feather hat. 1159: 11″ "Saratoga" in black and white stripe and white eyelet at hem. 1157: 11″ "Lady Ascot" in white with brown dotted over skirt and bodice and large ribbon on hat.

Our "Grandes Dames" — Collection combines the elegance of "European" couture with superb EFFANBEE craftsmanship to create a breathtaking effect, from the finely worked lace, to the touches of maribou, to the delicate designs . . . what could be more elegant? What could be more EFFANBEE?

By popular demand our collection has expanded! Now the Grandes Dames are available in 3 different sizes (11″, 15″ and 18″).

1757 — 18" OPAL
1756 — 18" DAPHNE
1558 — 15" GRAMERCY PARK
1557 — 15" COVENT GARDEN
*1158 — 11" PEACHES AND CREAM

1558: "Gramercy Park" in red with rows of lace and satin ruffles at hem, matching bonnet. 1756: 18″ "Daphne" all in rich brown with white lace mid-skirt and on sleeves. 1757: 18″ "Opal" all in white with antique color braid trim, pale brown sash and ribbon. 1156: 11″ "Francoise" is gowned all in deep peach with rose in hat and hem band above ruffled hem. 1158: 11″ "Peaches and Cream" is in pale peach with three tucks on skirt and wide lace at hem, on bodice. 1557: 15″ "Convent Garden" is blue floral print with blue pinafore style apron and matching bonnet. The "Peaches and Cream" was only one available in black.

1981

Petite Filles™ Collection

3641 – 16" DENISE

9541 – 18" BÉBÉ DENISE

3643 – 16" MARIANNE

9543 – 18" BÉBÉ MARIANNE

Effanbee has specially colored these vinyl faces to look like porcelain . . . and has mastered the unique painting techniques to reproduce that distinctive look of "old world" European craftsmanship. Each of the four lavishly dressed Bébés have an older sister to match.

9544 – 18" BÉBÉ NANETTE

3644 – 16" NANETTE

9542 – 18" BÉBÉ GENEVIEVE

3642 – 16" GENEVIEVE

The 1981 Petite Filles Collection had a complete change of faces with the "little girl" dolls having extra heavy painted eyes and darker brows. 3641: 16" "Denise" and 9541: 18" "Bebe' Denise" are dressed in white with antique color trim and ribbons. 3643: 16" "Marianne" and 18" "Bebe' Marianne" are in royal blue with white lace. The older girls have brown eyes and babies have blue eyes. 9544: "Bebe' Nanette" and 3644: 16" "Nanette" are dressed in blue with wide lace hems and blue ribbons. 9542: 18" "Bebe' Genevieve" and 3642: 16" "Genevieve" are in rust with pleated skirts and lace collars.

236

Pride of the South™ Collection

Return with us to the days of yesteryear in the "Old South". This collection of six 13" dolls evokes memories of elegant plantations, majestic riverboats and the smell of fragrant magnolias. Each one is elegantly attired for an afternoon of socializing and mint juleps . . . But watch out for the Riverboat Gambler!

3333 – MOBILE

3336 – CHARLESTON

3332 – NATCHEZ

3331 – RIVERBOAT GAMBLER

3334 – SAVANNAH

The Pride of the South Collection which is new in 1981 includes: 3333: 13" "Mobile" in pale pink and lace tiered skirt. 3336: "Charleston" in floral print with floral and stripe ruffles at hem. 3332: "Natchez" in pale peach with darker peach flower print. 3331: "Riverboat Gambler" in burgandy and black. 3335: "New Orleans" in pale green with overlace and long brim bonnet. 3334: "Savannah" in blue with white eyelet overskirt and straw hat.

The 1981 Smithsonian Institute doll made by the Effanbee Company was called "Lady With The Velvet Hat". In maroon taffeta with white collar and feather. Costume is based on a 19th century lithograph, "THE VELVET HAT" that is in the National Museum of American History. 14" and used the Caroline face. Photo is from the catalog offered to members of the Smithsonian.

Send In The Clowns™ Collection

A hush falls over the audience as the curtain goes up. Effanbee's new elegantly sophisticated Pierrots are ready to perform. Some stand erect waiting for the next curtain call, while their soft bodied companions pose in a dramatic fashion.

7745 – 18" PIERROT

5545 – 15" PIERROT

2245 – 11" PIERROT

4545 – 15" PIERROT – Soft Body

4745 – 18" PIERROT – Soft Body

The "Send In The Clowns Collection" was new in 1981. Some have plastic bodies and others have cloth bodies. All have sleep eyes, are dressed in white with red poms and tops of heads are black vinyl. They come in sizes 11", 15" and 18".

16″ "Hattie Holiday" using the Li'l Suzie Sunshine doll. Christmas is a red coat and bonnet with gold wrapped "gift", Easter is a pale blue dress, straw hat with flowers and tied with a blue ribbon, July 4th is a red and white Majorette outfit and Halloween is a multi color gown with black mask. The dolls can be bought in each outfit, or the Easter, July 4th and Halloween can be purchased separately. New for 1981.

The older set of the Four Seasons (discontinued in 1980) used the 11″ size "lady" doll, whereas the new 1981 set use the same doll that make up the "Days of the Week" Collection. Summer is dressed in white, Spring in yellow, Autumn in rusty red and Winter in white and plaid.

In 1981 Effanbee offered two witches in the Craftsmen's Corner Collection. Both designed by Faith Wick. The "Hearth Witch" has a lavender check poke bonnet, floral pattern cotton dress shawl with fringe and white apron, and carries a broom. The "Wicked Witch" is in all black with red lined shawl and carries an apple, plus basket. Both have same head with tongues out one corner of mouth.

16″ "Peddler Women" selling lace, yarn and flowers is part of the 1981 Craftsmen's Corner with face designed by Faith Wick. The bonnet and cape are red.

17″ "John Wayne" was made by Effanbee in 1981 and limited to one years production. He is the second in the Legend Series with the 1980 being W. C. Fields. A portion of the royalties paid will go to the John Wayne Memorial Cancer Fund. He comes with his exclusively recreated saddle carbine. Courtesy Marilyn Hitchcock.

11″ "Miss Amanda" made for the Amway Corporation is dressed in peach skirt, cream bodice and sleeves with peach yoke, lace at hem, and detachable lace collar. Feather on peach color ribbon tied in hair. Tan slippers. she has the smaller Nicole face.

The Legend Series was first introduced in 1980 with the "W. C. Fields" doll, and in 1981 Effanbee introduced the second in this extremely popular series, which was an older looking John Wayne, and in 1982 the younger John Wayne as "Guardian of the West". He is 18″ tall and authentically dressed in a Cavalry uniform. One third of the royalties paid for each John Wayne doll go to the John Wayne Memorial Cancer Research Fund at U.C.L.A. and each are produced for one year only.

The 1982 Legend Series include the "John Wayne" and "Mae West." The Mae West doll is 18″ tall, and looks just as she did on the vaudeville stage, and in early movies. She will be made for just one year, and is the fourth in the Legend Series.

13″ "Orange Blossom" is a Chinese little girl and was designed by doll artist Joyce Stafford. Effanbee has the exclusive rights to reproduce this fine porcelain doll in vinyl, and "Orange Blossom" joins the Craftsmen Corner of the Effanbee doll line.

11″ "Just Friends" series: top are the "Alpine Hikers" boy and girl, center left and lower left are the "Swiss Yodelers", and far right and lower right, the "Dutch Treat" set. They all come single or you can purchase a set. New in 1982.

11″ "Bobbsey Twins", Flossie and Freddie are based on the Bobbsey Twin storybooks and are new in 1982. The boy has molded hair and the girl has rooted hair, both have sleep eyes. They come in school plaid outfits, but four separately packaged outfits are available for them: top, Out West and Go A' Sailing. Lower, left, At the Seashore and Winter Wonderland.

13" Absolutely Abigail Collection, top: left is "Recital Time" and center is "Strolling in the Park." Lower left is the boy "Cousin Jeremy," center is "Sunday Best" and right: "Afternoon Tea." All are new for 1982. The boy has freckles under each eye.

The 1982 Faith Wick Originals include the 16" "Peddler Women" and 16" "Clown Girl." New in 1982 is the 16" "Billy Bum" and 18" "Santa Claus."

INDEX

The following listing (Chronology) is for quick reference by NAME of the doll to find the YEAR the doll was first introduced. From there you can get the complete information by checking that year in the CHRONOLOGY. You may also check the following years to see how long that particular doll was produced.

ABOUT PRICING & COLLECTING

A great number of Effanbee dolls have always been highly collectible, and as time goes on more will become so. The "Patsy" family and other compositions can be found in many collections, with some collectors working exclusively in that area. The really fine hard plastic Effanbee doll is so elusive that when found, it too, will most likely be in private collections. The vinyl and plastic have never been taken seriously, except by a few smart collectors. The current trends indicate that more and more will be sold and traded. Newer collectors will continue to seek out the dolls of certain "Collections" or "Series" and as the search continues it is very likely that the prices for the top lines of Effanbee dolls will continue.

There are three major eras of modern dolls: composition, hard plastic, and vinyl/plastic. The condition of each is most important in pricing.

COMPOSITION: It is rare to find a composition doll completely mint and in the original box. If you do, you can price that item way above book prices, as book prices are based on nice clean, near mint dolls. MINT means there are no cracks or crazing, the doll is extra clean and unplayed with, and has all its original clothes and tags. EXCELLENT: The doll may have very light crazing, the clothes may be washed, but otherwise it is a mint doll. GOOD: The doll may have a couple of small cracks, light crazing, original clothes are dirty, and it can be with or without original tags. FAIR: The doll is not original, the wig may or may not be original, it has extensive crazing, but only small cracks, and the shoes are gone. POOR: The doll may be nude and it has severe crazing and several cracks and chips.

HARD PLASTICS: Once is awhile a mint-in-the-box doll will be found and will command much higher than book prices. MINT: An unplayed with, all original doll with original tags. EXCELLENT: The wig may be slightly messed up, clothes original but washed, but it has original tags. GOOD: The original clothes may be dirty, wig mussed and undies may be missing. FAIR: The doll is not original, the wig maybe replaced, the hard plastic shows wear at the joints, and may even be slightly soiled. POOR: The doll may be nude, no wig or a replaced one, and may be dirty.

VINYL/PLASTIC: Many will be found mint in the box. MINT: Same as being in the box, but the box is missing. All original with original tags and unplayed with. EXCELLENT: Hair may be slightly mussed, clothes are original, but may have been washed. Doll has original tags, if any. GOOD: The hair may be mussed or slightly trimmed, clothes may be dirty and doll has no tags, or perhaps undies and shoes. FAIR: Dressed nicely, but not original, hair needs a lot of work, and the vinyl may be dirty, but washable. POOR: The doll may be nude, hair cut, and have felt tip marks on its head or body.

THIS PRICE GUIDE IS JUST THAT, A GUIDE NOT THE FINAL WORD. The prices are bound to rise on Effanbee dolls made of vinyl/plastic. Those of composition and hard plastic are already quite high priced. The later ladies of 16" – 21" will be of special interest to the collectors, as well as, all the characters and personalities.

Besides the *Effanbee Dolls, Dolls That Touch Your Heart* book by Patricia R. Smith, the author recommends *Effanbee, A Collector's Encyclopedia* by John Axe.

The Effanbee Doll Company enjoyed taking renowned artists and having them design for their doll line, listed in catalogs under the title "Craftmens Corner." The dolls are marked with the name of the designer.

FAITH WICK:	1979	Party Time Boy & Girl.
		Anchors Aweigh Boy & Girl
		Clown: two different,
		painted faces.
	1991 – 1992	Peddler Women
		Wicket and Hearth Witches
		Nast Santa
		Old Fashioned Billy Bum
	1982 – 1983	Bobbsey Twins (boy & girl)
ASTRY CAMPBELL:	1980	Baby Lisa
JOYCE STAFFORD:	1982	Orange Blossom, changed to Lotus Blossom in 1983
	1983	Little Tiger (boy)
JAN HAGARA:	1983	Christine
	1984	Laurel
	1985	Larry and Lesley, Belina and Bobby
EDNA HIBEL:	1984	Flower Girl and Contessa.

EFFANBEE VALUE GUIDE

ABRAHAM LINCOLN, 1983,18", Presidents Collection . . . 75.00
ABSOLUTELY ABIGAIL, 1982–1983, 13", includes Cousin Jeremy, Sunday Best, Recital Time, Strolling in the Park and Afternoon Tea. See the names for prices.
AFTERNOON TEA, 1982–1983, 13", Absolutely Abigail . .30.00
AGE OF ELEGANCE COLLECTION, 18", see the following for price: Buckingham Palace, Versailles, Victoria Station, and Westminster Cathedral, Roma, Gay Paree.
AIRMAN, 1919, 16", composition and cloth 195.00
ALICA, 1986, 15", Grande Dames Collection 50.00
ALICE, 1958
    15", hard plastic (Honey) . . . . 365.00 up
    19"–20", hard plastic (Honey) . . . . 500.00 up
ALICE IN WONDERLAND, 1977–1993
    11–11½" 30.00
    1977–1978, Disney exclusive, 14" 275.00
    1981–1982, huggable. 14", cloth body & limbs 25.00
    1986–1987, 19" 95.00
ALPINE HIKER, 1982, Just Friends (Half Pint) 40.00
ALYSSA, 1958–1963
    19", hard plastic/vinyl head 250.00
    23"–24", all vinyl, jointed elbows 385.00
AMANDA
    1982, 11", Grande Dames Collection 40.00
    1987–1989, 17", Little Old New York Collection . . 70.00
AMELIA, 1984, 15" Black, Grande Dames Collection . . . 65.00
AMERICAN BEAUTY COLLECTION, 1979, dolls wear velveteen dress with organdy apron
    11" Pun' Kin 20.00
    15" Chipper 25.00
    15" Black Chipper 40.00
    Li'l Suzie Sunshine 30.00
    15" Butterball 20.00
    18" Suzie Sunshine 40.00
    15" Buttercup 20.00
    18" Sweetie Pie 50.00
    20" Sugar Plum 40.00
    15" Little Luv 20.00
    20" Sugar Plum 40.00
AMERICAN CHILDREN, 1936–1940
    15", composition 650.00
    18" 700.00
    20"–21" . . . . 1,250.00 up.
    17" with music box, Birthday doll . . . . 850.00 up
AMERICANA, See Spirit of '76.
AMISH
    1939, 7"–8", composition 245.00
    1930s, 9", composition 255.00
    1930s, 12" 275.00
AMOSANDRA, 1936, 9"–10", black composition, three tufts hair 175.00
AMY
    1985, 15", Grande Dames Collection 75.00
    1986, 13", Little Women 70.00
    1989, 9", Li'l Innocent Collection 20.00
ANCHORS AWEIGH COLLECTION, 1972, dolls dressed in red, white, and blue
    17" Miss Chips 50.00
    20" Sugar Plum 40.00
    16" Baby Button Nose 30.00
    24" Precious Baby 45.00
    15" Chipper 30.00

ANCHORS AWEIGH BOY AND GIRL, 1979–1980, 16", sailor suits, designed by Faith Wick, character faces . . . . . 40.00 ea.
ANDREW JACKSON, 1990, 16", Presidents Series 85.00
ANNE OF GREEN GABLES
    14" All composition, 1937 . . . . .800.00
    15" 350.00
    18" 600.00
    21" 800.00
    22" 1,000.00
    28" 1,100.00
    Yarn hair and cloth body
    18" 550.00
    23" 775.00
    Hard plastic, 1950–1955
    15" . . . . 450.00 up.
    18" . . . . 600.00 up.
    21" 785.00
ANTIQUE BRIDE, 1979–1981, Keepsake Collection
    11" 20.00
    17" (Miss Chips) 40.00
APRIL
    1987, Rememberance Series, 11" 20.00
    1988–1990, 11", Special Moments of Month 20.00
ARGENTINA, 11", International Series 20.00
ART CARNEY AS ED NORTON, 1986, Great Moments on T. V. Series, 16¼" 75.00
ATLANTA, 1981–1982, 13", Pride of the South 35.00
AUDREY, 1989, 9", Little Innocents Collection 15.00
AUGUST
    1987, 11", Rememberance Series 20.00
    1989–1990, 11", Special Moments of Month 20.00
AUNT DINAH, 1916, 14", composition and cloth 285.00
AUNTIE EM, 1989–1990, 9", Wizard of Oz Collection . . 25.00
AUSTRIA, 1982, 11", International Collection 20.00
AUTO TRAIN HOSTESS, 1979, 15" (Chipper) 40.00
AUTUMN, 1976–1980, 11", Four Seasons Collection . . . 20.00
BABE RUTH, 1985, 16½", Great Moments Collection . . 85.00
BABETTE, 1980, 11" (Half Pint), Petite Filles 25.00
BABY BEAUTIES, 1973 (Sears)
    11" Black Butterball 35.00
    16" Baby Face 40.00
    14" Little Luv, cloth/vinyl 20.00
    11" Button Nose 20.00
    12" Baby Winkie 20.00
BABY BLANCHE, 1918, 15", cloth/composition 245.00
BABY BLUE, 1919, 12" 165.00
BABY BODKINS, 1915
    11" 225.00
    15" 365.00
BABY BROTHER & SISTER, 1940, composition
    9" 165.00
    11" 200.00
BABY BUDS, 1919 – 1920, 7", composition 145.00
BABY BUNTING, 1917, 16", cloth/composition 195.00
BABY BUTTERBALL, see Butterball.
BABY BUTTON NOSE, see Button Nose.
BABY CUDDLE-UP, 1953–1954, two lower teeth, cloth/vinyl
    20" 50.00
    23" 75.00
    27" 55.00
    1967 – 1968, 16", cloth/vinyl 30.00
    Black 40.00

Baby Cupcake, see Cupcake.
Baby Effanbee, 1925, 12", composition 185.00
Baby Evelyn, 1925, 18" 265.00
Baby Face, 1967–1969, 1973–1977, 1983, 16", toddler . . 40.00
Baby Face Collection, 1976–1977
    16" . . . . 40.00 ea.
    Black 55.00
Baby Grumpy, see Grumpy.
Baby Huggins, 1913–1925
    9" 165.00
    16" 290.00
Baby Lisa, by Astri, 1980–1982
    11", painted eyes 100.00
    In wicker case/layette . . . . 185.00 up
Baby Peaches, 1965, 16" (Sears) 40.00
Baby Pink, 1919, 12", composition 145.00
Baby Snowball, 1915, 12" 285.00
Baby Tinyette, 1932–1933, 8"
    Composition, baby 265.00
    Toddler 285.00
Baby Winkie, see Winkie.
Baby Wonder, 1935, 16" 265.00
Baby-Kin
    1940–1949, 9"–12", composition 185.00
    1952–1959, 10", hard plastic 100.00
    1966–1977, 8", vinyl 20.00
    1985, 14", Pretty as Picture Collection 30.00
    1986, 14", Gotcha Collection 30.00
Babyette, 1942–1946, composition
    12" 250.00
    16" 365.00
Ballerina, 1987 (Dancing School)
    11", Effanbee's Favorites Series, 1989 . . . . . . .30.00 ea.
    11", Joyous Occasions Series . . . . 30.00 ea.
Barbara, 1985, 15", Grande Dames Collection 50.00
Barbara Ann, 1930s, 18", composition . . . . 700.00 up
Barbara Joan, 1930s. 15", composition . . . . 600.00 up
Barbara Lee, 1924, 29" 360.00
Barbara Lou, 1936, 20"–21", composition . . . . . . 950.00 up
Baroness, 1976–1977, 17", Regal Heirloom Collection
    (Miss Chips) 45.00
Bea, 1940, 11", in trunk, composition 200.00
Beach Baby, 1923, 16", composition 190.00
Beautee-Skin Baby, 1944
    14" rubber/latex 45.00
    17" 65.00
    19" 85.00
Becky, 1989, 9", Bride, Li'l Innocents Collection 20.00
Becky Thacher, 1984–1985, Great Moments In
    Literature 50.00
Bedtime Collection, 1972, dolls dressed in red sleepwear
    15" Little Luv 20.00
    12" Baby Button Nose 15.00
    18" Suzie Sunshine 40.00
    11" Pun'kin 15.00
    13" Butterball 20.00
    14" Sissy Toddler 25.00
Belinda, 1985, Jan Hagara's Love-ables Collection . 185.00
Bessie, 1988–1989, 18", On the Prairie (Suzie) 50.00
Beth
    1985, Jan Hagara's Love-ables Collection 185.00
    1986, 13", Little Women Collection 70.00
    1989, 9", Currier & Ives Collection 15.00
Betsy Ross
    1976–1977, 11", Historical Collection 20.00

1983, 13", Women of the Ages Collection 30.00
Bettina, 1964–1965, 18", vinyl/plastic child 60.00
Betty Ann, 1938, 15", composition 225.00
Betty Bounce, 1913–1915
    11", composition 125.00
    15" 185.00
Betty Brite, 1933, 16", composition/fur wig 350.00
Betty Lee, 1924, 21", composition/cloth child 285.00
Beverly, 1989–1990, 9", Li'l Innocents Series 15.00
Bicentennial Boy and Girl, 1976, 11", composition .45.00 ea.
Big Sister and Baby, 1940, 9" & 11", composition . . .set 165.00
Billy Boy, 1915
    11", composition/cloth 185.00
    15" 250.00
Billy Bum, 1982, 16", designed by Faith Wick 45.00
Birmingham, 1984, 13", Pride of the South 35.00
Birthday, 1984–1985, 19", Baby's First Collection . . . 30.00
Birthday Baby, 1989–1990, 14", Joyous Occasions . . 20.00
Blessing, 1984–1985, 19", Baby's First Collection . . . 30.00
Blue Bayou, 1979, 15" (Chipper), Grande Dames 50.00
Blue Danube, 1978, 18" (Nicole), Grande Dames 70.00
Blue Heaven Collection, 1977, white organdy dresses
    over blue slips
    15" Little Lovums 25.00
    18" Lovums 35.00
    20" Sugar Plum 40.00
    1978, 11" Pun'kin 20.00
    16" Li'l Suzie Sunshine 30.00
    11" Butterball 20.00
    18" Sweetie Pie 40.00
Bo Peep, 1977, 1981–1982, 11" 20.00
Bobbsey Twins, 1982–1983, 11", by Faith Wick . . 45.00 ea.
Bobby
    1913, 11", composition 165.00
    1985, Jan Hargara Love-ables Collection 185.00
Bobby Ann, 1913, 12", composition 165.00
Bobby Bounce, 1913, 11", composition 200.00
Bottle Tot, 1934, 16", bottle molded to hand 145.00
Boudoir Doll
    1938, 24", composition/cloth 150.00
    29" 200.00
    1958, 28", nylon bodies/vinyl 185.00
Bridal Suite (Party), 1938, composition
    15" 225.00
    21" 400.00
    1973–1986, 11", Half Pint, ring bearer . . . . . . 30.00 ea.
    Black 60.00
    15" Chipper 60.00
    Black 85.00
    17" Miss Chips 75.00
    Black 100.00
Bridesmaid, 1977–1986
    15" (Chipper) 40.00
    Black 75.00
Brigette, 1980, 11", Half Pint, Petite Filles 30.00
Bright Eyes, 1916, 11", composition
    11" 265.00
    16" 300.00
    1939–1946, 20", cloth/composition 265.00
Bright Eyes, 1939–1940, composition/cloth
    15" 300.00
    20" 385.00
Bright Eyes, Jr., 1915, composition
    11" 265.00
    15" 300.00

BROADWAY, 1984, 14", Little Old New York Collection . . . 45.00
BROTHER, 1918, 14", composition 200.00
    1943, 12", composition/cloth, yarn hair 165.00
    16" 250.00
BROTHER & SISTER, 1969 (Toddletot), 13", vinyl . . . 20.00 ea.
BROWNIE SCOUT
    1959, 16" (Patsy Ann) 200.00
    1964 – 1965, 16" (Fluffy Face) 165.00
BRUSSELS, 1984, 18", Age of Elegance Collection 65.00
BUBBLES, 1924–1930s, composition/cloth
    12" 165.00
    16" 300.00
    20" 400.00
    26" 700.00
BUBBLES, walking, 1926, 14" 300.00
BUBBLES, Limited Edition Club (limit 4,470) 40.00
BUBBLES BABY, 1933
    11" 145.00
    20" 395.00
    25" 700.00
BUBBLES, Betty, 1924, 22" 425.00
BUBBLES, Charlotte, 1924, 20" 385.00
BUBBLES, New, 1932, all rubber . . . . N. P. A.
BUCKINGHAM PALACE, 1982, 18", Age of Elegance 125.00
BUCKWHEAT, 1990, 11¼", Little Rascals Collection 35.00
BUD, 1959–1960, 24", molded hair boy, jointed elbows . . 350.00
BUDAPEST, 1984, 18", Age of Elegance Collection 175.00
BUDS, 1915–1918
    11" 175.00
        Black 250.00
    15" 250.00
        Black 300.00
BUTTERBALL
    1971–1977, 13", with layette in suitcase. 165.00
    1972, in wicker hamper/wardrobe 185.00
    1987, 12", nurser (drink & wet), Effanbee Favorites . 25.00
    1988–1989, TO LOVE, 14", My Little Baby 25.00
    1990, 19" 40.00
BUTTERCUP
    1973–1974, 13" 25.00
    1979–1986, 15" 35.00
BUTTON NOSE
    1938–1943, 8", composition 225.00
    1968, 16" 30.00
    1971, baby, 12" 30.00
    1990, 12" 20.00
CANADIAN MOUNTIE, 1985–1986, 11", International . . . 25.00
CANDY ANN, 1954
    20", cloth/vinyl 65.00
    24" 85.00
    29" 135.00
CANDY KID
    1946, 12"–13", composition 325.00
        Black 475.00
    1954, 12", all vinyl, molded hair 145.00
CANDY LAND COLLECTION, 1973, in white/red stripe dresses
    11" Pun'kin 20.00
    15" Chipper 25.00
    17" Miss Chips 45.00
    13" Butterball 20.00
    15" Little Luv 20.00
CANDY WALKER, 1954–1956, 13", coated cloth body/vinyl . 35.00
CAPTAIN KIDD, 1983, 11", Storybook Collection 25.00
CARNEGIE HALL, 1980, 18", Grande Dames Series 70.00
CAROLINE,1976–1980, 1984, used for Internationals,

Storybook and several other series . . . . 15.00 up
CAROUSEL COLLECTION, 1974, white dress/multicolor stripe
    trim or full skirt, cut on bias
    11" Pun'kin 25.00
    16" Babyface 45.00
    14" Little Luv 25.00
    17" Miss Chips 50.00
    18" Suzie Sunshine 45.00
    20" Sugar Plum 45.00
CASSIE, 1986, 19" 55.00
CASTLE GARDEN, 1979–1980, 11", Currier & Ives 30.00
CELESTE, 1967, 18", Miss Chips/wardrobe exclusive for
    Marshall Fields . . . . 285.00 up
CENTRAL PARK
    1978, 11", Currier & Ives 30.00
    1985, 17", Little Old New York Collection 65.00
CHAMPAGNE LADY
    1957–1959, 18" (Lawrence Welk) 65.00
    1977–1978, 18" (Nicole), Grande Dames 70.00
CHANTILLY, 1981, 15" (Chipper), Grande Dames 50.00
CHARLEE, 1966–1967, 13" (Half Pint), eyes to side 35.00
CHARLESTON, 1981, 13", Pride of the South 30.00
CHARLESTON HARBOR, 1980, 11", Currier & Ives 30.00
CHARLOTTESVILLE, 1984, 13", Pride of the South 35.00
CHARLEY MCCARTHY, 1937, composition/cloth
    17" 600.00
    21" 725.00
    1950, hard plastic/cloth, 21" 165.00
CHARMING CHECKS COLLECTION, 1974, dressed in pale blue
    or pink check gingham/white apron except Baby Winkle
    in white on gingham pillow.
    11" Pun'kin 30.00
    18" Susie Sunshine 40.00
        Black 60.00
    16" Baby Face 40.00
        Black. 55.00
    12" Baby Winkle 20.00
    11" Butterball 20.00
    18" Sweetie Pie 40.00
CHERRIES JUBILEE, 1979, 15" (Chipper), Grande Dames . . 70.00
CHINA HEAD, 1986, Limited Edition Club, vinyl/cloth . 45.00
CHIPPER, 1965–1980, 15" 20.00–60.00
CHIPS, see Miss Chips.
CHIPS, without the "Miss," 1965, 18" 45.00
CHRIS, 1969, 18" (Miss Chips), for Marshall Fields
    wardrobe 300.00
CHRISTENING BABY, 1918
    25", composition/cloth 265.00
    29" 350.00
    1950, 20", hard plastic/cloth 175.00
CHRISTINA, 1988–1990, 9", Li'l Innocents Collection . . . 15.00
CHRISTMAS, 1984–1985, 19", Baby's First Collection . . . 40.00
CHRISTOPHER COLUMBUS, 1990, 14", New World 75.00
CINDERELLA, 1952 (Honey)
    14" 350.00
    18" 500.00
    21" 675.00
    1977–1983, 11", Storybook Collection 35.00
    1989, 17", painted eyes . . . . 150.00 up
CINDERELLA FOR DISNEY
    1977–1978, 14" exclusive 175.00
    1985, 13", Disney Doll Collection 100.00
CINDY, 1988–1990, 9", Li'l Innocents Collection 15.00
CIVIL WAR LADY
    1978–1979, 15", Passing Parade Collection 50.00

1985, 12", Through the Years Collection 25.00
CLARENCE CLOWN, 1984–1986, 11", Here Comes the
    Clowns 30.00
CLAUDETTE, 1982, 15" (Chipper), Grande Dames 50.00
CLEOPATRA, 1978, 11", International Series 45.00
CLIPPO CLOWN, 1938, 14" 175.00
CLOWN BOY, also see PIERROT. 1980–1981, 16", (girl
    1980–1983), designed by Faith Wick 50.00
COCO, 1980, 18", Grande Dames Collection 125.00
COLLEEN, 1989–1990, 9", Li'l Innocents Collection 15.00
COLONIAL LADY, 1977–1979, 15", Passing Parade 50.00
COLUMBIA, 1916, 12", composition 225.00
COMPOSITION BABIES–MAMA STYLE DOLLS, 1920s, early
    1930s, add more for original clothes, composition/cloth
    16" 525.00
    20" 375.00
    22" 400.00
    25" 475.00
    27" 525.00
COMPOSITION BABIES, 1930s–1940s, composition/cloth
    14" 225.00
    17" 275.00
    21" 350.00
    27" 450.00
COMPOSITION CHILDREN, 1920
    14" 285.00
    16"–17" 370.00
    22" 450.00
    25" 500.00
    29" 600.00
COMPOSITION CHILDREN, 1930s–1940s
    15" 275.00
    18" 325.00
    22" 400.00
    28" 500.00
CONTESSA
    1984, 15", Craftsmen Corner Collection 150.00
    1985, 13", Pride of the South Collection 35.00
CONVENT GARDEN, 1981, Grande Dames Series
    11" 45.00
    15" 50.00
COOKIE
    1968\1969, 16", baby, all vinyl 35.00
    1968, in suitcase/wardrobe, 16" 185.00
    1981, 16" 25.00
COQUETTE, 1977–1978, 15" (Chipper), Grande Dames . . . 50.00
COQUETTE, MISS, 1912–1918, molded hair
    10" $200.00
    14" $275.00
CORNWALL, 1986, 11", Victorian Miniatures Series 25.00
COSETTE, 1988–1989, 13", Broadway Footlights 95.00
COTTON CANDY COLLECTION, 1980, wears pink check
    gingham/white apron with embroidery trim, 11" boy has
    white knee length pants
    20" Sugar Plum 40.00
    11" Half Pint 25.00
    15" Chipper 25.00
        Black 40.00
    20" Floppy (cloth body and limbs) 30.00
    16" Li'l Susie Sunshine 30.00
    18" Sweetie Pie 35.00
    15" Black Chipper 40.00
    15" Buttercup 35.00
    13" Butterball. 20.00
COUNTESS, 1976–1978, 17", baby, Regal Heirloom 30.00

COUNTRY BUMPKIN' COLLECTION, 1977, wears country print
    accented with blue
    11" Pun'kin 20.00
    17" Miss Chips 40.00
        Black 55.00
    18" Suzie Sunshine 40.00
    14" Pint Size, cloth body/vinyl 25.00
    13" Butterball 20.00
    18" Sweetie Pie 40.00
        Black 55.00
COUNTRY COUSIN COLLECTION, 1974, dressed in multicolored
    "Pioneer" style outfits
    11" Pun'kin 20.00
    17" Miss Chips 45.00
    18" Suzie Sunshine 40.00
    16" Baby Face 40.00
    13" Butterball 20.00
    14" Little Luv 20.00
COUNTRY LOOK COLLECTION, 1973, patchwork pattern check
    clothes, made for JCPenney
    16" Baby Face with 9" baby 45.00
    15" Chipper with long white hair, full bangs 40.00
    13" Butterball 20.00
COUSIN JEREMY, 1982–1983, 13", Absolutely Abigail . . 35.00
COVENTRY, 1986, 11", Victorian Miniatures 25.00
COWARDLY LION, 1987–1990, 11" Wizard of Oz 25.00
CREAM PUFF COLLECTION, 1980, dressed in pastel colors
    16" Twinkie 20.00
    13" Butterball 20.00
    16" Baby Butter Nose 30.00
    18" Sweetie Pie 40.00
    20" Sugar Plum 40.00
CRISTINA, 1983, 15", Craftsmen Corner, by Jan Hagara . 195.00
CROCHET CLASSICS, 1973–1982, wears hand crocheted clothes
    11" Tiny Tubber 20.00
    12" Dy-Dee, New 25.00
        Black. 35.00
    12" Half Pint 35.00
        Black 40.00
    12" Butterball 20.00
    14" Little Luv, black 35.00
    22" Sweetie Pie 50.00
        Black 65.00
CROWN PRINCESS OR PRINCE, 11", Regal Heirloom 30.00
CROWNING GLORY, 1978, Limited Edition Club
    (limit 2,200) 100.00
CRYSTAL, 1979, 15", Grande Dames Series (Chipper) 50.00
CRYSTAL PALACE, 1980, 18", Grande Dames (Nicole) . . 70.00
CUDDLE-UP, 1953, two lower teeth
    20" 65.00
    27" 145.00
CUPCAKE, 1965, 12" 25.00
CURRIER & IVES COLLECTION, 1978–1980, 11" 30.00
DAFFY DOT COLLECTION, 1972, dressed in large dot cotton
    print dresses or aprons, pillows with babies that are in
    white with three rows trim near hem
    18" Suzie Sunshine 40.00
    14" Little Luv 20.00
    17" Miss Chips 45.00
    20" Sugar Plum 40.00
    24" Precious Baby 45.00
    16" Twinkie 20.00
    16" Gumdrop 30.00
    13" Butterball 20.00
    11" Pun'kin 20.00

DALLAS, 1983, 13", Pride of the South Collection 35.00
DANCING SCHOOL, 1986, 11", Dance Ballerina Dance . . 30.00
DANIELLE, 1978–1989, 15", Puttin' on the Ritz 40.00
DAPHNE, 1981–1989, Grande Dames (Miss Chips) 70.00
DAVY CROCKETT, 1977–1979, 11", Historical Collection . . 30.00
DAY BY DAY COLLECTION, 1980–1982, freckles 20.00
DEBBIE, 1990, 18", Precious Toddlers Collection 35.00
DEBORAH, 1987, 18", Prom Night Collection 70.00
DEBRA, 1985, 11", Masquerade Ball Collection 35.00
DECEMBER, 1981, 11", Rememberance Dolls 20.00
DENMARK, 1985, 13", International Brides Collection . . . 20.00
DEWEES COCHRON, 1977, Limited Edition Club
    (limit 3,166) 100.00
DIANE, 1983, 15", Grande Dames Series 50.00
DISNEY COLLECTION, 1985
    13" Cinderella, Poor Cinderella, Mary Poppins . 100.00 ea.
    15" Prince Charming 165.00
DOLL HOUSE DOLLS, 1952, set of four, marked 200.00
DOLLY DUMPLING, 1918, 14", composition/cloth 245.00
DOROTHY
    1985, 11", Storybook Collection, 1987–1990, Wizard of
    Oz Collection 35.00
    1984, 15", Legend Series 100.00
DOROTHY DAINTY, 1916, 16", composition/cloth 250.00
DOUGLAS MACARTHUR, 1991, 16", History's Great
    Heroes 160.00
DOVER, 1986, 11", Victorian Miniatures 25.00
DUBLIN, 1985, 18", Age of Elegance Collection 65.00
DUCHESS, 1976–1978, 18", Regal Heirloom Collection . . . 40.00
DUCK, DUCK GOOSE COLLECTION, 1975, dresses are cotton
    with ducks and geese embroidered on skirt
    18" Suzie Sunshine 40.00
    15" Baby Face 40.00
        Black 55.00
    12" Butterball 20.00
    11" Pun'kin 25.00
    16" Twinkie 25.00
DUFFY SQUARE, 1985, 17", Little Old New York 65.00
DUTCH, 1937–1943, 9", composition 250.00
DWIGHT D. EISENHOWER, 1987–1989, 16", Presidents . . . 150.00
DY DEE BABY, 1930s
    11"–12" . . . . 125.00 – 200.00
    15" . . . . 150.00 – 250.00
    20" . . . . 175.00 – 300.00
    1940s, 1950s, 15" . . . . 165.00 – 200.00
    16" 75.00
    20" . . . . 175.00 – 300.00
    1960s, 1970s, 12" 45.00
    20" 90.00
    Darlin', 1967–1969, 1971, 16"–17" 170.00
    Ette, 1933, 1940–1943, 11" 150.00
    Educational Doll, 1971–1976, 20" 250.00
    Ellen, 1940–1954, 15" .100.00
    Jane
        1940–1943, 20", composition/rubber 200.00
        1955, hard plastic/vinyl 165.00
    Kin
        1933–1940, 13" 125.00
        1955, 20", hard plastic/vinyl 150.00
    Lou
        1940, 20", composition/rubber 275.00
        1955, 20", hard plastic/vinyl 150.00
    Louise
        1940, 20", composition/rubber 275.00
        1954–1955, 20", hard plastic/vinyl 150.00

New, 1975
    12" 20.00
        Black 35.00
    16" 45.00
        Black 60.00
    Wee, 1933, 9", composition 100.00
    1955, 9", vinyl 65.00
EAST END AVENUE, 1988–1989, 17", Little Old New York
    Collection 65.00
EDNA HIBEL, Craftsmen Corner, see Preface.
ELEANOR ROOSEVELT, 1985, 15", Great Moments in History
    Collection 95.00
ELIZABETH
    1938, 29", composition/cloth 350.00
    1982, 1985–1986, 1990, 11", Grande Dames 40.00
ELLA, 1938, 24", composition/cloth 275.00
ELMER CLOWN, 1984–1986, 24", Here Comes
    the Clown 55.00
EMERALD, 1986, 17" Jewels Collection 70.00
EMERALD ISLE, 1979, 15", Grande Dames (Chipper) . . . 50.00
EMILY, 1990, 18", Precious Toddlers 55.00
EMILY ANN, 1937, 14" 200.00
ENCHANTED GARDEN COLLECTION, 1973–1974, dressed in
    pastel print trimmed in organdy/lace
    20" Sweetie Pie 45.00
    13" Li'l Darlin' 30.00
    13" Butterball 20.00
    11" Pun'kin 25.00
    20" Sugar Plum 40.00
    16" Twinkie 30.00
    1982, dressed in floral print
    Black Sweetie Pie 55.00
    Black Pun'kin 35.00
    15" Chipper 35.00
        Black 45.00
    21" Floppy 45.00
ENGLAND, 1985–1986, 11", International Series 15.00
ERIKA, 1984, 11", Grande Dames Series 40.00
ERIN, 1985, 15", Grande Dames Series (Chipper) 50.00
FAIR BABY, 1969–1974
    14" 30.00
    20" 65.00
FAIRY PRINCESS, 1935, 9" 165.00
FAITH WICK, see Craftsmen Corner in Preface.
FALL, 1976–1980, 11", Four Seasons Collection 20.00
FEBRUARY, 1987–1989, 11", Rememberance Dolls 20.00
FEMME FATALE, 1979–1980, 1979–1980, 11", Through the
    Ages with Gigi 35.00
FIFTH AVENUE, 1985, 17", Little Old New York 65.00
FINLAND, 1986, 11", International Series 15.00
FIONA, 1986, 15", Grande Dames Series (Chipper) 50.00
FLAPPER, 1977–1979, 15", Passing Parade Collection . . . 50.00
FLOPPY
    1964, 21" Clown, vinyl/cloth body & limbs 75.00
    1975, Ragamuffins Collection, 1976, Granny's Corner
    Collection, 1977, Yesterdays Collection, 21" 60.00
    1980, 20", Cotton Candy, 1981, Over the Rainbow,
    1982, Enchanted Garden Collection 45.00
FLORENCE
    1938, 31", composition/cloth 350.00
    1984, 18", Age of Elegance 65.00
FLORENCE NIGHTINGALE
    1977, 11", Historical Collection 35.00
    1983, Women of Ages Collection 35.00
FLOSSIE, 1982–1983, 11", Girl of Bobbsey Twins 45.00

FLOWERGIRL
    1973, 1979, 1985–1986, 11" 35.00
    1984, designed by Edna Hibel 185.00
FLOWER GIRL OF BRITTANY, 1984, Craftmens Corner . 125.00
FLUERETTE, 1977–1978, 18", Grande Dames Series . . . 70.00
FLUFFY, 1954–1965
    8"– 10" 35.00
        Black 45.00
    12" 40.00
        Black 50.00
FORTUNE COOKIE, 1983, 11", Just Friends Collection 40.00
FOUR SEASONS COLLECTION
    1976–1980, 11" 20.00
    1981–1983, New Doll, freckles 20.00
FRANCE, 1987, 11", International Series 15.00
FRANCOISE, 1981, 11", Grande Dames Series 40.00
FRANKLIN D. ROOSEVELT, 1985, 16" 100.00
FREDDIE, 1982–1983, 11", Boy of Bobbsey Twins 45.00
FRONTIER, 1985, 12", Through the Years Collection . . . 25.00
FRONTIER SERIES, 1970–1971, dressed in calico cotton with
    white aprons or white dress with calico apron
    11" Pun'kin 20.00
    14" Little Lov 20.00
    15" Chipper 25.00
    16" Gumdrop 30.00
    17" Miss Chips 45.00
    18" Suzie Sunshine 40.00
    20" Sugar Plum 40.00
    25" Precious Baby 45.00
GABRELLE, 1980, 16", Petite Filles Collection 40.00
GARDEN PARTY, 1983, 13", Absolutely Abigail 35.00
GAY PAREE, 1983, 18", Age of Elegance Collection 125.00
GAY NINETIES, 1979, 15", Passing Parade Collection . . 50.00
GENEVA, 18", Age of Elegance Collection 65.00
GENEVIEVE, 1981, 16", Petite Filles Collection 35.00
GENI, 1984–1985, 11", Storybook Series 20.00
GEORGE WASHINGTON, 1983, 16", Presidents Collection . . 75.00
GERMANY, 1987–1989, 1990, 11", International Series . . . 15.00
GIBSON GIRL, 1977–1979, 1990, 15", Passing Parade 50.00
GIGI, 1979–1980, 11", Through the Ages with Gigi 35.00
GINGER CURLS, 1938, 21", composition 300.00
GIRL SCOUT, BROWNIE, ETC., 1957–1960 . . . .$145.00 up
GIRL WITH WATERING CAN
    1981, Limited Edition Club, (limit 3,875) 70.00
    1959–1960, 15", Fluffy Free, freckles . . . . 145.00 up
    1964–1965, 16", freckles . . . . 145.00 up
GISILLE, 1980, 16", Petite Filles Collection 35.00
GLORIA ANN, 1936, 21", composition 350.00
GOLDILOCKS, 1979–1983, 1986, 1987, 1990, 11"
    Storybook Series 30.00
GOOD WITCH, 1986, 1987, 1990, 11", Storybook 25.00
GRACE, 1984, 15", Grande Dames Series 50.00
GRAMERCY PARK, 1981, 1986, 17", Little Old New York . . 65.00
GRAND MERE. 1979, 1980, 11", Through the Years with
    Gigi 35.00
GRANDE DAMES COLLECTION, 1976–1983, see individual listings:
    Amanda, Blue Bayou, Blue Danube, Carnegie Hall,
    Champagne Lady, Chantilly, Cherries Jubilee, Coco, Coquette,
    Convent Gardens, Crystal, Downing Square, Elizabeth,
    Emerald Isle, Francoise, Fluerette, Hyde Park, Jezebel,
    Katherine, Lady Ascot, Lady Ashley, Lady Grey, La Vie en
    Rose, Lorraine, Ma Chere, Madame Du Barry, Magnolia,
    Mam'selle, Mint Julep, Nicole, Night at the Opera, Peaches
    and Cream, Priscilla, Robyn, Ruby,Saratoga, Southern
    Belle, Suzanne, Vicki, Victorian Lady, Violette.

GRANDMA, 1934, 10", composition 175.00
GRANNY'S CORNER COLLECTION, 1975–1976, 1983, dressed in
    paisley print, old fashioned styled dresses except boy who
    has velveteen pants and lace trimmed shirt
    11" Pun'kin 20.00
    15" Chipper 25.00
    17" Miss Chips 45.00
    18" Suzie Sunshine 40.00
    16" Twinkie 20.00
    11" Butterball 20.00
    15" Little Lov 20.00
    20" Sugar Plum 40.00
GREAT MOMENTS IN HISTORY, 1984, 1985, see individual listing:
    Winston Churchill, Eleanor Roosevelt
GREAT MOMENTS IN LITERATURE, 1983, 1984, see individual
    listings: Mark Twain, Huckleberry Finn, Becky Thatcher
GREAT MOMENTS IN MUSIC, 1984, Louis "Satchmo" Armstrong
GREAT MOMENTS IN SPORTS, 1985, 1986, see individual listings:
    Babe Ruth, Muhammad Ali
GREAT MOMENTS IN TELEVISION, 1986, see individual listings:
    Jackie Gleason as Ralph Kramden, Art Carney as Ed
    Norton.
GREECE, (Soldier) 1980, 11", International Series 20.00
GRETEL, 1981–1990, 11", Storybook Series 25.00
GROUCHO MARX, 1983, 17", Legend Series 85.00
GRUMPY, 1913–1930s, composition/cloth
    12" 265.00
    14" 300.00
    18" 400.00
    20" 425.00
    Baby, Jr., 1915, 12" 265.00
    Black, 1913–1930s, 12" 30.00
    14" 375.00
    18" 485.00
    20" 500.00
    Lady, 1918, 14" 300.00
    1985, Limited Edition in porcelain (limit 2,800) . . . 165.00
    1988, Limited Edition Club, vinyl (limit 5,000) 60.00
GUINEVERE, 1982, 15", Grande Games Series 50.00
GUM DROP, 1962–1977, 16", all vinyl toddler 30.00
HAGARA, JAN, see Preface under "Artists."
HALF PINT, 1966–1980, 11", vinyl and plastic/vinyl . . . 25.00
HALF PINT COLLECTION, 1975–1977, 11", four toddlers in four
    costumes, all have velvet shoes with spats 30.00
HANS BRINKER, 1982–1983, 11", Storybook Series 25.00
HANSEL, 1982, 1990, 11", Storybook Series 25.00
HAPPY BOY, 1960, 10½", molded tooth, freckles 45.00
HAPPY FAMILY, see "Most" listing.
HARMONICA JOE, 1924, 15" 285.00
HARRY S. TRUMAN, 1988–1990, 16", Presidents 75.00
HATTIE HOLIDAY, 1981–1982
    16" (Li'l' Suzie Sunshine) 35.00
    Gypsy or Majorette 45.00
HEARLD SQUARE, 1986. 11", Little Old New York 35.00
HEART TO HEART COLLECTION, 1981–1982, dressed in flowers
    and hearts print with the Effanbee signature in the
    background
    11" Pun'kin 25.00
        Black 35.00
    11" Tiny Tubber 20.00
        Black 30.00
    With pillow 40.00
    With blanket 45.00
        Black with pillow 45.00
    16" Twinkie 25.00

Black 45.00	
12" Baby Winkie Black 30.00	
12" Baby Button Nose 25.00	
12" Lovums 20.00	
13" Buttercup 30.00	
18" Sweetie Pie 40.00	
20" Sugar Plum 40.00	

HEARTBEAT BABY, 1942, 17", composition/cloth 185.00
HEARTH WITCH, 1981–1982, 18", cloth/vinyl, by Faith
    Wick 70.00
HEATHER, 1989–1990, 21", Little Girl Collection 85.00
HEAVEN SCENT COLLECTION, 1982, dressed in sheer dotted
    Swiss pastel dresses with smocked bodices
    11" Butterball 20.00
    12" Baby Button Nose 20.00
    15" Little Lovums 25.00
    18" Louvums 35.00
    13" Buttercup 30.00
    20" Sugar Plum 40.00
HEIDE, 1980–1983, 11", Storybook Series 25.00
HER ROYAL HIGHNESS, 1976–1979, 17" (Miss Chips) 95.00
HESTER, 1982, 15", Grande Dames Collection 50.00
HIBEL, EDNA, see Preface under "Artists."
HIGHLAND FLING COLLECTION, 1973, dressed in red plaid
    trimmed with organdy
    11" Pun'kin 20.00
    17" Miss Chips 45.00
    18" Suzie Sunshine 40.00
    16" Baby Face 40.00
        Black 55.00
    13" Butterball 20.00
    14" Little Luv 20.00
    20" Sugar Plum 40.00
HISTORICAL DOLLS, 1930s, composition, painted eyes, add
150.00 for mint original clothes
    14" 500.00
    21" 1200.00
    1976, see individual listing: Paul Revere, Betsy Ross,
    Martha Washington
    1977, Davy Crockett, Pavlova, Florence Nightingale,
    Pocahontas
    1978, Cleopatra
HOLLAND, 1987, 1989, 1990, 11", International 15.00
HOMER CLOWN, 1984–1986, 15", Here Comes the Clowns
Collection 55.00
HONEY, 1948–1949, composition, add 50.00 for flirty eyes
    14" 250.00
    18" 395.00
    21" 450.00
    24" 600.00
    1950s, hard plastic, 14" 250.00
    18" 450.00
    21" 500.00
    24" 700.00
    1951, clothes designed by Schiaparelli, 14" . . 550.00 up
    Jointed ankles/knees, 17" 385.00
    Cinderella, 1950s, 17" 475.00
    Majorette, 17" 435.00
    Walker, 1949–1955, head turns, 14" 275.00
    17" 475.00
    20" 575.00
HONEY ANN, 1952, 24", hard plastic walker, has one dark,
    painted lash from corner of eyes. 400.00
HONEY BUN, 1967, 18", baby 30.00
HONEY BUNCH, 1923, 16", composition/cloth 265.00

HONEY-KINS, 1954, 12", all hard plastic, sleep eyes. . . .20.00
HOURGLASS LOOK, 1978 – 1979, 15", Passing Parade . .500.00
HOUSTON, 1985, 13", Pride of the South Collection 35.00
HOWDY DOODY, Puppet, composition/cloth, 1947
    20" 300.00
    23" 400.00
    1952, hard plastic/cloth
    20" 200.00
    23" 350.00
HUCKLEBERRY FINN, 1983, 13½", Great Moments in
    Literature 80.00
HUG ME, see Rosemary for prices.
HUGGABLES COLLECTION, 1981–1982, vinyl head, body and
    limbs cloth, 14" 45.00
HUMPHREY BOGART, 1989, 15", Legend Series 80.00
HUMPTY DUMPTY, 1985, 1988–1990, 14", Once Upon a
    Time . . . . .70.00 up
HUNGREY, 1985, 13", International Brides Collection 20.00
HYDE PARK, 1980, 15" (Chipper), Grande Dames Series . .50.00
ICE QUEEN, 1938, 15", composition, open mouth . . . .600.00 up
ICE SKATER, 1989–1990, 11½", Joyous Occasions 30.00
INGENIE, 1979, 11", Through the Years with Gigi 25.00
INNOCENCE COLLECTION, 1978–1979, babies in embroidered
    batiste dresses, ladies in tiered batiste gown,
    embroidered over skirts, toddlers in short batiste
    dresses, both lady and toddler have straw hats
    11" Caroline (used for International dolls) 20.00
        Black 35.00
    15" Chipper 25.00
    16" Li'l Suzie Sunshine 35.00
    17" Miss Chips 45.00
    18" Suzie Sunshine 40.00
        Black 60.00
    16" Twinkie 20.00
    11" Half Pint 25.00
    15" Little Lovums .25.00
    18" Sweetie Pie 40.00
        Black 55.00
INTERNATIONAL COLLECTION, 1976–1983, see individual dolls,
    Miss Ancient Egypt, Miss Argentina, Miss Austria, Miss
    Black America, Miss Brazil, Miss Canada, Miss Czecho
    slovakia, Miss India, Miss Denmark, Miss France, Miss
    Greece, Miss Germany, Miss Holland, Miss Hungary,
    Miss Ireland, Miss Israel, Greece Soldier, Miss India,
    Miss Italy, Miss Mexico, Miss Norway, Miss Poland, Miss
    Romania, Miss Russia, Miss Scotland, Spain (Boy), Miss
    Spain, Miss Sweden, Miss Switzerland, Turkey, Miss
    U. S. A.
JACK, 1979–1983, 11", Storybook Series 20.00
JACKIE GLEASON AS RALPH KRAMDEN, 1986, 16½", Great
    Moments of Television Series 75.00
JACKSONVILLE, 1985, 13", Pride of the South 35.00
JACQUELINE, 1984, 11", Grande Dames Series 40.00
JAMBO
    1940, 14", composition puppet 175.00
    1952, 14", hard plastic. 200.00
JAN CAROL, 1929, 24", composition/cloth 385.00
JANE, 1983–1984, 11", One World Collection 20.00
JANUARY, 1987–1989, 1990, 11", Remembrance Dolls . . .20.00
JAPAN, 1986,1987, 1989, 1990, 11", International 15.00
JEAN, 1985, 15", Grande Dames Series 40.00
JENNA, 1986, 16", Lynn Hollyn American Countrytime . .50.00
JENNIFER, 1988–1989, 9", Way We Were Series 30.00
JENNY, 1990, 21", Thank Heavens For Little Girls . . .160.00
JETHRO CLOWN, 1984–1986, 18", Here Comes the Clowns .75.00

JEZEBEL, 1980, 15", Grande Dames Series 50.00
JILL
    1979–1983, 11", Storybook Series 20.00
    1987–1990, 11", Nursery Rhymes Collection 20.00
JO, 1986, 13", Little Women Collection 70.00
JOAN, 1988–1989, 11", On the Prairie Collection 20.00
JOAN CAROL, 1929, 20", composition/cloth 365.00
JOHN F. KENNEDY, 1986, 16", Presidents Series 80.00
JOHN WAYNE, 1981–1982
    Cowboy 265.00
    Soldier 245.00
JONATHAN, 1990, 9", French Country Collection 15.00
JOY, 1990, 9", Li'l Innocents Collection 15.00
JOYOUS BALLERINA, 1988–1989, 1990, 17" 70.00
JR. MISS, 1958
    15" Bride, hard plastic/vinyl 200.00
    21" Bridesmaid 365.00
    15" Ballerina, jointed knee, ankle walker 250.00
    21" 400.00
JUDITH, 1985, 11", Masquerade Ball Series 20.00
JUDY, 1928, 18", composition/cloth child 325.00
JUDY GARLAND AS DOROTHY, 1984, 14½", Legend 90.00
JULY, 1987–1989, 11", Remembrance Dolls 20.00
JUMBO INFANT, 1915–1920, 20", composition/cloth 300.00
JUNE, 1987–1989, 11", Remembrance Dolls 20.00
JUST FRIENDS, 1982–1983, see individual names. Dressed in
    Provincial costumes: 11" Dutch boy/girl, Swiss Yodeler
    boy/girl, Alpine Hiker boy/girl
KALI-KO-KATE, 1933, 18", printed oilcloth 375.00
KATERINA, 1986, 15", Dance Ballerina Dance 45.00
KATHERINE, 1982–1990+, 11", Grande Dames Series . . .40.00
KATIE (KATY), 1954–1957, 8", all vinyl, molded hair . . .35.00
KATIE KROOSE, 1918, 15", cloth/felt 300.00
KEEPSAKE COLLECTION, 1979–1980, see individual names:
    Antique Bride, Old Fashioned Baby, boy or girl
KIKI, 1990, 18", Precious Toddlers Series 55.00
KILROY
    1940, 14", composition .300.00
    1952, 14", hard plastic .185.00
KIM, 1983–1984, 11", One World Collection, Oriental . . .25.00
KOREA, 1986, 11", International Series 15.00
LA VIE EN ROSE, 1980, 18", Grande Dames Series 75.00
LADY ANGELIQUE, 1988–1989, Eugenia Dukas 195.00
LADY ASCOT, 1981, 15", Grande Dames Series 50.00
LADY GABRIELLE, 1988–1989, 18", Eugenia Dukas 195.00
LADY GREY, 1978, 15", Grande Dames Series 50.00
LADY IN RED VELVET HAT, exclusive for Smithsonian . . .95.00
LADY JACQUELINE, 1988, 18", Eugenia Dukas 195.00
LADY NICHOLE, 1989, 18", Eugenia Dukas Collection . . .195.00
LADY SNOW, 1979, 18", Grande Dames Series 70.00
LADY STEPANIE, 1987, 18", Eugenia Dukas Collection . . .195.00
LANA, 1985, 11", Masquerade Ball Collection 35.00
LARRY, 1985–1986, 17", Jan Hagara Collectibles 165.00
LAUREL, 1984–1985, 15", Jan Hagara Collectibles 195.00
LEGEND SERIES, 1980–1990, see individual names: 1980 W. C.
    Fields, 1981 John Wayne as cowboy, 1982 John Wayne as
    soldier, 1982 Mae West, 1983 Groucho Marx, 1984 Judy
    Garland as Dorothy, 1985 Lucille Ball, 1986 Liberace,
    1987 James Cagney, 1989 Humphrey Bogart, 1990
    Claudette Cobert.
LENOX, 1919–1920, 20", porcelain head, jointed body . . .500.00
LES INFANTS COLLECTION, 1981, babies in pastel dresses
    16" Twinkie 20.00
    12" Baby Button Nose 20.00
    13" Butterball 20.00

    15" Little Lovums 25.00
    18" Lovums 35.00
    13" Buttercup 30.00
    18" Sweetie Pie 40.00
    20" Sugar Plum 40.00
LESLEY, 1985–1986, 15", Jan Hargara Collectable . . .140.00
LIBERACE, MR. SHOWMANSHIP, 1986, Legends 200.00
LIFE IN THE COUNTRY, 1978–1979, 11", Currier & Ives . . .35.00
LI'L DARLIN'
    1949, 16", puckered face, painted eyes 85.00
    1959–1963, all vinyl/nurser 40.00
    1965–1968, 18", cloth/vinyl 35.00
LI'L JOHN JOHN, 1988–1989, 9", On the Prairie 15.00
LI'L JUDY, 1988–1989, 9", On the Prairie Collection . . .15.00
LI'L SUZIE SUNSHINE, 1978–1981, 1983, 16", freckles . . .30.00
LI'L SWEETIE, 1967, 16", no lashes or eyebrows 60.00
LILI, 1980, 16", Petite Filles Collection 35.00
LILLIAN RUSSELL, 1984, Women of the Ages Collection . . .55.00
LIMITED EDITION CLUB, see Preface.
LISA, 1987, 1989–1990
    18", Prom Night Collection 70.00
    9", My Little French Country Collection 25.00
    7", Baby Collection 20.00
LISA GROWS UP, 1983, 11", toddler, all vinyl 30.00
LITTLE BO PEEP
    1977–1982, 11", Storybook Series 25.00
    1981–1982, 14", Huggables., cloth/vinyl head 35.00
    1986–1987, 19", Fantasyland Collection 95.00
LITTLE BOY BLUE, 1912, 12", composition 250.00
LITTLE GIRL WITH A CURL, 1984–1985, 11", Storybook 25.00
LITTLE GUMDROP, 1964–1967, 14", all vinyl toddler 30.00
LITTLE LADY FLUFFY
    1960s, marked with name, 10½" 40.00
    1939–1946, composition, 15" 300.00
    17" 385.00
    21" 450.00
    27" 800.00
    1943, 21", yarn hair 450.00
    Magnets in hands, 18" .465.00
    Black, 21" 650.00
    1950s, 19", hard plastic/vinyl head 300.00
    Birthday, 1941, 21", music box in doll 700.00
    Jig saw puzzle, 1943 . . . . .25.00
    15", toiletries by Helene Pessel, all vinyl, narrow bangs,
    long curls in back. 165.00
LITTLE LOV, 1970–1977, 14"
    Baby 20.00
    Black 30.00
LITTLE LOVUMS, 1977–1986, 15", cloth/vinyl 25.00
LITTLE MERMAID, 1984, 11", Storybook Series 25.00
    1985, 9", Fairy Tale Collection 20.00
LITTLE MILK MAID, 1985, 11", Storybook Series 20.00
LITTLE MISS MUFFET, 1983, 11", Storybook Series 20.00
LITTLE RED RIDING HOOD
    1977–1983, 11", Storybook 20.00
    1981–1982, 14", Huggable, cloth/vinyl head 45.00
    1986–1987, 19", Fantasy Land Collection 95.00
LITTLE TIGER, 1983, 13", Craftsmen Corner 60.00
LITTLE WALTER, 1912, 16", composition/cloth 350.00
LITTLE WOMEN, See individual name, Jo, Meg, Beth, Amy
LIZA LEE, 1937, 14", composition 265.00
LONDON, 1985, 18", Age of Elegance Collection 65.00
LOTUS BLOSSOM, 1983 (Orange Blossom in 1982), 13" 50.00
LOUIS ARMSTRONG, 1984, 16½", Great Moments in Music .90.00
LOUISVILLE, 1985, 13", Pride of the South Collection . . .35.00

LOVE & LEARN SET, 1965, 22", Sweetie Pie, all vinyl, box contains
　　record explaining the "How & Why" of a Mother's love:
　　Complete 150.00
　　Doll only 50.00
LOVEY MARY, 1926
　　14", composition. 300.00
　　19" 400.00
　　25" 600.00
LOVUMS , 1928, composition/cloth
　　16" 275.00
　　21" 375.00
　　24" 475.00
LOVUMS COLLECTION, 1975–1979, 18", cloth/vinyl baby
　　Dressed in nine different outfits . . . . .40.00 ea.
　　In wicker basket 125.00
LUCIFER, 1938, 14", Black marionette 285.00
LUCILLE BALL, 1985, 14", Legend Series . . . . .85.00.
LUCINDA
　　1952–1959, 18", hard plastic 300.00
　　1964, 12" (Baby-kin), wardrobe/trunk 135.00
LUV, 1970, 18", all vinyl toddler, puckered style mouth . . .60.00
LYNN, 1969, 14", toddler for Marshall Field 60.00
MA CHERE, 1976, 15", Grande Dames Series 50.00
MACAWFUL THE SCOT, 1948, 14", composition 200.00
MADAME BUTTERFLY COLLECTION, 1983, white Oriental faces,
　　dressed in kimonos
　　11" 20.00
　　15" 35.00
　　17" 45.00
MADAME DU BARRY, 1977–1978, 15", Grande Dames . . .50.00
MADELEINE, 1980, Petite Fillies Collection 30.00
MADISON PARK, 1985, 17", Little Old New York 65.00
MAE STARR, 1928, 29", record player in body 475.00
MAE WEST, 1982, 18", Legend Series 80.00
MAGNOLIA, 1979–1980, 15", Grande Dames Series 50.00
MAID MARION, 1978, 1984–1985, 11", Storybook Series . .30.00
MAMA, 1979–1980, 11", Through the Years With Gigi . . .40.00
MAMA'S BABY, 1983–1985, 25", cloth/vinyl 40.00
MAM'SELLE, 1976–1977, 17", Grande Dames Series . . .70.00
MARCH
　　1987–1989, 11", Rememberance Collection 20.00
　　1990, Special Moments Dolls of the Month 15.00
MARGARET, 1987, 18", Prom Night Collection 70.00
MARGIE
　　1921, 16", composition child 285.00
　　1990, 9", Li'l Innocents Four Seasons (Spring) 15.00
MARIA, 1989–1990, 9", Li'l Innocents Collection 15.00
MARIANNE, 1981, 16", Petite Filles Collection 35.00
MARIETTA, 1938, 27", composition/cloth child 450.00
MARILEE, 1924, marked with name, composition/cloth
　　17" 300.00
　　27" 550.00
MARK TWAIN, 1983–1985, 16", Great Moments in
　　Literature 80.00
MARLENE, 1987–1989, 15", Puttin' on the Ritz 40.00
MARSEILLES, 1984, 18", Age of Elegance Collection 45.00
MARTHA WASHINGTON
　　1976, 11", Historical Collection 45.00
　　13", 1983–1984, Women of the Ages Collection . .40.00
MARVEL-TOT, 1934, 16", baby, molded bottle in hand . . .300.00
MARY ANN, 1923–1937, composition/cloth
　　16" 300.00
　　18" 350.00
　　24" 400.00
　　1986, 15", Jan Hargara Collectibles 165.00

MARY HAD A LITTLE LAMB, 1981–1983, 1987, 11" 25.00
MARY JANE
　　1917–1923, 20" 325.00
　　1923–1931, 18" 285.00
　　　24" 395.00
　　1959, 32", freckles .475.00
　　1959, with baby sister in bassinette 650.00
　　1960–1962, 30", flirty eyed walker 460.00
　　1963, 32", in nurse uniform 500.00
　　1963, toddler, vinyl, 13" 45.00
MARY LEE, 1930–1935, composition/cloth
　　14" 240.00
　　17" 350.00
MARY POPPINS
　　1982, 1989, 11", Storybook Series 25.00
　　1985, 13", Disney Doll Collection 100.00
MARY SUE, 1927, composition/cloth
　　18" 300.00
　　21" 385.00
　　1988–1990, 9", Li'l Innocents Series 15.00
MARY LOU, 1924, 20" .365.00
MARY, MARY, 1977–1983, 11", Storybook Series 25.00
MARYANNE, 1988–1990, 9", Li'l Innocents Collection . . .15.00
MAUREEN, 1986, 15", Grande Dames 50.00
MAY, 1987–1989, 11", Day by Day, Rememberance and
　　Special Moments of the Month Collections 20.00
MEG, 1986, 13", Little Women Series 70.00
MEGAN, 1986, 16", Lynn Hollyn American Countrytime .50.00
MELAINE, 1986, 15", Grande Dames Series 50.00
MELISSA, 1989, 21", Little Girls Collection 85.00
MELODIE, 1953–1956, 30", hard plastic/vinyl head,
　　recorder 365.00
MEMORIES COLLECTION, 1978, dressed in white organdy,
　　trimmed with velveteen, boys have print shirt,
　　and velveteen pants/caps
　　11" Pun'kin boy/girl .20.00 ea.
　　15" Chipper 25.00
　　16" Li'l Suzie Sunshine 30.00
　　17" Miss Chips 45.00
　　18" Suzie Sunshine 40.00
　　11" Half Pint 25.00
　　11" Butterball 20.00
　　15" Little Lovums .25.00
　　18" Sweetie Pie 40.00
　　20" Sugar Plum 40.00
MEMPHIS, 1984, 13", Pride of the South Collection 35.00
MEREDITH, 1990, 9", Li'l Innocents Four Seasons (Autumn) .15.00
MICHELLE, 1988–1990, 21", Little Girls Collection 85.00
MICKEY (ALL AMERICAN BOY), 1952–1962, 11", some with
　　molded caps, all vinyl, painted eyes 70.00
MICKEY BABY, 1939–1949, composition/cloth
　　15" 300.00
　　20" 390.00
　　22"–23" 450.00
　　1950–1969, vinyl/cloth
　　15" 125.00
　　20" 175.00
MIMI
　　1927, 15", Patsy type, marked with name. 485.00
　　1980, 11" (Half Pint), Petite Filles 35.00
MINT JULEP, 1976, 17", Grande Dames Series 70.00
MISS AMANDA, made for Amway Products, 11" 35.00
MISS ANCIENT EGYPT
　　1978, 11", Historical Collection 35.00
　　1979, 11", International Series 35.00

20" Floppy (cloth body and limbs) 30.00
11" Half Pint boy or girl 25.00
11" Butterball 20.00
13" Buttercup 30.00
18" Sweetie Pie 40.00
20" Sugar Plum 40.00
PAJAMA KID COLLECTION, 1972–1976, dressed in floral print
   flannel sleepwear
   18" Suzie Sunshine 40.00
   11" Pun'kin 20.00
      Black 35.00
   11" Tiny Tubber 30.00
   18" Sweetie Pie 40.00
      Black 60.00
   8" Babykin 20.00
PAPA'S PET, 1979–1980, 11", Through the Years with
   Gigi 35.00
PARADE OF WOODEN SOLDIERS, 1982
   11" 25.00
   15" 35.00
   18" 50.00
PARK AVENUE, 1985, Little Old New York Collection . . .65.00
PARTY BOY OR GIRL, 1979 – 1980, Age of Innocence . . .65.00
PARTY TIME COLLECTION, See individual name: Civil War,
   Colonial Lady, Gibson, Flapper, Frontier, The 70s
   Women.
PAT-O-PAT (CAKE)
   1924, composition/cloth, hands made to clap 200.00
   1939, 18", composition/cloth, hands held together . .165.00
   1980, 15", Once Upon a Time Collection 40.00
PATRICIA, 1932
   14", all composition 450.00
      Black 600.00
PATRICIA-KIN, 1932, 14", composition 350.00
PATRICIA WALKER, 1954, hard plastic
   15" 225.00
   21" 400.00
   Vinyl head/hard plastic
   19" 300.00
   25" 475.00
PATSY (FIRST), composition shoulder plate/cloth, 15" 400.00
PATSY, 1926–1930s
   14" 385.00
   Magnets in hands 425.00
   Music box in body 500.00
   1964–1965, 11", one-piece vinyl body/limbs 50.00
   1976, 16", Limited Edition Club (limit 1,200) 285.00
   1986, 14", Once a Star...Always a Star 60.00
   1987, 14" (limit 7,500) .75.00
PATSY ANN, 1958–1960
   15", Fluffy style face, freckles 85.00
   Girl Scout 100.00
   1988–1990, 9", Christmas Eve Together 35.00
PATSY BABY, 1932
   Cloth body, can have straight legs 300.00
   11" Black or Brown 385.00
PATSY BABYETTE (BABYKIN), 1932–1947, 10" 275.00
PATSY, BLACK, 1946, 14" 600.00
PATSY FLUFF, 1932, 14" 400.00
PATSY JOAN, 1930s, 1946
   16" 465.00
   Black 645.00
PATSY JR. 1930, 11" 325.00
PATSY LOU, 1929–1930s, 22", composition 525.00
PATSY MAE, 1934, 30" 750.00

PATSY RUTH, 1936, 26" 800.00
PATSY, WEE, 6"–7" 325.00
PATSYETTE, 1930, 9" 300.00
PATSYKINS, 1930, 11" 325.00
PAUL REVERE, 1976–1977, 11", Historical Collection . . .30.00
PAVLOVA
   1977–1979, 11", Historical Collection 30.00
   1979, 11", Storybook Series 30.00
PEACHES BABY, 1965–1966, 16", cloth/vinyl 25.00
PEACHES & CREAM, 1965, sold through Sears, each dressed
   in white with peach color blanket/coat or trim (not in
   Effanbee Catalog)
   16" DyDee 30.00
   18" Sweetie Pie 40.00
   16" Gum Drop 35.00
   1976, 15", Grande Dames Series 50.00
   1981, 15", Grande Dames Series 50.00
   11" Black 65.00
PEDDLER WOMEN, 1981–1982, 16", Faith Wick design . . .60.00
PEGGY LOU, 1936, 21", composition/cloth girl 325.00
PENNSYLVANIA DUTCH, 1936–1936, 9" . . . . .250.00 ea.
PETER PAN, 1982–1983, 11", Storybook Series 30.00
PETEY, 1990, 4½", sitting dog, Little Rascals set. 15.00
PETITE FILLIES COLLECTION, see individual names: Babette,
   Brigitte, Bebe Genevieve, Bebe Denise, Bebe Marianne,
   Bebe Nanette, Denise, Gabrielle, Genevieve, Gisille, Lili,
   Nanette, Madeleine, Mimi, Monique
PHILLIPINES, 1987, 11", International 15.00
PIERROT CLOWNS, 1981–1984, 11", Storybook Series . . .30.00
PIMBO
   1940, 14", composition 165.00
   1952, 14", hard plastic 100.00
PINOCCHIO
   1981–1983, 1990, 11", Storybook Series 30.00
   1982, Huggables Collection
   Cloth body and limbs 35.00
PINT SIZE, 1975–1977, 1983
   14", flannel covered body and vinyl head 30.00
   1975, 1976, Ragamuffin Collection 25.00
   1976, Granny's Corner Collection 25.00
   1977, Yesterdays Collection, in stripe and floral print
      trimmed in black and white 30.00
   1977, Country Bumpkin Collection, has blue trim on
      pale blue print 25.00
   1983, in old fashioned looking eyelet, Granny's Corner
      Collection 25.00
PIONEER COLLECTION, 1969, in floral print on black skirt/bon-
   net with bodice and lining in yellow
   16" 30.00
   18" 45.00
PLAINS COUPLE, 1939, 9", composition 300.00
PLYMOUTH LANDING, 1978–1980, 11", Currier & Ives . . .30.00
POCAHONTAS, 1977–1978, 11", Historical Collection . . .30.00
POLAND, 1987, 11", International Series 15.00
POLKA DOTTIE, 1954, oil cloth body
   21" 185.00
   Vinyl head/latex body, 11" 70.00
POLYANNA, 1983, 11", Storybook Series 20.00
POOCHIE, 1937, 14", composition 300.00
POOR CINDERELLA, 1984–1985, 1990, 11" Storybook . . .25.00
POPEYE, 1933, 16", composition 450.00
PORTRAIT DOLLS, 1940–1949, 11", all composition, two ladies
   in gowns, Little Bo Peep, Majorette, Bride & Groom
   Set . . . . .265.00 – 250.00
PORTUGAL, 1985–1986, 11", International Series 15.00

PRAIRIE NIGHTS COLLECTION, 1976, dressed in beige with lace
 and blue ribbon trim
   11" Pun'kin 20.00
   18" Suzie Sunshine 40.00
   13" Butterball 20.00
   1" Tiny Tubber 150.00
   5" Chipper 35.00
OUS BABY, 1962–1975
   24", cloth/vinyl 50.00
   1975, Limited Edition Club (limit 872) 300.00
RESIDENTS, 1983, see individual names: George Washington,
 Abraham Lincoln, Theodore Roosevelt, John F. Kennedy,
 Dwight D. Eisenhower, Harry Truman, Thomas Jefferson,
 Andrew Jackson.
PRIDE OF THE SOUTH COLLECTION, 1981–1983, see individual
 names: Riverboat Gambler, Natchez, Mobile, New Orleans,
 Savannah, Charleston, Atlanta, Richmond, Dallas
PRIMA BALLERINA (NATALIA), 1990, 18", Eugenia Dukas .200.00
PRINCE, 1978, 11", Regal Heirloom Collection 40.00
PRINCE CHARMING, 1952, hard plastic
   14" 350.00
   18" 500.00
   1978–1983, 11", Storybook Series 30.00
   1985, 15", Disney Collection 165.00
PRINCESS, 1976–1978, 17", baby, Heirloom Collection . .65.00
PRINCESS DIANA, 1982, Limited Edition Club
   (limit 4,220) 85.00
PRISCILLA
   1983, 11", Grande Dames Series 40.00
   1987–1988, 11", Little Old New York Collection 35.00
PUERTO RICO, 1986, 11", International Series 15.00
PUN'KIN, 1966–1983
   11" 20.00–25.00
   Black 30.00–35.00
QUEEN ELIZABETH, 1983–1984, 13", Women of the Ages .55.00
QUEEN ISABELLA, 1990, 14", New World Collection 50.00
QUEEN MOTHER, 1977– 1978, 18", Regal Heirloom 45.00
QUEEN OF HEARTS
   1986, Storybook Series 35.00
   1987, Nursery Rhymes Collection 40.00
RABBIT, 1931, 11", all composition, Patsy type body 300.00
RACHEL, 1990, 21", Thank Heaven for Little Girls 160.00
RAGAMUFFIN COLLECTION, 1975–1976, vinyl head, cloth body
 and limbs, removable dress/bonnet or hat
   12" Baby Button Nose 20.00
   14" Half Pint 25.00
   21" Floppy 45.00
RAINBOW PARFAIT COLLECTION, 1979, in pastel organdy dresses
   11" Pun'kin 20.00
      Black 35.00
   16" Li'l Suzie Sunshine 30.00
   13" Butterball 20.00
   13" Buttercup 30.00
   20" Sugar Plum 40.00
   18" Lovums 35.00
RALEIGH, 1984, 13", Pride of the South Series 35.00
RAPUNZEL
   1982–1983, 11", Storybook Series 20.00
   1989–1990, 9", Storybook Series 15.00
REBECCA OF SUNNY BROOK FARM, 1983, Storybook 15.00
RECITAL TIME, 1982–1983, 13", Absolutely Abigail 35.00
RED BOY, 1985. Limited Edition Club (limit 4,470) 75.00
REGAL HEIRLOOM COLLECTION, 1976–1979, see individual
 names: Crown Princess, Her Royal Highness, Baroness,
 Dutchess, Queen Mother, Princess, Countess

RENOIR, see Girl With Watering Can.
RHAPSODY IN BLUE COLLECTION, 1980, dressed in dark
 blue/white.
   11" Pun'kin 20.00
   15" Chipper 25.00
   16" Li'l Suzie Sunshine 30.00
   13" Buttercup 20.00
   17" Miss Chips 45.00
   18" Sweetie Pie 40.00
   20" Sugar Plum 40.00
RICHMOND, 1983, 13", Pride of the South Collection . . .35.00
RING BEARER, 1985, 11", Bridal Suite Collection 20.00
RING BOY, 1977–1979, 1986, Bridal Suite Collection 20.00
RIVER BREATHERN, 1936–1939, composition
   7" 245.00
   9" 300.00
RIVERBOAT GAMBLER, 1981, 13", Pride of the South 40.00
ROARING TWENTIES, 1990, 18", Ladies of Fashion 85.00
ROBIN HOOD, 1978, 1984–1985, 11", Storybook Series . .30.00
ROBYN, 1982, 11", Grande Dames Series 40.00
ROMA, 1983, 18", Age of Elegance Collection 125.00
ROMPER BABIES, 1918, 15", cloth/composition 225.00
ROOTIE KAZOOTIE, 1954
   11", vinyl head/latex body 70.00
   21", vinyl head/oilcloth body 185.00
   21", hard plastic body/vinyl head 265.00
ROSEMARY, 1925, cloth/composition
   14" 250.00
   17" 275.00
   25" 435.00
   29" 550.00
RUBY, 1980, 1986
   15", Grande Dames Series 50.00
   Black 65.00
RUSSIA, 1987
   11", International Series .15.00
   9", Li'l Innocents International Series 15.00
RUSTY, 1955 (Danny Thomas Show), 19", all vinyl, molded
   hair 250.00
RUTH ANN, 1936–1939, composition/cloth 365.00
70'S WOMEN, 1977–1979, 15", Passing Parade 50.00
S & H GREEN STAMP DOLL, 1964–1966, 1970 . . . . .40.00
SALVATION ARMY LASS, 1921, 16", composition 400.00
SALISBURY, 11", Victorian Miniatures 25.00
SALLY, Black doll, 1985, 11", Sunday Best Collection . .30.00
SAM, Black doll, 1985, 11" ,Sunday Best Collection 40.00
SAN ANTONIO, 1984, 13", Pride of the South 35.00
SANDY, 1988–1990, 9", Li'l Innocents Collection 15.00
SANTA CLAUS
   19", composition 950.00
   1982, 18", vinyl 85.00
SAPPHIRE, 1986, 17", Jewels Collection 65.00
SARA, Black doll, 1985, 16", Sunday Best Collection . .35.00
SARAH, 1990, 18", Precious Toddler Collection 40.00
SARATOGA, 1981, 11", Grande Dames Series 40.00
SATURDAY, 1980–1982, 11", Day by Day Collection 20.00
SAVANNAH, 1981–1982, 13", Pride of the South 35.00
SCARECROW, 1983, 6", Craftsmen Corner, Faith Wick
   Design, ...50.00
SCHAIPARELLI, 1951–1953, 18", dressed in clothes designed by
 Schaiparelli, hard plastic Honey Doll
   14" . . . . .400.00 up
   18" . . . . .550.00 up
SCHOOL DAYS
   1913, 11", composition .250.00

15" 325.00
1979–1980, 11½", Special Moments Collection 30.00
SCHOOL GIRL WRITING, 1963, 18", Suzie Sunshine made for
   Sears, has right hand molded to hold a crayon/pen . .55.00
SCHOOL TIME, 1986, 18", Age of Innocence Collection . .65.00
SCOTLAND, 1987, 11", International 15.00
SCOTT, 1989, 9", Currier & Ives 15.00
SEND IN THE CLOWNS COLLECTION, 1981–1983, dressed a
   Pierrot in white costumes with red trim
   11" 30.00
   15" 45.00
      15", with cloth body 40.00
   18" 75.00
      18", with cloth body 60.00
SEPTEMBER
   1987–1989, 11", Rememberance Dolls 15.00
   1989, 13", Special Moments of the Month 15.00
SEWING KIT DOLLS, 1942, composition
   5½" 100.00
   9½" 135.00
SHAUNA, 1981, 15", Grande Dames Series 50.00
SHEER DELIGHT COLLECTION, 1983, babies dressed in pastel
   "frosted" gowns and bonnets
   16" Twinkie 20.00
   13" Butterball 20.00
   14" Button Nose 20.00
   15" Little Lovums 25.00
   18" Louvums 35.00
   13" Buttercup 30.00
   18" Sweetie Pie 40.00
   20" Sugar Plum 40.00
SHERLOCK HOLMES, 1983, Limited Edition Club
   (limit 4,470) 90.00
SHERRY
   1955, 19", vinyl head/hard plastic body, walker 250.00
   1984,11", Grande Dames Series 40.00
   Black 55.00
SHIP AHOY COLLECTION, 1979, in red/white/blue outfits,
   offered by special flyer and not in catalog
   11" Half Pint boy or girl 30.00
   15" Chipper 30.00
   16" Li'l Suzie Sunshine .35.00
   11" Tiny Tubber 25.00
   14" Little Lov 25.00
SIR WINSTON CHURCHILL, 1984, Great Moments in
   History 65.00
SISSY, 1972–1984
   14", all vinyl, Bedtime Story Collection 25.00
   1985, Black, Sunday Best Collection 30.00
SISTER, 1943–1958
   10", all vinyl, from Most Happy Family set 35.00
   12", composition/cloth, yarn hair 165.00
   16" 250.00
SKATERS, boy or girl, 1978–1980, 11", Currier & Ives . .30.00 ea.
SKIPPY
   1927–1943, all composition, painted eyes, 14" . . .485.00
   1979, Limited Edition Club (limit 3,488) 400.00
   Composition
   As Soldier, Sailor, Safari, Farmer 525.00
   As Aviator, Cowboy 550.00
SLEEPING BEAUTY, 1977–1978, Disney exclusive
   14" 275.00
   1980–1983, Storybook Series 30.00
   1984, 9", Storybook Series 20.00
SMITHSONIAN, see Lady in Red Velvet hat.

SNOW QUEEN
   1986, 11", Storybook Series . . . . .30.0⬚
   1987, 11", Fairy Tales Collection . . . . .30.0⬚
SNOW WHITE
   1977–1978, 14", Disney exclusive . . . . .3⬚
   1977–1983, 11", Storybook Series . . . .
   1987, Fairy Tales Collection . . . .
SNOWBALL, 1913
   12" . . . . .24⬚
   18" . . . . .450.0⬚
SNOWMAN, 1986, 11", Storybook Series . . . . .30.0⬚
SOFT 'N SWEET COLLECTION, 1979, floral print dress with
   velveteen bow
   11" Pun'kin 20.00
   15" Chipper 25.00
   L'il Suzie Sunshine 30.00
   17" Miss Chips 45.00
   18" Suzie Sunshine 40.00
   11" Half Pint 25.00
   13" Butterball 20.00
   15" Buttercup 25.00
   18" Sweetie Pie 40.00
   20" Sugar Plum 40.00
SOLDIER, 1918, 16", composition 275.00
SONJA ON SKATES, 1938, 17", all composition child 345.00
SOPHIA, 1984, 15", Grande Dames Series 50.00
SOUTHERN BELLE, 1976, 15", Grande Dames Series 50.00
SPAIN BOY, 1980, 11", International Series 20.00
   Girl, 1978–1982, 11", International Series 15.00
SPANKY, 1990, 11½", Little Rascals collection 40.00
SPIRIT OF '76 COLLECTION (Americana), 1976, each dressed in
   blue or pink gingham check apron over white dress with
   matching bonnet
   11" Pun'kin 20.00
      Black 30.00
   15" Chipper 25.00
      Black 35.00
   18" Suzie Sunshine 40.00
      Black 60.00
   13" Butterball 20.00
   15" Little Luv 20.00
   20" Sugar Plum 40.00
SPRING
   1976–1980, 11", Four Seasons Collection 20.00
      Black 30.00
   1981–1983, 15", Four Seasons Collection 25.00
   1984, Four Seasons, 11" 20.00
   15" 25.00
   1985–1986, 17", Four Seasons 85.00
STEPHANIE, 1983, 15", Grande Dames Series 50.00
STORYBOOK COLLECTION, see individual names: Alice In Won-
   derland, Caption Kidd, Cinderella, Cowardly Lion,
   Dorothy, Goldilocks, Gretel, Hans Brinker, Hansel, Heidi,
   Jack, Jill, Little Bo Peep, Little Milk Maid, Little Miss
   Muffet, Little Red Riding Hood, Maid Marion, Mary Had
   A Little Lamb, Masry, Mary, Mary Poppins, Mother
   Goose, Mother Hubbard, Mrs. Santa Claus, Strawman,
   Musketeer, Old Women In The Shoe, Rapunzel, Rebecca
   of Sunnybrook Farm, Robin Hood, Pavlova, Pinocchio,
   Peter Pan, Polyanna, Prince Charming, Sleeping Beauty,
   Snow White, Sugar Plum Fairy, Tin Man, Tinkerbelle.
STRAWBERRY PATCH COLLECTION, 1972, dressed in pink and
   white with strawberry print or decoration
   16" Gumdrop 30.00
   18" Sweetie Pie 40.00

11" Pun'kin 20.00
18" Suzie Sunshine 40.00
13" Butterball 20.00
Black 30.00
16" Twinkie 20.00
STRAWMAN
1985, 11", Storybook Series 25.00
1987–1990, 11", Wizard of Oz Collection 25.00
STROLLING IN THE PARK, 1982, Absolutely Abigail 35.00
SUGAR BABY, 1936–1940
20", composition/cloth 250.00
24" 300.00
1959–1963, 14", all vinyl 35.00
18" 50.00
SUGAR PIE
1959–1969, 18" 50.00
In bassenette/layette 185.00
SUGAR PLUM, 1969–1986 (17 years) 40.00
SUGAR PLUM FAIRY
1976–1983, 11", Storybook Series 25.00
1987, 11", Fairy Tales Collection 25.00
SUMMER
1976–1983, 11", Four Seasons Collection 20.00
1984–1986, 11", Four Seasons Collection 20.00
15" 25.00
SUNDAY, 1980–1982, 11", Day By Day Collection 20.00
SUNDAY BEST, 1982–1983, 13", Absolutely Abigail 35.00
SUNNY, 1969–1974, 19", all vinyl girl 85.00
SUSAN B. ANTHONY, 1980, Limited Edition Club
(limit 3,485) 70.00
SUTTON PLACE, 1987, 17", Little Old New York 70.00
SUZANNE
1940, 14", all composition 285.00
1983, 11", Grande Dames Series 40.00
SUZETTE
1939, 12", all composition 260.00
1959. 15", all vinyl 85.00
1961–1965, 15", all vinyl 85.00
SUZIE (Susie) SUNSHINE, 1961–1979 (18 year)
18", freckles 40.00
Black 60.00
SUZIE SUNSHINE COLLECTION, 1983, 18", in three gowns with
one in floral print, in embroidered and long gown with
apron 45.00
SUZIE SUNSHINE WRITING DOLL, see School Girl Writing.
SWAN LAKE, 1984, 13", Dance Ballerina Dance 40.00
SWEET DREAMS COLLECTION, 1977–1982, floral print night clothes
11" Pun'kin 20.00
15" Chipper 25.00
18" Suzie Sunshine 40.00
13" DyDee 25.00
12" Butterball 20.00
12" Baby Button Nose 20.00
15" Little Lovums 25.00
SWEET NOSTALGIA COLLECTION, 1973, all wearing long gowns
of pastel print and trimmed with ruffles
11" Pun'kin 20.00
18" Suzie Sunshine 40.00
16" Twinkie 20.00
16" Baby Face 40.00
15" Little Luv 20.00
SWEET SIXTEEN, 1989–1990, 13", Joyous Occasions 35.00
SWEETHEARTS, THE, 1918, 16", composition/cloth . .250.00 ea.
SWEETIE PIE
1938–1948,14", composition/cloth 150.00

1952, 18", hard plastic/latex/cloth 135.00
1957, 22", hard plastic/vinyl 185.00
1960s, 22", vinyl 135.00
Black 60.00
1969–1986 (17 years) .40.00
SWISS YODELER BOY OR GIRL, 1982–1983, Just Friends . . .40.00
TANGO KIDS, 1914
12", composition 165.00
16" 225.00
TERESA, 1988–1989, 11", The Way We Were 25.00
TESSA, 1986, 16" Lynn Hollyn American Countrytime .50.00
THEODORE ROOSEVELT, 1984, 17", Presidents 95.00
THOMAS JEFFERSON, 1989–1990, 16", Presidents 60.00
THREE PIGS, 1934, 10", all composition . . . . .200.00 ea.
THROUGH THE YEARS WITH GIGI, 1979–1980, represent six
stages in the life of a French woman. 1830–1900, see
individual name, Ingenue, Mama, Papa's Pet, School
Girl, Femme Fatale, Grand-Mere.
THUMBLINA, 1984–1985, 11", Storybook Collection 25.00
THUMKIN, 1965–1966, 18", cloth/vinyl baby 40.00
THURSDAY, 1980–1982, 11", Day By Day Collection 25.00
TIN MAN, 1985
11", Storybook Series .25.00
11", Wizard of Oz Collection 25.00
TINKERBELLE, 1978–1983, 11", Storybook Series 25.00
TINTAIR, 1951–1952, hard plastic (Honey) with hair color set
14" 300.00
16" 365.00
18" 425.00
TINY TAD, 1912, 1916–1918, 7", composition 175.00
TINY TUBBER, 1955, 1958, 1981–1986
11" 20.00
Black 30.00
TODAY, 1985, 12", Through the Years Collection 25.00
TODAY'S GIRL, see Little Lady, yarn hair.
TODDLE TOT, 1858, 1960s, 1970', 22" 50.00
TODDLETOT, 1968–1970, 13", all vinyl 20.00
TOMMY TUCKER, 1939–1949
15" 300.00
20" 385.00
24" 450.00
TOONGA
1940, 14", composition 200.00
1952, 12", hard plastic
TOOTH FAIRY, 1985, 13", Once Upon a Time 30.00
TOPAZ, 1981, 17", Grande Dames Series 70.00
TOUCH OF VELVET COLLECTION, 1973–1983, dressed in burgundy velveteen dress and white eyelet trimmed white
apron.
11" Pun'kin 20.00
15" Chipper 25.00
Black 35.00
18" Suzie Sunshine 40.00
Black 60.00
15" Little Luv 25.00
18" Sweetie Pie 40.00
20" Sugar Plum 40.00
TOUSLE TOT, 1939–1941, 16", composition/cloth 250.00
TOUSLEHEAD, 1928–1939, composition/cloth
15" 250.00
22" 300.00
28" 450.00
15", Black, 1943 . . . . .300.00
22" 365.00
TRACEY, 1989, 13", Currier & Ives 20.00